Conventional Realism and Political Inquiry

Conventional Realism and Political Inquiry

Channeling Wittgenstein

JOHN G. GUNNELL

The University of Chicago Press
Chicago and London

The University of Chicago Press, Chicago 60637
The University of Chicago Press, Ltd., London

Published 2020
Printed in the United States of America

29 28 27 26 25 24 23 22 21 20   1 2 3 4 5

ISBN-13: 978-0-226-66127-8 (cloth)
ISBN-13: 978-0-226-66130-8 (e-book)
DOI: https://doi.org/10.7208/chicago/9780226661308.001.0001

Library of Congress Cataloging-in-Publication Data
Names: Gunnell, John G., author.
Title: Conventional realism and political inquiry : channeling Wittgenstein / John G. Gunnell.
Description: Chicago : University of Chicago Press, 2020. | Includes bibliographical references and index.
Identifiers: LCCN 2019038474 | ISBN 9780226661278 (cloth) | ISBN 9780226661308 (ebook)
Subjects: LCSH: Wittgenstein, Ludwig, 1889–1951. | Political science—Philosophy.
Classification: LCC JA71 .G865 2020 | DDC 320.01—dc23
LC record available at https://lccn.loc.gov/2019038474

♾ This paper meets the requirements of ANSI/NISO Z39.48-1992 (Permanence of Paper).

Contents

Introduction

> Here we strike rock bottom, that is, we have come down to conventions.
>
> Grammar tells us what kind of object anything is. . . . *Essence* is expressed in grammar.
>
> WITTGENSTEIN

This book, in its most general sense, consists of an exploration of the relationship between philosophy and political inquiry as well as an assessment of what that relationship has been, currently is, and what it should be. My purpose is to explain certain dimensions of how political science and political theory have understood and deployed philosophy. When, however, social scientists and social theorists turn to the work of philosophers for intellectual authority or when they criticize certain philosophers, what they extract is often selective and in the service of some prior agenda. The philosophers whose work I discuss have all in various degrees been objects of the conversation of political theory, but close acquaintance with that work is often limited and derivative. My goal is to initiate a more genuine conversation with certain philosophers and political theorists, including those with whom I agree as well as those with whom I disagree.

I have, for many years, been deeply involved with Ludwig Wittgenstein's texts, but what I speak of as "channeling Wittgenstein" is neither a rhetorical strategy nor simply a case of philosophical fealty. What I have found in his work is inspiration and, what I believe to be, insight. My more detailed analysis of his work and my argument about its general implications for thinking about social inquiry were presented in my 2014 book *Social Inquiry after Wittgenstein and Kuhn: Leaving Everything as It Is.* I argued that for Wittgenstein philosophy was, in effect, a form of social inquiry and that his work contained the basis of a theoretical account of social phenomena and the epistemological and methodological implications of such a theory. I also argued that Thomas Kuhn's *Structure of Scientific Revolutions* exemplified Wittgenstein's image of philosophy as an interpretive endeavor, and I discussed how Kuhn, in his later work, reflectively addressed this hermeneutical approach and its epistemological and practical entailments. Kuhn, who began his career as a physicist but became a historian and philosopher of science, acutely understood what I will stress as the difference between the perspective of a participant in a practice and that of an interpreter of a practice.

Although I am, by job description, a political theorist, my 2014 book was conceived and published as primarily a contribution to the philosophy of social science and did not specifically discuss political inquiry. The present volume is devoted to significantly extending and elaborating my philosophical argument but in the context of applying it to some specific issues in the study of politics. I am committed to my interpretation of Wittgenstein, but my argument stands on its own, whether or not a reader might conclude that it conforms to his work. The consolidating thesis that defines this book is what I refer to, oxymoronically some may believe, as *conventional realism.* This phrase should not be confused with what, in the philosophy of science, is sometimes referred to as theoretical conventionalism and the claim that scientific theories are heuristic constructs rather than, themselves, reality claims. Although I have referred to "conventional realism" in previous work, it was part of an argument for the autonomy and logical parity of conventional phenomena, but it is now an argument for what might be characterized as *conventional universalism* or the proposition that everything we designate as "real," whether natural or social, is both rendered and accessed conventionally. I reject what has been, and continues to be, the widely accepted distinction between what is natural and what is conventional as a way of demarcating natural science and social science, which is a distinction that has touched all dimensions of political inquiry. Although I had once subscribed to this distinction, I now argue that it always partakes of some form of what Wilfrid Sellars dubbed the "myth of the given." I maintain that all phenomena are conventional in that they are specified in language, constituted by human agreement, and located in what I refer to as *first-order practices.* These practices give content and meaning to what we tend to speak about abstractly and summarily as "reality" or the "world" and, in their various manifestations, are the basic subject matter of interpretive *second-order* discourses such as social science and philosophy.

My oppositional emphasis is directed toward what is often referred to as representational philosophy, which is rooted in the work of individuals such as Descartes and Locke but, in various forms and degrees, perpetuated by many contemporary philosophers. Despite the criticisms that have been directed toward this genre of philosophy, the residue of its assumptions has persistently informed not only our everyday folk psychology but the theory and practices of social science. I focus particularly on what I will speak of generically as "mentalism" and traditional forms of "realism," which claim that the mind is the source and repository of meaning, that language is primarily a vehicle of thought and a means of communication, and that reality resides in some physical or metaphysical realm that stands behind our discursive practices. A basic question being posed in this volume is why and how so many philosophers, political theorists, and political scientists have come to believe that the criteria of truth, reality, objectivity, and meaning are to be found outside rather than within our practices. My argument is that the foundations of knowledge reside within our practices. What we refer to as the "mind" is basically our linguistic abilities and learned linguistic conventions, rather than an invisible receptacle containing mysterious pre-linguistic mental objects and processes, and the terms "reality" and "world" have no meaning outside the contexts of substantive theoretical claims and assumptions about what exists and how it behaves. It is only in language, and therefore conventions, that the terms "world" and "reality" become objects. What this entails in part is that there is no presumptively authoritative external philosophical basis for judging the validity of claims about what is real and true.

Although the imprint of realism and mentalism as attempts to exceed the limits of convention is still apparent in all the social sciences, it has, for reasons I will attempt to make clear, especially influenced political theory and other aspects of political science. Consequently, it is particularly important for these fields to understand fully the nature of these philosophical arguments but also the challenges mounted by Wittgenstein, Gilbert Ryle, and J. L. Austin, as well as others who, I will claim, are, in various respects, their successors. In the *Investigations*, Wittgenstein most thoroughly pursued a critique of mentalism, but the basic argument had already been evident in his earlier work and explicitly and most prosaically stated in *The Blue and Brown Books*. And in *On Certainty*, his rejection of traditional philosophical realism was unequivocally articulated.

Even some contemporary critics of representational philosophy have found it difficult to extricate themselves from the terms and assumptions that have characterized forms of that philosophy. They still often speak of "mind" and "reality" as if referring to something that itself is not representable but the ground sustaining various discourses ranging from natural science to what Sellars referred to as the commonsense "manifest image." Although it has become popular to advocate some version of what is often referred to as "direct realism," which is claimed to bypass the problems of representational philosophy, this can be misleading if it is taken to mean that the world causally determines our concepts or that there is some immediate pre-conceptual phenomenal access to the "world." Peter Winch put it in a manner on which

I cannot substantially improve: "Our idea of what belongs to the realm of reality is given to us in the language we use" and consequently "the world *is* for us what is presented in these concepts. That is not to say that our concepts do not change; but when they do, that means that our concept of the world has changed too" (1958, 23, 61–62).

As I will make clear in the following chapters, it would be a mistake to construe my argument for conventional realism as a form of "linguistic idealism," if that phrase, which has been used in a number of ways, and usually pejoratively, has any intrinsic meaning. Arguments such as that of Wittgenstein, Winch, and Kuhn have often been interpreted by some philosophers as claiming that the world is in some way a product of language or a linguistic construction. This was not, however, what Wittgenstein, Winch, and Kuhn were saying, and it is not my position. Classic idealism was basically the claim that reality is ultimately ideational. Although I personally do not read Plato as this kind of idealist/realist, his work is often cited as the paradigm case of such a position. George Berkeley claimed that physical objects are collections of ideas in the mind of perceivers, and for much of German idealism, reality was either a product of mind and thought or something only indirectly accessible through the categories of the mind. My argument, however, is not that language is the ontological foundation of reality but simply that reality is what is presented in natural science and other first-order conceptions of some dimension of the constitution of the "world," and when these change, what we mean by "reality" changes accordingly.

I argue that the very distinction between real and unreal is dependent on language and that human awareness and thought, even of particular things, requires language and attending concepts. It would be misleading to say literally either that *the* world changes or that our perspective on *the* world changes, because what changes is actually our *conception* of to what the word "world" refers. Although we often speak of people as having different views of the world, this can be misleading if it is taken to mean that there is some pre-conventional world on which they have different perspectives. Although a natural scientist, for example, assumes, and actually must assume, that they are living in, exploring, and representing a given world, the content of that "world" is specified and defined by their theoretical conception. As philosophical and social scientific interpreters of "worlds," the assumption of an unrepresentable reality that stands outside discursive presentations of what is claimed to be real is as meaningless as assuming that the content of what we often speak of as the human mind is anything more than our linguistic capacities and repertoire of conventions.

A fundamental problem with terms such as "world," "mind," and "reality" is that they are so often used as if they denoted something particular when they are actually used in a variety of ways, and, outside of a particular theoretical context, do not refer to any specifiable object. It is not like talking and having various beliefs about what is agreed to be some discovered yet not fully explored terrain. The diversity of, and transformations in, what is taken to be "true" and "real" about the "world" has led some philosophers and social theorists to worry that the concepts of truth, reality, and objectivity have been endangered. And such arguments have been popularized by claims such as those of the investigative documentary filmmaker Errol Morris whose diatribe against Kuhn's argument about "scientific revolutions" was first published (2011) as a series in the *New York Times* "Opinionator" section and more recently as a book (2018) with the subtitle "Or the Man Who Denied Reality" (for a full critical discussion of Morris's argument, see Gunnell 2014b, ch. 1). Whether or not Morris's interpretation was motivated by his admitted personal grudge against Kuhn, he egregiously distorted what Kuhn had said as well the arguments of Wittgenstein, which he associated with Kuhn. Kuhn's historical account of how scientists have changed their views about to what the term "reality" refers was not in any way a dismissal of the concept of reality. What Morris construed as reality was something that must underlie all scientific conceptions but which itself could not be described. I want definitively to put to rest arguments such as that of Morris as well as that of philosophers who have been a source of support for such arguments.

Morris did not understand that words such as "reality" and "truth" are not in themselves names for anything, nor did he understand the difference between the practice of science and the interpretation of that practice. There are two basic "reality" and "truth" issues: first, that of what is the case with respect to some particular state of affairs and, second, that of what is the case with respect to a general concept of a state of affairs. Although in the following chapters, I will be attempting to clarify both issues, what Kuhn actually denied, and properly so, was the belief that truth and reality are transcendental objects of which human practices in various degrees partake. Abstract holistic claims about the "world," "truth," and "reality," like those of "beauty" and "justice," are only an extrapolation from the various and diverse contexts in which the words have been applied. What Kuhn did, in effect, was to return the criteria of scientific truth and reality to scientists and to other seekers of the truth about some particular matter, such as, ironically, Morris himself.

My book is not a research monograph designed to survey the wide range of secondary literature that, in both political science and the philosophy of social science, might be considered relevant to the issues I discuss. The philosophical and social scientific claims that I defend as well as those I critically assess are meant to be exemplary of my argument and contending positions. I do not carry on an auxiliary bibliographical dialogue in footnotes or explore in detail all the areas of social science and political theory (Straussian natural right, arguments for deliberative democracy such as those associated with Jürgen Habermas, recent arguments for material naturalism such as those derived from cognitive science, etc.) in which vestiges of traditional mentalism and realism still hold sway. Mentalism and realism are the basis of an equal opportunity rhetoric adopted and deployed by both the ideologically right and left. Although Wittgenstein is in some respects featured and, as the epigraphs indicate, channeled, in each chapter, this is not primarily a book about Wittgenstein. The identity of the manuscript is thematic and argumentative, that is, the argument for conventional realism and the critique of mentalism and realism. What I speak of as conventional realism is my argument and not a position advocated by any particular philosopher, even though I believe it as an implication of Wittgenstein's work.

Chapter 1 consists of an expanded overview of the general argument that I have summarized above as well as of my approach to analyzing the issues involved, and it is designed to guide the reader through the subsequent chapters. In order to make the discussion more concrete and inclusive, I also offer a very brief and selective account of forms of mentalism and realism in the history of American political science and political theory. Current issues in political inquiry cannot be disjoined from the past political and philosophical contexts from which they emerged. I emphasize that it is particularly important to recognize the extent to which a concern with the practical goal of affecting political life has structured the discourse of political science and particularly the subfield of political theory and how this has perpetuated the search for philosophical grounds of epistemic validation. Chapters 2 and 3 analyze illustrative contemporary cases of mentalism and realism in the study of politics. Chapter 2 focuses on a distinct and pervasive instance of the problems associated with what I refer to as the "mind-first" attitude. I critically discuss the manner in which, in both philosophy and political inquiry, concepts have typically been conceived as mental objects, and, as part of my argument for conventional realism, I advance an alternative analysis of concepts as forms of linguistic usage. This chapter also examines the persistent, but, I claim, futile, search for the theoretical universality of politics. Chapter 3 explores the problems that have characterized claims about realism in the study of politics. In order to focus the discussion, I analyze a particular philosophical rendition that has been derived primarily from the philosophy of natural science and that has at various points surfaced in contemporary social science but recently has been advanced as a basis of theory in the study of international politics. The next two chapters turn to a detailed examination of the philosophical literature that has been devoted to a critique of representational philosophy and particularly mentalism and traditional forms of realism. These chapters provide the ground for my thesis of conventional realism. Chapter 4 explores the role of Wittgenstein, Ryle, and Austin in initiating this critique, and chapter 5 discusses the contributions to, as well as some of the difficulties in, contemporary anti-representational literature. These chapters seek to give students of politics a clear account of a literature that is relevant to political inquiry and often cited but seldom well understood. Chapter 6 defends a distinction between the concepts of presentation and representation, which is important both to my argument for conventional realism and to understanding the difference between natural and social inquiry. I argue that social inquiry is basically a representational and interpretive activity while natural science is presentational, even though each shares a form of the other. An important caveat is that when I speak of representation in this chapter, it should not be confused with what I have characterized as representational philosophy. I undertake illustrating the difference between representation and presentation somewhat indirectly through an interpretation of Wittgenstein's *Tractatus* and by an analysis of the persistence of this distinction in his later work. Although Wittgenstein's name often appears in the literature of political theory, there are very few political theorists who are familiar with the actual content of the *Tractatus* and with exactly what changed as well as did not change in his later work. Chapter 7 is devoted to a fuller account of conventional realism and of what Wittgenstein said about conventions. I begin that chapter, however, with a detailed analysis of how the philosophers and social theorists John Searle and Charles Taylor, who had been deeply involved in the defense of mentalism and realism, have recently acknowledged some of the problems with these positions and embraced some of the criticisms. They have, however, proceeded by trying to solve the problems attributed to mentalism and realism rather than rejecting the framework in which the problems have arisen. Chapter 8 begins with a brief case study of how social theorists have often sought a ground of philosophical realism that would provide a basis for both interpretation and critical judgment. The principal subject of the chapter is an argument by the philosopher Cora Diamond. Although she had once described and defended what she believed to be a "realistic spirit" in Wittgenstein's work, which she interpreted as going against the grain of traditional realism, she nevertheless later argued that it was possible to elicit from that work a philosophical realist basis for what she referred to as "criticizing from outside." As in the case of a number of other philosophers and social theorists (see Gunnell 2011), this attempt to enlist Wittgenstein in vouchsafing the critical and epistemic authority of some philosophical or social position is a fruitless venture. In a brief conclusion, instead of summarizing what has gone before, I suggest what might be the normative democratic implication of conventional realism.

There are parts of the book that might to be hard going for some students of politics. They might wonder if I am actually a political theorist or a philosophical bootlegger, but political science has been consuming philosophical commodities since its inception. I believe that philosophy only becomes relevant when directed toward how to study substantive practices, but it is time for political scientists to be more philosophically discriminating and for philosophers to understand their impact on other fields.

1

Representational Philosophy and Conventional Realism

Je pense, donc je suis.

Idées, où l'on considère seulement la réalité qu'ils nomment objective.

DESCARTES

There is a kind of general disease of thinking which always looks for (and finds) what would be called a mental state from which all our acts spring as from a reservoir.

The idea of "agreement with reality" does not have any clear application.

WITTGENSTEIN

The Argument: An Overview

This volume, and my argument for conventional realism, could be understood as largely an elaboration of the above quotations from Wittgenstein and as substituting "*je parle*" for Descartes's "*je pense*," and "*langue*" for his "*idées*." I begin, however, with a discussion of Richard Rorty's *Philosophy and the Mirror of Nature*. When this seminal critique of representational philosophy was published in 1979, it not only precipitated a significant conversation in philosophy but in the field of political theory as well. Some political theorists either embraced or rejected his anti-foundationalist message, but that message was often shallowly understood. Much of the discussion actually focused on his defense of liberalism and pragmatism as well as the extent to which his book might support a more interpretive, qualitative, post-behavioral approach to political inquiry. It is, however, important to remember that Rorty's basic goal was to call into question much of the enterprise of contemporary academic professional philosophy and the manner in which it was organized around the problems of how mind could represent reality and how language could represent the contents of mind. There may be reasons to doubt Rorty's suggestion that American pragmatism was, on the whole, a rejection of representational philosophy, as well as his equation of Wittgenstein and Dewey as both embracing "epistemological behaviorism" (174), that is, the claim that "society" provides the criteria judgment. But his challenge to philosophy was also in effect a challenge to much of social inquiry, which had absorbed the basic tenets of representational philosophy.

Rorty's purpose was to criticize philosophical pretensions to be able to specify the general nature and foundations of knowledge and truth and to have the authority to either underwrite or invalidate claims to knowledge in spheres such as science, morality, politics, and everyday life. He wished to reorient philosophy and encourage a more egalitarian "edifying" role in the general "conversation of mankind." Exactly what this role would involve and how it would be effected was unclear, but his principal point was to allay the fear that "if we deny that there are foundations to serve as a common ground for adjudicating knowledge claims, the notion of the philosopher as guardian rationality seems endangered" and that consequently there would be "no such thing as rational argument and disagreement" (317). The mistake all along had been to believe that philosophy, and also social inquiry, had some special access to the foundations of knowledge and rationality and that they were intrinsically qualified to stand in judgment of truth-claims in various substantive practices ranging from science to politics. Although Rorty suggested that the roots of representational philosophy reached back to the Greeks, his focus was on seventeenth-century thinkers such as Descartes and on what he claimed was the transmission forward of the problems associated with this literature. Among many political theorists, across the ideological academic spectrum, there were, as in the field of philosophy itself, worries about Rorty's critique and what many believed, and often still believe, to be its relativistic and historicist implications. What so many failed to comprehend, however, was that his argument, like that of Kuhn, was not primarily directed at science and other practices, including common sense, but at philosophers who identified themselves as the guardians and arbiters of truth.

Rorty sought support in the work of a number of philosophers such as Wittgenstein, Sellars, Austin, W. V. O. Quine, Kuhn, and Donald Davidson, but it would be very difficult to gain from his book a sufficient understanding of their arguments. Another problem with his analysis was that he tended to provide a somewhat one-dimensional view of the history of philosophy and gave short shrift to the rhetorical context in which much of past philosophy was situated. And his references to the arguments of philosophers such as Wittgenstein were often summary, with limited attention to textual detail. Although I hope to ameliorate these limitations, they did not diminish the importance of his basic argument. Another relevant book published in 1979 was Stanley Cavell's *Claim of Reason*, the first half of which largely consisted of his already widely read but unpublished Harvard dissertation. His arguments, and his focus on conventions and the work of Austin and Wittgenstein, complemented Rorty's efforts, but the book did not become as prominent in the conversation of political theory.

By the early 1980s, discussions in political science had become diverted from fundamental theoretical issues about the nature of political inquiry and instead dominated by often competing epistemological and methodological claims that were not actually specific positions but abstractions detached from a variety of philosophies from which they had been derived as well as from their deeper roots in practices such as science. A prime example was the debate between so-called positivist and post-positivist images of inquiry or what was often referred to as scientific as opposed to interpretive or qualitative methods, and sometimes even more broadly parsed as a difference between explanation and understanding. This trend has continued in confrontations such as that between empiricism and constructivism, but the important question is why social inquiry had been so entranced by these epistemological ideologies, which were often also assumed to constitute general approaches to, and even methods of, social inquiry. The subtext in these controversies was actually the residue of an issue that had been endemic to political science from its inception. An essential part of the explanation of this syndrome is that it involved a search for cognitive authority as an avenue to the achievement of practical goals. This issue has been, and continues to be, common to both philosophy and social inquiry, and consequently it is necessary to be concerned with both the history of philosophy and the history of social science. Metaphysical philosophy was seldom pursued merely for, so to speak, its own sake. Its original and typical concerns, from at least the time of Plato, were practical, normative, and prescriptive, and this was also the case with modern social science, which had its origins in nineteenth-century moral philosophy and social reform movements. Anthropology, for example, was the outgrowth of missionary work.

We lose sight of what philosophy and social science had been all about when we approach them as the prehistory of contemporary academia. And we misconceive the history of much of American political science and political theory if we interpret it as other than an extended defense of, and argument about, the nature of democratic values and the path to their realization (Gunnell 2004). The first systematic use of the term "social science" in the United States was by the nineteenth-century American Social Science Association, which was an, often religiously inspired, organization devoted to a wide range of social causes that it believed could be best pursued if backed by the increasing authority of science. It was from this association that most of the particular social scientific disciplines eventually differentiated and emerged.

A dilemma facing the early modern social sciences, in England, Europe, and the United States, was that, despite some instances to the contrary, their external, and often critical, perspective alienated them from the social practices to which they wished to speak. Their purpose was often political, but they did not occupy a position that carried political authority. Because in most contexts their arguments usually possessed very little inherent practical purchase, their claim to public recognition was primarily based on assertions of some sort of epistemic privilege. Their conceptual and practical distance from their subject matter was especially pronounced by the end of the century, when the social sciences, in search of a scientific identity, became professionalized and formalized as particular disciplines situated in institutions of higher education. This not only separated them further from their envisioned audience but tended to transform their priorities from practical to academic. Nevertheless, the problem of their practical relationship to their object of inquiry remained a defining, even if sometimes latent, preoccupation of these fields, which increasingly submerged that problem in various epistemological arguments. Even at those relatively recent points in the history of political science, such as the 1960s and the early years of the twenty-first century, when enthusiasm for becoming politically relevant has been particularly pronounced, the arguments have often turned on offering epistemological solutions directed toward political science becoming either less scientific or more scientific.

The practical purposes—or now often the institutional memory of these purposes manifest in the residual language and structure of social science—have contributed to the adoption of rhetorically motivated philosophical claims and, particularly, to an enchantment with various forms of philosophical realism and to a fixation on the issue of how to access the meaning putatively concealed behind language and action. Because these concerns have persisted in many elements of philosophy, those elements have continued to capture the imagination of many of those who study politics and who are often intent on specifying what they take to be the nature of politics and on offering assurances of their access to that nature. This has led to what I have referred to as the "alienation of political theory" (1986) or the manner in which the field increasingly, from the 1970s to the present, has chased after a variety of philosophical images that would sustain the persistent dream of finding an external ground for explaining and judging the practices of politics. And it has entailed the persistence of what I have referred to as a "dislocated rhetoric" (2006, 2011), that is, the displacement of political arguments by epistemological claims.

Among the social sciences, political science and political theory have remained especially haunted by their normative origin and heritage and by a concern with speaking *to* as well as *about* their subject matter. I am not in any way suggesting that political inquiry should refrain from taking a normative stance but only that this has often led to a fruitless and misleading search for some ultimate ground of philosophical validation. Although only a careful study of the history of these fields fully reveals the source of these difficulties, it can be partly explained by the fact that, unlike the more abstractly specified subjects (such as society, culture, the economy, etc.) of many other social sciences, politics, no matter how notationally or functionally conceived and universally ascribed by many of those who study it, refers, in the first instance, to a specific and historically concrete element of social life. Although, for example, sociologists might attempt to locate politics as a subsystem within what they refer to as the general social system, societies are usually encompassed by a particular political regime, and politics stubbornly stands out as unamenable to conceptual sublimation. Contemporary political science, with its propensity to employ aggregate analysis, has, like most of the social sciences, become increasingly removed from the particulars of political life, but it is still often difficult to study politics without addressing, and making judgments about, specific values, individuals, groups, policies, and institutions. And this relationship cuts both ways. It would be odd to suggest, for example, except in some metaphorical sense, that the study of economics has ever been threatened by the economy or that anthropology must be wary of culture, but the study of politics has occasionally, and in some significant instances, precipitated pointed political retaliation.

Although political science has sometimes attempted to close the conceptual and practical gap between itself and its subject matter by seeking a common identity and adopting the name "Politics" or "Government," it has more frequently claimed autonomy and priority on the basis of possessing either a "science" of politics or some special capacity or position that allows for superior understanding and judgment. I have argued that if political theory wishes to speak to politics, it is an illusion to believe that it can achieve its practical goals by philosophical posturing. But this continuing search for epistemic authority has led to a debasement of theorizing and a flight to the foundational promises of philosophy as well as to an image of social inquiry as a form of mind reading.

Although I argue that some philosophical work, such as that of Wittgenstein, can contribute to the theory and practice of social inquiry, engagement with philosophy must be approached with caution. One of the principal reasons that social scientists should pay attention to philosophy is simply because social science has, since its inception, already paid attention to philosophy—and often absorbed assumptions that are in need of further philosophical scrutiny. Contrary to many ideologically and philosophically diverse contemporary academic theorists, I have argued, and continue to claim in this volume, that there is nothing *theoretically* unique about politics and what is now often referred to as "*the* political." There cannot be a general theory (ontology) of politics per se, or of any other particular class of social facts, but only a theory of the *kind* of phenomena of which politics is one historical and cultural form. Consequently, the study of politics should first be approached in terms of theoretical issues that are involved in all forms of social inquiry. This entails the need for a general theory of social phenomena, which, at the deepest level, must, I argue, be predicated on what I will speak of as a theory of conventionality and what I refer to as conventional realism.

When confronting the general theoretical issue in social inquiry, engagement with the field of philosophy is not only inevitable because of the interactions between them, but essential because philosophy and social science are logically comparable enterprises. Although philosophy, in the form of metaphysics, has often been conceived, as Wittgenstein noted, as a kind of super-science, philosophy is, at least as featured in his work, as well as that of someone such as Kuhn, primarily an interpretive endeavor that belongs to the same order of inquiry as social science. At the core of what I take from Wittgenstein is not only that social inquiry is interpretive, and therefore presupposes the conceptually pre-constituted nature of its subject matter, but that it is necessary to reject the assumption that the meaning of human language and action is grounded in something that stands outside these phenomena and that provides a basis for judging them. Such an assumption was what led Wittgenstein to speak of the "dogmatism" of metaphysics. What he particularly challenged, and the residue of which I critically examine with respect to the study of politics, are varieties of what I refer to as mentalism and realism. It was Wittgenstein's critique of mentalism that primarily inspired his well-known rejection of the universality of the object-designation account of meaning as well as his argument about the impossibility of a private language. And the message of *On Certainty* was that the term "reality" has no specific referent that stands outside the variety of theoretical contexts in which it is employed and gains meaning.

The framework of much of what I have to say in the following chapters is predicated on distinguishing between the kinds of practices constituting what I have referred to as the "orders of discourse" (Gunnell 1998). The basic distinction is between *first-order* practices and discourses and various levels of *meta-practical* interpretive analysis. My use of the terms "practice" and "discourse" are simply taxonomic or categorical and a way of discriminating various historical types of linguistic domains. Despite the widespread use of the phrases "practice theory" and "discourse theory," there can be no theory or ontology of practices and discourses themselves, which can range from something only analytically circumscribed and designated to something more generally recognized but still quite amorphous, such as politics, as well as to something more formal and institutional such as the discipline of political science. A discourse can exist apart from, and prior to taking the more institutionalized form of, a practice. There were, for example, discourses about nature and about politics before, respectively, the emergence of the natural sciences and the practices of social science.

First-order practices *present* the "world," and logically and temporally, their priority must be assumed. All meta-practices are supervenient and, one might say, parasitic on their subject matter. Unlike my distinction between practices and discourses, my distinction between first-order practices and meta-practices and between different levels of meta-practice, are not simply analytical. They are what both Wittgenstein and Austin might have viewed as different ways of doing things with words. Although social science and much of philosophy (such as the philosophy of natural science, the philosophy of religion, and ordinary language philosophy) are *second-order* practices, they do embody a first-order presentational dimension, because they entail, either implicitly or explicitly, a general theory of social phenomena. The practice of the philosophy of social science, as well as self-reflective discourse internal to the practice of social science, is an example of *third-order analysis.* And the very act of making these distinctions, as I am doing, could be construed as a *fourth-order* activity and mode of analysis. But for clarity about what one is doing or saying, it is always essential to locate discussions within this scheme. Although there is a logical relationship between the orders of discourse, it is necessary to recognize that there is no necessary practical relationship—or *lack* of such a relationship, which is an empirical and historical matter, such as the relationship between political science and the first-order practice of politics or the relationship between the philosophy of social science and political theory. It has not been uncommon for political theorists to blur the distinctions and suggest, or even argue, that, for example, academic political theory is a mode of political action or that the distinction between them is negated if a political theorist engages in a political act. Such claims have sometimes surfaced in literary criticism and other fields, but these logical lapses and rhetorical ploys only underscore the fact that relationships do not presuppose an identity between the things that are related. Quite the opposite, there can be no meaningful discussion of relationships without these distinctions, but blurring the distinctions has typically been a way of avoiding directly dealing with the issues involved.

Although the basic vector of the relationships between the orders of discourse might be considered "vertical" in the sense that meta-practices exist by talking about their subject matter, this does not mean that first-order practices do not on occasion respond to meta-analysis or that second-order practices do not borrow from third-order practices such as the philosophy of social science. There are instances of political actors responding to political science, natural scientists responding to the philosophy of science, and social scientists responding to the philosophy of social science. The relationships are also sometimes "lateral," such as the case of instances in which political scientists have often attempted to derive epistemological and methodological guidance from the philosophy of natural science.

No matter how we may judge the viability and justifiability of the practical concerns and motives of social inquiry, its definitive, initial, and principal task, like that of philosophy as conceived by Wittgenstein, is to understand, interpret, and represent historically and socially variable realms of language and action. This requires recognizing how these realms have conceived the world they inhabit, including their place in that world. Despite the continuing efforts of some philosophers and social theorists, there is no authoritative philosophical basis for either justifying or falsifying the content of first-order discourses and practices, which range from politics to more institutionalized symbolic forms such as religion and natural science. When we speak of the "world," it is, if meaningful, always a conception indigenous to a first-order practice, and it is futile for interpretive inquiry to posit a world that stands outside such practices. To do so is in effect to embrace a theological perspective and to believe in believing rather than in any identifiable object of belief. As a regulative ideal in fields of natural science, it is pragmatically useful, and even necessary, to assume a "world" that stands outside, and both enables and constrains, all past and present first-order articulations, and to which science is devoted to progressively revealing, but as a philosophical and interpretive claim, such "realism" is a chimera and adds nothing to our understanding of how things are.

In chapter 6, I will discuss more fully the distinction between *presentational* or theoretical practices and *representational* or descriptive practices. When Wittgenstein wrote the *Tractatus* he was still under the spell of representational philosophy, but he was strangely prescient and recognized that although there is a logical connection between the propositions of what Kuhn would later refer to as "normal science" and the "world," this did not obtain in the case of scientific theories, which were not representations of the world but presentations of the world, or what Wittgenstein referred to as "shown." He was adumbrating a distinction that would be at the core of the conception of philosophy in his later work. First-order practices do not literally represent anything at all but instead present the framework within which representation take place.

Part of what characterizes first-order practices is that there is no fundamental distinction between their general conception of the world and their account of the particularities of that world. There is no ontological distinction between universals and particulars. For example, despite arguments such as that characteristic of positivism, scientific theories cannot be checked against an independent realm of facticity. Theory and fact are logically and internally related. The "facts" studied and represented by natural science have already been conceptually specified and defined in terms of the theories of natural science. And the facts of one theory cannot be the basis for definitively judging or explaining another. All this has, however, created a problem for both philosophy and social inquiry with respect to mounting a critical analysis of their subject matter. There is no external, second-order, neutral, and decisive basis for adjudicating conflicts between incommensurable first-order practices, between theoretical disputes within those practices, and between second-order investigations and first-order practices. In each case, as Wittgenstein argued, and Kuhn described in the case of natural science, conflict resolution is an internal matter of bringing to bear various forms of persuasion. There may be many reasons to put one's faith in the domain of facts presented by the theories of natural science, as opposed to other first-order discourses, but the reason cannot be that scientific facts stand outside convention and that what science takes to be true at any particular time is immutable.

What frightens many philosophers and social theorists is what they often refer to as the danger of relativism, the fear that there is not some realm of discourse that is self-validating, but although the label of relativism has occasionally been self-ascribed, it is not an actual philosophical position. It is only the "other" conjured up by philosophical foundationalism and a reflection of the self-induced fear that philosophy or social inquiry will lose cognitive authority. The foundations of first-order practices reside, as Wittgenstein, Kuhn, and others have stressed, within those practices rather than in some philosophical netherworld. These practices may circumstantially come into conflict, as in the case of science and common sense, but they are also often compartmentalized and simultaneously embraced without significant cognitive dissonance.

In the case of second-order studies, the "facts" constituting the objects of investigation, no matter how they may be theoretically conceived and presented in those studies, are conceptually autonomous. Consequently, second-order practices have not only an *epistemic* relationship to their object of inquiry but, at least potentially, a contingent *practical* relationship. The *relational* character of these practices entails that there is an ineluctable practical and epistemic distance from the object of inquiry, but this is what philosophers and social theorists have attempted to overcome by searching for a philosophical ground of apodictic certitude. One of the positive implications of this relational condition of social inquiry is, however, that such inquiry cannot think about the identity of its subject matter without internal *third-order* reflection on its own identity and how it relates, both practically and epistemically, to that subject matter. This is what brings it into contact with the formalized external third-order field of the philosophy of social science, where, however, there are both dangers and benefits.

An internal realm of historical and philosophical meta-theoretical reflectivity is largely absent from contemporary natural science and other first-order practices. The philosophy of science, for example, is not normally part of either a scientist's education or subsequent activity. This is in part a consequence of the particular history of these fields, which I will speak more about in chapter 3, but it is also because the typical scientist, like many citizens of the commonsense conception of the world, does not really possess a language for engaging in such reflection. When such reflection does occur among scientists, it is usually in the memoirs of older practitioners or in textbooks where the substantive information is often prefaced by what is assumed to be the need to say something about the nature of science or the "scientific method." These statements are often expressed in terms derived in a secondary or tertiary manner from the philosophy of science. Self-reflection is not an inherent aspect of first-order inquiry, because it is only in a somewhat metaphorical respect that we can speak, for example, of the relationship between natural science and nature, since, in Western society, science is largely constitutive of what we mean by "nature." Such reflection is, however, inherent in second-order studies, but not because, as sometimes suggested, they are still immature sciences. It is simply part of the both epistemic and practical relational dimensions of these studies. Here, as opposed to a first-order field such as natural science, there are, so to speak, two "theories" to be considered—the theory of social phenomena that informs inquiry and the "theory" that is indigenous to subject matter. And internal third-order reflection in social science is the principal site of *theorizing* about the nature of social phenomena and about the entailed approach to understanding and representing such phenomena. Because of its relational character, such theorizing, whether viewed, as in the case of political science, as a somewhat distinct activity and subfield or, as in some other fields of social science, as only more analytically distinguishable, is a necessary aspect of social inquiry. An account of the nature of social phenomena and entailed epistemology cannot, any more than in the case of theories in natural science, simply be left to philosophy.

The philosopher John Searle, in various publications and particularly in his *The Construction of Social Reality* (1995) and the *Making of the Social*

World (2009), is one of the few philosophers who have attempted to formulate what he referred to as "a general theory of the ontology of social facts and social institutions." He noted that his project addressed "problems in the foundations of the social sciences" that "one might suppose . . . would have been addressed and solved already in the various social sciences" (1995, xii). As I will make clear later, I fundamentally disagree with Searle's particular formulation and his distinctions between what is natural and what is conventional and between what is mental and linguistic. But I endorse his concern with articulating a general theory of social phenomena, and I concur with his observation that this matter has not been adequately confronted within the social sciences themselves. In these fields, epistemology, which should be an appendage of ontology, has become a disembodied substitute for it.

In whatever manner social science has approached social phenomena, whether as naturalistically explicable or as sui generis, there has been little dissent from the assumption that such phenomena are conventional. Consequently a theory of social phenomena must be based on a theory of *conventionality*, but in both philosophy and social inquiry, attention to such a theory has been very limited. This is partly because conventions, as opposed to what has been construed as natural, have been typically viewed as ephemeral, artificial, and as resting on some prior ground. This has been the case not only with someone such as Searle but also with social critics who claim that conventions mask underlying realities, either in the "mind" or the "world." Many theorists are seeking something behind or beyond conventions and on which conventions are grounded and in terms of which they can be understood and judged. But it is this assumption that I am challenging. It is not simply social facts that are conventional. As human beings, conventionality is our natural habitat, and my argument is that in an important sense "every-*thing*" is conventional and that the *basic distinction should be between the conventions in which social facts are specified and those in which natural facts are specified. Both social and natural phenomena are species of conventionality.* Many philosophers and social theorists, such as Searle, continue to seek a reality that is pre-conventional, whether located in natural science, metaphysics, or some form of "brute fact" open to immediate experience of the "world."

Wittgenstein sometimes talked about the relationship between our concepts and the general "facts of nature," and he raised questions about what that relationship might be. Although these passages have been interpreted in quite diverse ways, and sometimes, even by someone such as his student and translator G. E. M. Anscombe, as suggesting that social facts are somehow grounded in natural facts, I will argue that on the whole his work makes it clear that such facts depend on the grammar of the concepts belonging to the conventions of a particular form of discourse, that is, the conventions in which a vision of the natural world is articulated and the conventions that compose what we speak of as the social world. He stressed that it is impossible to use language to get outside language. Whether it is a philosopher, such as Kuhn, studying the history and practice of natural science or whether it is a political theorist studying the history and practice of politics, both must come to grips with the theoretical issue of conventionality.

Our concepts often do specify *what we take to be* the general facts of nature and what Wittgenstein once referred to as what we may at any point assume to be the "unassailable" limits of the human constitution and condition, but it is not that there is some natural datum that stands outside our conceptual universe. For example, when the theories of natural science change, our conception of what constitutes natural facts changes accordingly. When social scientists call upon natural facts in support of their claims, it is hardly a matter of pointing to some theoretically neutral and persistent criterion. The assumption that, in some general manner, natural facts explain conventional facts is simply wrong. At most it could be an attempt to demonstrate that social facts are made possible by certain natural conditions and capacities. But my argument is not that conventions explain natural facts. It is simply that nature is always linguistically and conceptually specified.

Although Wittgenstein is often, and correctly, viewed as placing a great deal of emphasis on what can be achieved by "ordinary language," he also devoted considerable attention to how the idioms of that language can lead us astray and create pictures that hold us captive as well as to how philosophers have often attempted to reinforce the bases and biases of those pictures. In everyday life, people cling to the assumption that language is a way of expressing pre-linguistic thoughts, and this assumption has a variety of philosophical counterparts, even among philosophers who in other respects may sharply disagree with each other. Although it is reasonable to say, for example, that we often think before we act and that we act in view of our beliefs, our thinking and believing are already linguistic and not something pre-conventional. There is a tendency to have an image of belief as a shadowy mental state that explains, or can be detected behind, what we say and do, but the term "belief" simply refers to what a person claims or assumes to be the case with respect to some state of affairs. The assumption of the primacy and autonomy of thought is of course true in the limited sense that we may silently rehearse what we are going to say or do. But much of what we say and do requires no such rehearsal. And it is a mistake to assume that the thinking takes place in a pre-conventional non-linguistic medium.

The persistent intuition that, despite what I claim is the basic identity of language and thought, there must be a kind of non- or pre-verbal thinking has in part led to the current popularity of arguments, often inspired by recent work in cognitive science, that claim that there is unconscious prelinguistic physiologically based thought, "thinking without thinking," that sometimes even functions better than deliberation and reasoning. What is actually involved in some of these pop-science claims, such as that of Malcolm Gladwell (2005), as well as in the work of some cognitive scientists, who talk about the underlying "gut" judgments of everyone from art assessors to chicken sex-sensing experts, is simply what Ryle spoke of as the difference between "knowing that" and "knowing how," which is evident, for example, in the ability to play music by "ear" and by benefit of "muscle memory," without relying on notation.

Although there is what might be called unreflective thought, the notion of unconscious thought is as conceptually problematic as what Wittgenstein criticized as a belief in a private language. The common idiomatic rendering of the relationship between thought and language is simply in part a consequence of our useful experience of, and attachment to, folk psychology, but that psychology has been reinforced by the residue of varieties of philosophical mentalism and the assumption that action and speech are the expression and symptoms of ontologically prior mental states and processes that compose the "mind." Just as it is a mistake to assume that the term "reality" has any particular privileged application, even though we cannot, in a variety of contexts, do without a concept of what is real and objective, "mind," "idea," "thinking," and other mental terms, have many uses in our language, but they should not be confused with a concept that specifies a particular thing. On reflection, we probably often realize all this, but it remains very difficult to extricate ourselves from a manner of speaking that uses these terms referentially.

Forms of mentalism and realism tend, in effect, to deny the autonomy of both social phenomena and social inquiry, divert attention from what is actually said and done in a sphere of speech and action such as politics, and, most importantly, suppress theoretical concern with the basic kind of the phenomena that social inquiry seeks to explain. I agree with Nelson Goodman's claim (1978, 20) that the search for a transcendental concept of the "real world" is futile and, as Rorty also insisted, a concept that is "well lost," and my argument is that the concept of mind as it has been typically conceived should also be jettisoned. When we use the word "mind," are we referring to the vague commonsense image of some place in our heads where thinking takes place, the cognitive scientist's claim that the mind is the brain, the Kantian account of mind, the Freudian mind, and such? And when we talk about the "world," is it our particular cultural conception, the world as conceived by religion, the various dimensions of the world specified by the natural sciences, and so on? It will simply not do to suggest that these are perspectives on some world that cannot itself ultimately be described and represented. The philosophical problems of how the mind makes contact with the world, how the realities of the world impact the mind, and how language can represent the content of mind are pseudo-problems and the result of inventing metaphysical phantoms such as mind and world and then pondering the relationship between them. These arguments do not explain anything. Would we want to say that the reason that we, for example, now accept the plate tectonic theory of mountain formation rather than the previous geosyncline account is that the mind made better contact with the world or that the world suddenly made a better causal impact on the mind or that we found a more suitable way to express in language the ideas in our mind? But these phantoms continue to haunt both philosophy and social inquiry. Wittgenstein's critique of metaphysics, and particularly of mentalism and realism, was at the core of his work, which recognized the need to face up to the reality of conventionality. Mentalism and realism are, however, as I will attempt to demonstrate, often deeply entangled with one another. As Austin said about idealism and realism, they take in each other's washing.

Since the last half of the twentieth century, there has been a growing philosophical critique of mentalism and realism. Those, such as Rorty, associated with this general critique do not, any more than those who have propagated the mind-first attitude and realism, speak with exactly the same philosophical voice, but they are in accord as far as calling into question some of the basic premises of mentalism and realism and offering an alternative vision, which, in effect, constitutes an important challenge to the assumptions behind much of the contemporary theory and practice of political inquiry. It is difficult to pinpoint the beginning of this basic challenge, but there is good reason to suggest that in an important respect its lineage began with Wittgenstein's later philosophy. In chapter 4, I will recapitulate my earlier (2014b) textual interpretation of Wittgenstein's critique of mentalism, but much of my focus in chapters 4 and 5 will be on the work of philosophers such as Ryle, Austin, Sellars, Hilary Putnam, Davidson, John McDowell, and Daniel Dennett. Their arguments are by no means unproblematic, but, in various ways, they reinforce Wittgenstein's critique of mentalism and realism. Once we disabuse ourselves of mentalism and traditional realism, we are left with the truth of conventional realism.

If the typical distinction between natural and conventional cannot be sustained, it is, however, difficult to avoid the question of how to demarcate natural and social science. There have been many answers to the demarcation question, but I suggest that the *difference does not reside in a basic dichotomy between what is natural and conventional but, instead, in the content of the respective concepts, the relational and interpretive character of social inquiry, and the difference between first- and second-order practices.* What I have said at this point suggests another basic difference between natural and social inquiry. While there is actually no such thing as a universal theory of natural objects, there is a need for a universal theory of conventional objects.

In 1927, Arthur Eddington, a well-known astrophysicist, gave the Gifford Lectures at the University of Edinburgh, which would be published the following year as *The Nature of the Physical World.* He began by saying that he had drawn up his "chairs to my two tables" to write about how "scientific developments provide new material for the philosopher." He wished to demonstrate why "we must bid good-bye to" the first table, that "strange compound of external nature, mental imagery and inherited prejudice—which lies visible to my eyes and tangible to my grasp" as a "commonplace object of that environment which I call the world." He claimed that "modern physics has by delicate test and remorseless logic assured me that," despite the fact that "modern physics will never succeed in exorcising that first table," "my second scientific table," the one composed of invisible particles, "is the only one which is really there" as part of a "wholly external world" (1928, ix).

Eddington's mistake was to assume that the fundamental elements of matter are in effect a theory of everything and provide the criteria for specifying and judging what is real. There was, in fact, no *second* table in the world of particle physics. There was only the "commonplace" table that belonged to the reality presented in the commonplace first-order conception of the world. But it is difficult to exorcize the myth that behind all claims about what is real, there is a universal reality of which all reality claims ultimately partake and in terms of which they can be assessed. Despite Eddington's apparent material reductionist position, he also defended what might seem to be the contradictory idealist assumption that what we speak of as the objective world is ultimately, in his words, "mind-stuff" and that our only access to that world is what is reflected in our consciousness. And although he is credited with providing one of the confirmations of Einstein's general theory of relativity, he was also, as opposed to Einstein, a defender of Heisenberg's uncertainly principle in quantum mechanics and the claim that there is a basic indeterminism in nature. So in Eddington's work we can see the persistent dilemmas and melding of mentalism and realism that have characterized representational philosophy.

Despite the occasional search in natural science for what the cosmologist Stephen Hawking spoke of as a "theory of everything," even he finally concluded that there is no such theory. Those who seek something such as the "god particle" are, in the first place, not really positing *theories* of everything, that is, theories that encompass biology, chemistry, and so on, but rather an ultimate *ground* of everything. But this is neither a substitute for, nor an explanation of, the theory of evolution, the theory of tectonic plates, the theory of DNA, and so on. The theories of natural science are constitutive of various particular domains of natural phenomena, which together compose the abstraction that we speak of as the natural "world." Here the parable of the blind men and the elephant does not apply, because in that case the men were providing representations of or perspectives on what we know in advance was an elephant, while in the case of the common use of "world," we cannot point to a specifiable object that underlies all scientific theories. There is no general scientific theory of what we often speak of as natural objects, but for interpretive inquiry, *there must be a general theory of social objects that informs second-order practices.* In the case of social science, as well as in the study of something such as the history of natural science, there is a need to confront the "nature" of these discursive objects and what is involved in interpreting and representing them. In second-order investigations, there must be something, whether assumed or explicitly stated, comparable to a theory of everything, a general ontology of the kind of objects that underlie the singularity and historicity of various forms of social life, whether it is science, politics, or some other part of the social sphere. This is a theory of conventionality, but an account of such a theory has been inhibited by the dominance of mentalism and realism.

Although, as I have already noted, it will surely seem to some readers that I am subscribing to a form of linguistic idealism and claiming that nothing is real except conventions, what I am actually saying is that it is in the conventions of first-order discourses that the criteria of what is real reside. I am not saying *only* first-order practices, because, as I have already stressed, social inquiry must, either explicitly or implicitly incorporate a theory or ontology of the phenomena it studies even if it is at odds with that of its subject matter. Just as Wittgenstein emphasized that it is not possible get outside language, we can paraphrase Martin Heidegger and say that conventions are the house of reality.

What I am arguing should also not be confused with the claims and implications often associated with postmodernism, poststructuralism, and deconstructionism, which suggest that the meaning of social phenomena is a function of how they are interpreted. There was a correct intuition in this position, that is, that we cannot get outside language and that it is conventions all the way down, but it is not interpretation all the way down. Interpretation comes up abruptly against what is interpreted. An interpretation is, in effect, an argument and therefore always contestable and a view from somewhere, but interpretations presuppose the priority and autonomy of what is interpreted. For example, an interpretation of the history of a practice does not become that history any more than depictions of an object replace the object. Variations on the kind of argument that I speak of as *interpretism* are as problematic as mentalism and realism. They belie the relational dimension of social inquiry and displace meaning from its location in speech and action. In social theory, claims about interpretation as the source of meaning are also another manifestation of the propensity to seek an authoritative basis of both epistemic and practical privilege and to assume that meaning ultimately belongs to judgments external to the object that is interpreted.

Semiotics, according to Saussure, was, supposedly, the study of representation and of how signs or signifiers stand for something that is signified. A problem with Saussure's work, however, was that it still reflected the persistent mentalist implication that what we directly know are only our own ideas or sense impressions. He claimed that while the signifier was part of a socially constructed system of signs, the signified was not an external object but a concept, which he construed as a mental entity. This position revealed the idealist implication of empiricism, which is still manifest in poststructural and postmodernist claims about how everything is already interpretation. The argument implies a certain kind of identity between an interpretation and what is interpreted. It is claimed that such identity is apparent in such things as empty and floating signifiers and about how certain signifiers lose their criteria of reference. But the fact is that if something like this takes place, the signifiers lose their role as signifiers rather than embodying something signified. They in effect become pseudo-presentations masquerading as representations. It is not, however, easy for second-order inquiry to find an adequate language of interpretation and representation. Because there is no necessary logical relationship between a representation and what is represented, there is the constant danger of reifying the language of representation. The basic problem was articulated by René Magritte when he said of his picture, "this is not a pipe" (whether he was referring to the image in the painting, the painting itself, the sentence "Ceci n'est pas une pipe," the word "this," etc.).

I am also wary about associating my arguments with those who speak of conventional phenomena as "socially constructed" and with political scientists who refer to themselves as "constructivists." There are definite problems with the phrase "socially constructed." It seems to imply that there are things that are somehow simply given and that conventions are constructed of something that is not conventional. Wittgenstein sometimes spoke of conventions as arbitrary, but he only meant that they rest on agreement within a form of life and particular language-games, which can and do change. Constructivism and other varieties of what is often referred to as an interpretive approach to social inquiry are largely a reaction against various forms of positivist and naturalistic explanation. Constructivism stresses the role of values and institutions, but it has remained a theoretically porous position, and it draws broadly, but often strategically, on a variety of philosophical claims, which are not always compatible. And, like most of the history of political inquiry, it continues to remain under the shadow of mentalism and realism. There are things that we might classify as linguistic constructions, such as what I refer to in the next chapter as categorical and analytical concepts, which are constructed out of concepts that refer to particular things that have been theoretically presented in the concepts of first-order discourses.

It is important to situate the basic problems I have discussed in concrete past and contemporary dimensions of political inquiry. From its inception, political science has, from various philosophical standpoints, consistently searched for political explanation and meaning outside what is said and done in politics. The search has always been for something behind politics and located either in the mind or in some deeper form of reality. But in each case, this has been part of the constant pursuit of a definitive basis of judgment that exceeds the criteria belonging to its subject matter. Consequently, I begin with a brief and very selective overview of the history of American political science, which I have discussed more fully elsewhere (e.g., 1993, 2004).

Realism and Mentalism in the History of Political Science

The assumption of a gap between the "mind" and language and between language and "reality" has, from the *Federalist Papers* to the present, been endemic to American images of a "science of politics." In *Federalist* 37, James Madison noted a dilemma that reflected the paradoxes of what amounted to his Cartesian/Lockean empiricist image of the relationship between mind, language, and world. He stated that a limitation of what he viewed as the wisdom behind the applied "science of politics" that informed the formulation of the proposed Constitution was that in addition to

> obscurity arising from the complexity of objects, and the imperfection of the human faculties, the medium through which the conceptions of men are conveyed to each other adds a fresh embarrassment. The use of words is to

> express ideas. Perspicuity therefore requires, not only that the ideas should be distinctly formed, but that they should be expressed by words distinctly and exclusively appropriated to them. But no language is so copious as to supply words and phrases for every complex idea, or so correct as not to include many, equivocally denoting different ideas. Hence it must happen, that however accurately objects may be discriminated in themselves, and however accurately the discrimination may be conceived, the definition of them may be rendered inaccurate, by the inaccuracy of the terms in which it is delivered. And this unavoidable inaccuracy must be greater or less, according to the complexity and novelty of the objects defined. When the Almighty himself condescends to address mankind in their own language, his meaning, luminous as it must be, is rendered dim and doubtful, by the cloudy medium through which it is communicated.

This was a classic restatement of the dilemmas conjured up by seventeenth-century mentalism and realism and the assumption that in some mysterious manner the mind is influenced by an unknowable reality and that ideas are the residual representations lodged in the mind, expressed in language, and thereby communicated, but often poorly, among people. It was these amorphous philosophical connections between reality, mind, and language that opened up grounds of skepticism and at the same time propelled the continuing search for certainty, which has marked the history of political inquiry.

At the core of the defense of the proposed Constitution was the issue of what the founders spoke of as "political reality." The *Federalist Papers* had retained the rhetoric of traditional republicanism, which included the assumption that behind the observable facts of political life there was the deeper reality of an intentional invisible virtuous community of the "people" functioning in a sovereign capacity. The authors argued that the Constitution was the product of this "great body of the American people," which had been obscured by the image of state sovereignty that had informed the *Articles.* But now the new national government would be the representative of this latent "united people," which through its voice of "public opinion," both limit and enable government action. They described the visible surface reality of political life, however, as lacking any underlying sense of unity and as consisting of not only somewhat institutionally autonomous States but, socially, of an infinite plurality of contentious factions and self-interested individuals whose passions threatened not only political cohesion but harbored the danger of the rise of a populist majority tyranny. The tension between these two images of political reality persisted throughout American history, and the mythology of a hidden actual reality behind the virtual reality of political practice would remain a consistent part of the American tradition of the study of politics.

Alexis de Tocqueville confronted the same problems that were noted in the *Federalist.* He worried about how such an apparently pluralistic society could both sustain what he assumed to be the necessity of a general democratic community and yet avoid the danger of a tyranny of a self-interested majority. He nevertheless persisted in believing that despite the diversity of American society there was at least an underlying mental world of "public opinion" that emanated from a people with shared principles and that constituted a sovereign power with moral authority. He suggested that even if it turned out that such opinion was what he referred to as an "empty phantom," an image of its presence would at least have a constraining effect. The task of giving theoretical substance to claims about the existence of an American people and a public mind fell, however, to those who created the discipline of American political science. But the problem of finding a unity beneath the diversity remained.

What became the subject of nineteenth-century political science was a concept designated as the "*State*," but this was not the concept by the same name that heretofore had been part of the currency of European and American political discourse. It was an image drawn from the literature of German idealism by the émigré Francis Lieber, who can reasonably be called the "founder" of the discipline of American political science. The basic concept of the State that Lieber adapted to the American context was embraced by other academicians and, by the point of the Civil War, accepted by a wide range of public intellectuals and political actors. At the core of this argument, which would transcend American ideological differences, was the claim that the State was not the government but an invisible organic "aboriginal" community grounded in the mind of the people. It constituted, in Lieber's words, a "*res communis,*" "*res publica,*" and "*res populi,*" which had created and authorized the Constitution, functioned as a limit on the institutions of government, and gave meaning to the concept of popular sovereignty. Although, like Tocqueville, he recognized and applauded the plurality of association in the United States, he maintained that behind it American citizens composed an "organism," which through its expression of "public opinion" represented the will of a "community" and functioned in a sovereign manner.

Lieber was quite conscious of the fact that he was grafting a construction of German philosophy onto an indigenous, and largely English, tradition of philosophy and politics. He claimed, however, that in the United States an ideal metaphysical reality had finally become empirically real. A number of those who followed Lieber continued to adapt German philosophy to the American academy. Most prominent among these scholars was John W. Burgess who succeeded Lieber at what became Columbia University and who, along with Herbert Baxter Adams at The Johns Hopkins University, created the core structures of the discipline of American political science and political theory. Burgess continued to predicate political science, and the study of what by then had become valorized as the theory and practice of American "democracy," on a study of the State as the ultimate tangible historical manifestation of "the political idea." He accentuated still further the distinction between the government and the State, and argued that the Idea of the State found full expression in the Hegelian "march of reason" and its "advance toward its own perfection," which, despite its "Aryan" origins, had finally become manifest in American history.

By the later part of the century, the conditions and events of American politics had made this vision of political reality and the political mind difficult to sustain. Woodrow Wilson and other founders (in 1903) of the progressively oriented American Political Science Association followed their conservative forebears in defending the existence and power of the national state, but the State was now fast becoming equated with the government, and the "mind" behind politics would become increasingly internalized in the psychology of political actors. Wilson argued that the time had come to turn away from theoretical abstractions and to study the "actual practices" of politics and government, and he claimed that the image of "the sovereign mind" that had animated the theory of the State was nowhere to be found. His influential book *The State* (1889) was actually about government, and the "people," as formerly conceived, largely disappeared from his analysis.

The English scholar James Bryce was one of the first to take on the task of empirically studying particular aspects of American politics and institutions, but he continued to perpetuate the remnants of the assumption that American democracy rested on the reality of a general "mind or consciousness" expressed in "public opinion." But both theoretically and practically, the belief was becoming increasingly threadbare. The language of traditional State theory persisted, such as in the work of W. W. Willoughby, another founder of the APSA, but in his work the theory increasingly deconstructed itself and ended in arguments that in effect endorsed the assumption that "state" was simply another word for government. This occasioned a crisis in democratic theory and the rise of a new vision of democracy, but it was one in which the dialectic of realism and mentalism persisted.

By the beginning of the twentieth century, the real was no longer the ideal, and the effort now became one of finding an ideal in the real. Increasingly what came to be understood as the facts of politics was what Arthur Bentley in the *Process of Government* (1908) described as the behavior of interest "groups" and the "forces" arising from group interaction. This was the "raw material of politics," which Charles Beard claimed was even behind the framing of the Constitution. For Bentley, and many others, the "state" now explicitly referred to nothing but the government, which served as an instrument for helping to achieve an "adjustment" among group interests and maintaining a social "equilibrium." It was not only the concept of a sovereign people that was deemed mythical but also the concept of sovereignty itself, including popular sovereignty, along with other elements of what Bentley referred to as nineteenth-century "soulstuff." But a new soulstuff was emerging in this talk of interest and other psychological factors.

Explaining the facts of group politics drew political scientists not only methodologically to the fields of sociology and economics in search of what was perceived as a more truly scientific basis of inquiry but to psychology and an account of the mind as the font of political action. What was behind the observable facts of politics was believed to be unobservable mental states. It was these subjective factors that were the focus of Charles Merriam, and his student Harold Lasswell, who contributed to a refounding of the discipline and set the stage on which what was claimed to be the "scientific" study of politics in the United States would be played during the rest of the century. As one prominent political scientist asked in 1923, "So, then, if political science is not psychology, what is it?"

Walter Lippmann was one of most adamant in challenging the claim that there was a public opinion of the kind previously conceived, and by the mid-1920s, what came to be called the "democratic dogma," which had been based on what he spoke of as a "phantom public," was severely eroded. Lippmann maintained that politics was based on diverse and ultimately unfathomable individual motives, but he claimed that it was nevertheless possible to discern the potential for a realizable "ideal" even if it was not the "unattainable" mythical ideal of the "public interest." What Lippmann imagined, and imaged, was a society characterized by what he referred to as a "deep pluralism" in which there was no "organic unity or purpose," but he believed that the actions of individuals, with the aid of government control and education, constituted an underlying self-sustaining and self-correcting system.

In his early work, John Dewey, who despite his Progressive politics and pragmatist philosophy had remained influenced by German philosophy, continued, as in the case of his *The Public and Its Problems* (1927), to defend the idea of a public or people behind government. He argued that what had actually happened was that there had once been a real public that had existed behind the observable facts of political life but that, in the modern era, had been "eclipsed." Like Lippmann, Merriam, and others, he claimed that the task was a creative restoration of that public through education informed by science, and particularly the science of politics, and this was largely the same kind of nostalgia evident in the work of conservatives such as William Yandell Elliott. By the early 1930s, however, this vision had run its course, and the theory of pluralist democracy as the reality of political life was increasingly formalized. This theory was at the heart of what came to be understood, beginning in the 1930s, as America's basic political identity—liberalism. The behavioral era in political science, beginning in the 1950s, is often defined methodologically in terms of a commitment to emulate the natural sciences, but it was to a large extent in the service of the theory of pluralist democracy as re-articulated shortly before World War II by individuals such as Pendleton Herring and in the postwar period in the extensive work of Charles Lindblom and Robert Dahl. It was predicated on what Bernard Berelson referred to as an invisible "system" that, as the historian Daniel Boorstin suggested, constituted the inherent "genius" of American politics hidden beneath the surface of what often seemed to be a chaotic striving for group interests. The postwar resurrection of this image was, however, largely a response to a new wave of criticism directed at both social pluralism and science.

By the 1930s and in the wake of Hitler's ascendancy in Germany, a large, and both ideologically and philosophically diverse, number of émigré scholars joined American faculties of political science. The subfield of political theory was the most profoundly affected and in a manner that set the field against what had become mainstream political science and both its scientific and historical self-images. These critics ranged from conservatives, such as Leo Strauss, to members of the neo-Marxist Frankfurt School, and others, such as Hannah Arendt, who were less easy to characterize ideologically. What most had in common, however, was that in many ways they resurrected, complemented, and perpetuated the mentalism and realism that was already indigenous.

The study of political theory, as part of the political science curriculum, had emerged as a history of political "ideas." From the earliest examples, such as in the work of William Archibald Dunning, to George Sabine's paradigmatic text published 1937, political theory was largely the study of the history of political "thought," which was supposedly manifest in writings of the canonical theorists and which was considered to be what animated politics. This was, however, congruent with the rest of political science and its search for the ideas that explained political life. Political reality was still conceived underneath as basically ideational, and both historians of political theory and political scientists identified their business as basically one of accessing those ideas. This basic perspective was reinforced in the last half of the twentieth century by the new wave of European philosophy, but this philosophy was inimical to what had become the American science of politics.

Politics was still conceived as essentially an emanation of a world of ideas, but while the history of political theory had been understood as largely a history of progress both in the science of politics and in the evolution of liberal democracy, that history was presented by this new literature as a tale of declination marked by the demise of any fundamental ground of reality on which political judgment could be based. The image of science behind the American claim to a science of politics had, however, from the beginning been notoriously vague and consisted of little more than a collage of arguments extracted from early positivism, pragmatism, and methods of quantification typical of natural science. Although there were sporadic attempts to apply specific theories of natural science, ranging from physics to Darwinism, to the study of politics, scientific naturalism was basically a vague methodological ethic. In seeking a new defense of science, political scientists increasingly turned to another group of émigré scholars who paralleled the arrival of the political theorists.

The remnants of the Vienna Circle and the schools of logical positivism and logical empiricism were transplanted to the United States and became the basis of the emerging field of the philosophy of science in American universities. The work of Carl Hempel and others, as well as a large secondary literature retailing their arguments, gave new life to a defense and deployment of a scientific approach to the study of politics. But it was one in which reality was conceived as consisting of observable facts, while scientific theories were conceived as mental constructs for organizing and generalizing about those facts. Similarly, what political scientists equated with "theories" were what they referred to as "conceptual frameworks."

By the 1960s, it might be fair to say that the central debate in political science was between reprises of European prototypes in which forms of mentalism and realism persisted. Despite the growing distance between political "science" and political "theory" after midcentury, as well as the diversity within each camp, they in many ways remained epistemologically united. While the mentalism inherent in empiricist factual realism was at the core of behavioral political science, the critics of science focused on ideas and ideology as proximate causes of behavior. And just as the study of the history of political theory continued to be devoted to the task of recovering the thought and ideas behind the classic texts, mainstream empirical political science persisted in seeking the mind behind politics.

In the following chapters, I will be examining more fully particular examples of mentalism and realism in contemporary political studies, but the emphasis will be on a critique of, and alternative to, the vestiges of these philosophical persuasions, which have for so long dominated the assumptions embraced by students of politics. My argument is that both political reality and the political mind are located in, rather than outside, the conventions that constitute political phenomena. I will clarify and challenge the dominant philosophies that characterize the study of politics and focus on presenting an alternative theoretical formulation. The next chapter explores the general character of the mind-first attitude in political studies, which is nowhere more prominent than in the treatment of concepts.

2

Mentalism and the Problem of Concepts

The word "concept" is by far too vague.
WITTGENSTEIN

When Woody Allen, in the film *Annie Hall*, said "Right now it's only a notion, but I think I can get money to make it into a concept . . . and later turn it into an idea," we probably caught the sense of what he was saying, but it also demonstrates just how elusive and variable the meaning of these terms may be. And it also should raise suspicion about whether, despite the many uses of such words, they inherently refer to any particular thing at all. And this ambiguity extends to both philosophy and the social sciences. *Political Concepts: A Critical Lexicon* is a recent multidisciplinary web-based journal sponsored by several major United States universities. It is devoted to entries focusing on "a single concept with the express intention of resituating it in the field of political discourse by addressing what has remained unquestioned or untaught in that concept." The journal, however, explicitly states that it "does not predetermine what does or does not count as a political concept" (http://www.politicalconcepts.org). This is only one example of the general failure to engage thoroughly the issue of the nature of concepts and of the circumvention of the issue of what is distinctive about political concepts. If one asks a student or even a professional political scientist what they are talking about when they so frequently talk about concepts, there is likely to be at best a very equivocal answer or a response similar to that of US Supreme Court Justice Potter Stewart when faced with attempting to define "hard-core pornography." The problem of achieving clarity about concepts is not only evident in the discipline of political science and the subfield of political theory but in the social sciences as a whole, and philosophy has not done much better.

While there are few words in the vocabularies of social theory and social science that appear more frequently than "concept," there are also few words that are more amorphously, elliptically, diversely, and unreflectively used.

The ontology of concepts, that is, what kinds of things they are, has been hotly debated among some philosophers, but there remains little consensus about the use of the word "concept." What tends to predominate, however, and what has been passed on to social scientists by philosophers as well as by our everyday manner of speaking, is the image of concepts as mental objects, which are expressed in language and action. This image and its implications deserve careful scrutiny.

The Mind-First Attitude

There is little need, and it is not my purpose, to document in detail the pervasive hold of this mind-first attitude on various forms of political inquiry, but it ultimately results in the view that such inquiry is largely a form of clairvoyance. Historians of political theory, as philosophically and methodologically diverse in some ways as Leo Strauss and Quentin Skinner, remained captured by the assumption that their subject matter is basically a history of *thought*, and they have been committed to recovering what they conceive as the *ideas* behind the texts of the classic canon as well as the ideas that have animated politics. Language is treated as a path to and from the mind. Strauss attempted, by a careful scrutiny of a text, to decipher the "intention," "purpose," and real meaning of an author such as Machiavelli. This approach was, however, actually designed to rhetorically convince a reader of the credibility of Strauss's story of the history of political philosophy.

Despite Skinner's formidable challenge to certain aspects of Strauss's work, and to the traditional study of the history of political theory as a whole, he remained indebted to the idealist premises of R. G. Collingwood. Although he attempted to enlist philosophical support from the work of individuals such as Wittgenstein and Austin, who were actually dissenters from the mind-first premise, Skinner claimed that the task of the historian is to recover, by a detailed examination of the historical context of political language, what he referred to as, the "mentalities," that is, the "writer's mental world" of concepts, thinking, intentions, motives, beliefs, and ideologies expressed in texts and political life (e.g., 1972, 1978; for a more detailed discussion of Strauss and Skinner, see Gunnell 1979, 1998).

Mentalism characterizes what political theorists have embraced as what they conceive as more interpretive and qualitative modes of inquiry, and although there continues to be a significant estrangement of political theory from empirical political science, they share both a common history and the same basic view about the relationship between thought and language. Both camps tend to accept the same underlying epistemological assumptions, that is, that the task of inquiry is, as defended by the literary critic E. D. Hirsch Jr., to recover from objectified "intentional acts" an "original meaning" located in the "contents of mind" (1976, 79–80). One might argue, in retrospect, that behavioral political scientists were on the right track when they focused on what political actors said and did, but this work still remained deeply committed to the mind-first perspective. Most political scientists assume that terms such as "ideology," "beliefs," "attitudes," "preferences," and other constituents of our mental vocabulary refer to mental states, which are not directly known, but can be detected in, and inferred from, behavioral and linguistic manifestations and in that manner at least operationally defined. Behavioral political scientists did not reject the assumption that mental states were the cause of speech and action but only assumed that those states could not be directly empirically accessed.

One of the places in which the image of concepts as mental phenomena remains supported in philosophy are varieties of what is commonly referred to as the representational theory of the mind (RTM) and its basic image of the relationship between language and thought. The core of this dualistic image is the assumption that thought is ontologically autonomous and prior to language. Although the origins of this theory are often attributed to the work of Plato and Aristotle, it was formalized by Descartes and John Locke, passed on in the nineteenth century to both empiricism and idealism, and has remained influential. Although Locke, who is often deemed the classic empiricist, maintained that what he referred to as simple "ideas" originated from experiencing the external world, he argued that all we actually directly know are these ideas, which gain identity and meaning as representations in the "mind" and which are then expressed in language and social behavior. Bishop Berkeley, however, simply drew the logical conclusion that was immanent in empiricism, that is, that the experienced world really consists of ideas. Kant tempered Berkeley's radical idealism by positing an invisible noumenal reality that was reflected in phenomenal experience, but he claimed that such experience ultimately gained meaning by the imposition of innate categories of the mind. Locke and Hume's associational psychology was expanded and formalized in James Mill's *Analysis of the Phenomena of the Human Mind* and nicely summed up:

> We have now seen that, in what we call the mental world, Consciousness, there are three grand classes of phenomena, the most familiar of all the facts with which we are acquainted,—SENSATIONS, IDEAS, and the TRAIN OF IDEAS. We have examined a number of the more complicated cases of Consciousness; and have found that they all resolve themselves into the three simple elements, thus enumerated. We also found it necessary to shew, for what

> ends, and in what manner, marks were contrived of sensations and ideas, and by what combinations they were made to represent, expeditiously, trains of those states of consciousness. (1)

As much as Marx may have ostensibly rebelled against Hegel and German idealism, and insisted that ideas were reflections of material conditions, he not only remained as vague as Locke about exactly how experience of the material world was translated into ideas but claimed that ideology was the immediate explanation of human action and historical change. He remained as much a mentalist as a materialist. In contemporary philosophy, variations on this basic picture of the relationship between thought and language/action are reflected in H. P. Grice's influential intention-based semantics and account of the primacy of "non-natural" or psychological meaning; John Searle's argument that although the mind is an emergent property of the brain, it is autonomous and that the intentionality of language is a secondary manifestation of the mind's "original" mental intentionality; Noam Chomsky's Cartesian linguistics, which claims that humans are endowed with an abstract mental super-grammar containing a basic syntactic and semantic structure, which underlies, and allows the acquisition of, a natural language; and related arguments such as those of Jerry Fodor (1975) and Steven Pinker (2007) who claim that there is a primal innate and universal language of thought that they refer to as "mentalese," which is a semantic system composed of mental representations and which assumes there can be thought without language, even though thought is typically translated into a natural language. There is considerable variation among those who subscribe to some version of RTM, but Fodor may be the most vigorous defender of the position that it is the "right theory of mental states" and that concepts are the "constituents of mental states." Although he recognizes that RTM is not "canonical" and believes that some theories of concepts in cognitive science do not "fill the bill," he argues that all versions of RTM include the claims that psychological experience is nomic and intentional in that it is directed toward objects, that mental representations are bearers of intentional content, that thinking is computational and informational and takes place "in the head" (1998, 23). He views concepts as "atomistic" mental particulars, many of which are learned and public in character, and function as causes and effects of human behavior. This formulation epitomizes the philosophical dimension of the mind-first attitude.

The term "concept" first appeared in the mid-sixteenth century, and, from the beginning, it has been prominently identified with mental phenomena. Although Locke did not actually use the word, he spoke about the clear and distinctive perception of an idea as an "appearance or conception in the mind," which could then be mentally manipulated, made more complex, and expressed in language. Standard dictionaries continue to define a concept as a "thought," "something conceived in the mind," "a notion," or an "abstract or generic idea." But what constitutes a mind, a thought, or an idea, let alone a notion, is even more difficult to specify than the meaning of "concept." We do not have much difficulty identifying what kind of things words are, because they are physical signs and elements of language, which are used in various ways to say and do certain things. Although it is generally agreed that in some manner concepts are elements of thought, there have been various views about exactly how they relate to language. Although the influential philosopher Gottlob Frege (1848–1925), who was one of the founders of modern logic, did not claim that concepts are actually psychological states, he defined them as abstract objects of thought, which he referred to as "senses" that mediate between language and the specific objects to which language is applied. For example, claims about Venus and the evening star would respectively have different senses or meanings but denote or refer to the same thing.

Despite the persistence of variations of the mind-first attitude, it has, as I will demonstrate in chapters 4 and 5, been challenged in significant elements of twentieth-century philosophy, and this challenge has important implications for how we should approach the study of concepts. It may, however, be instructive to note that the word "concept" originally derived from the Latin noun "*conceptus*," which meant, literally, a thing conceived, such as an embryo, and, as opposed to the ideational aura that has often come to be associated with the German word *Begriff* and the typical English use of "concept," it implied something observable. We might say, then, that before its idealization, "concept" basically referred to objects—but not mental objects.

Although in the *Investigations*, Wittgenstein never explicitly disambiguated the meaning of "concept," he had once in the *Tractatus*, and occasionally in later remarks, employed the term "concept-word" (*Begriffswort*), which was largely identical to what he would subsequently simply refer to as a "concept." This indicated that *when we talk about concepts, we are talking about a certain kind of word usage*. Ryle pointedly claimed that concepts are not in themselves specific things and that it is "not true that in any natural sense 'there are concepts'" (1931, 140), and Austin maintained that they are not, any more than ideas, universals and "palpable objects" that are part of the "furniture of the mind" and that one can acquire or possess (1961, ch. 1). As long as the mind-first perspective dominated and the general assumption was that concepts were mental things expressed in words, the relationship between words and concepts seemed unproblematic. But after the challenge to the mind-first perspective, the question of this relationship, and the nature of concepts, has been left hanging.

My answer to this question is that "concept" refers to a class of words that are used either to denote particular things or kinds of things, whatever the ontological status of those things may be: observables (such as physical objects); human norms; theoretically posited entities (e.g., dark energy); fictional, imaginary, or virtual things and creatures, and so on. Although we often use an individual word to name a concept, "word" is not merely a synonym for "concept." Many words are not concept-words, more than one word can refer to the same thing, and different things may be referred to by the same word. When Wittgenstein said in *On Certainty* that if people did not understand a "concept," he could teach them to use the "words," he was indicating that although words and concepts are not the same, they are related, because "when language games change, then there is a change in concepts, and with the concepts the meaning of words change" (1969, 65). To say that people possess and deploy concepts, primarily means that they have the ability to use a concept-word intelligibly.

Political Science and the Treatment of Concepts

Political scientists and political theorists often find themselves all tangled up in their discussion of concepts and the use of words such as "power," "state," "equality," and "justice." Some of the confusion is the consequence of not distinguishing between concept-words that refer to specific things and those that refer to kinds or categories of things, but what often creeps into discussions of concepts is a tendency to reify general terms and assume an idealist image of concepts as super-things or abstract mental objects, which have particular empirical manifestations. A word such as "equality," for example, is a general term that has gained its meaning from positing similarities among particular things, but the instances are not tokens of some transcendent form of equality. Confusion also sometimes arises from not distinguishing between words and the things to which they may refer. Many books are written about the history of a particular concept, such as, for example, the state or liberalism, when what such a book is often really about is a history of the word "state" or "liberalism" and the different, and sometimes incommensurable, things or concepts to which the word has been applied.

When social theorists analyze a concept such as representation or power, they often approach it as if they were talking about a particular, but abstract and often mental, complex object, composed of various aspects that can be viewed and defined from various perspectives. They suggest that if all aspects of this object are accounted for, we can gain a complete account of the concept. In her influential book on the concept of representation, Hanna Pitkin treated representation in this manner, but, in a later edition, she stated, in a footnote, that after reading Wittgenstein she had come to realize that her analysis was in some respects "profoundly misleading about concepts and language" (1972a, 255). Although she neither revised her account nor specified why it was so misleading, it was misleading because there actually is no such thing as "*the*" concept of representation that lies behind various uses of the word. Steven Lukes (1974), among others, has talked about the different "faces" of power, as if power were a distinct object, which could be described in various terms depending on one's perspective. "Power," however, like "representation," is a word used to refer to a variety of things that are often viewed in some manner as similar. Such categorical similarity is not usually determined by positing the existence of an underlying theoretical sameness between components of the category but by what an observer might, on the basis of some criteria, construe as what Wittgenstein referred to as "family resemblances."

While some theorists, such as Pitkin and Lukes, assume that the problem of understanding concepts resides in their complex and abstract nature, an equally common but related, and probably even more pervasive, mistake has been to claim that the problem is somehow located in the very nature of concepts, or at least certain concepts. The argument is that concepts such as representation, democracy, or power are difficult to deal with because their meaning is in some way necessarily inconclusive or indeterminate. It is argued that this is especially a problem with normative concepts such as justice. The classic statement of this position was the essay by the philosopher W. B. Gallie (1956) on "essentially contested concepts," which has been a continuing source of both hope and confusion among political theorists and political scientists. I say "hope" because it seems for many, from James Madison on, to explain the complexity and diversity of political life as well as difficulties in the study of politics.

Gallie claimed to be isolating certain concepts, such as democracy, which, he argued, have a number of distinctive intrinsic attributes (such as the character of being evaluative, internally complex, and capable of different descriptions) and which together *necessarily* give rise to disputes about their genuine meaning when, in fact, the very nature of such concepts prevents any determination of uncontested meaning. One central problem with Gallie's argument was that he tended to use "word" and "concept" interchangeably, but, on the whole, he actually seemed to be talking about words and simply noting that because certain words can, and have been, conventionally used in many ways, it is often difficult to agree on how to narrow the usage. But he nevertheless concluded that concepts such as democracy are somehow inherently contestable and ambiguous, no matter how one may choose to use them or how they function in various discursive practices.

For many political theorists, Gallie's argument was, for a number of reasons, appealing. It seemed to provide insight into the conflictual character of politics and political discourse as well as the multiple perspectives that often inform social scientific discourse about politics. It appeared particularly useful to those who rejected quantitative behavioral methods and insisted that political inquiry is an interpretive endeavor and who were wary of the attempts of some social scientists to construct the kind of precise definitions that seemed to characterize the natural sciences. Gallie's formulation has explicitly found its way into many discussions of political and legal analysis (e.g., Freeden 2008; Collier, Hidalgo, and Maciuceanu 2006; Mason 1990; Grafstein 1988; Koselleck 2002; Swanton 1985; Lukes 1974; Rawls 1971; Dworkin 1972).

An early major proponent of this position was Alasdair MacIntyre (1973) who argued that a basic difference between natural science and social science is the "open texture" of the concepts both employed and studied by social scientists, which entails an "essential incompleteness" and "essential contestability" that cannot be solved by definitions and other such strategies. What many political theorists, such as William Connolly (1993) took from Gallie was not only what they saw as an explanation of the peculiarities of the "terms of political discourse," which made political inquiry so different from the methodology of natural science, but a justification for what they defended as the inherently pluralistic character of politics. The response to the kind of argument that Gallie advanced was often, as in the case of individuals such as Giovanni Satori (1984) as well as Theodore Lowi and Mario Calise (2011), to call for a yet greater reduction in terminological fluidity and debate; conduct an inventory of social scientific concepts; settle on more precise meanings of words applied to concepts; sort out the elements of various concepts; and prescribe a variety of formal concepts for organizing empirical research. Some, however, such as Jeremy Waldron, have defended and accentuated Gallie's basic claim and argued that in discussions of law, many references to Gallie's argument have tended to neglect his radical point about the necessary indeterminacy of certain concepts and mistakenly to understand him as making the weaker claim that the use of some concepts are often disputed and not well defined (2002). It is, however, just as questionable to assume that strict word usage is the answer to agreement in politics and political inquiry as it is to assume that the nature of certain concepts is the explanation for disagreement in such matters.

The recent infatuation with applying research in cognitive science to the study of politics is an example of the perennial search for a biological or physiological foundation for social scientific inquiry, and this has influenced the treatment of concepts. George Lakoff's work in cognitive linguistics focused on how rhetoric, persuasion, and emotion function in political discourse, but this work constitutes yet another version of RTM. Building on the assumption that concepts are basically categories, he attempted to explain them as prototypical models located in the brain. He argued that experimental evidence indicated that a "concept is instantiated in the synapses of the brain" and arises from an interaction between the mind / brain and world (2008, 40). The general argument that the synapses of the brain underlie our capacity to use language, or in Lakoff's words "no brain, no concepts," is credible, but, absent the brain, we would be without many things. And although it might be reasonable to suggest that there is an interaction between the brain and the world, he, no more than Locke, explained how this gives rise to concepts. The notion that there are concepts *in* the synapses of the brain is not experimentally demonstrable, and what Lakoff actually tended to discuss was how contestation arises from the manner in which people inevitably use various "frames" for cognitive mapping, which involves "clusters" of idealized "metaphors" peculiar to various cultural settings and from which spring a series of "radial categories." He argued that a contested concept such as democracy is such a radial category and that it is open to contention, because it may be either oversimplified or in competition with other members of a cluster. This was, however, little more than a complicated way of saying something with which hardly anyone would disagree, and it did not depend on a study of the anatomy of the brain.

There is simply no such thing as an *essentially* contested or indeterminate concept, and even if Gallie had actually been referring to words, he would have been incorrect in claiming that the meaning of some words is essentially contested. The proper use of many words may, or may not, be contested, but this does not provide an answer to the question of concepts. What is involved in most disputes about, for example, democracy is disagreement about the state of affairs to which the word "democracy" should refer. Debates about democracy do not, for the most part, emanate from the nature of a word, even though there are instances in which a failure to distinguish between the uses of a word may give rise to controversy. People might argue about the appropriate use of a word, such as in the case of the controversy about whether the American polity is a democracy or a republic. The parties to the controversy might not disagree about the nature of the United States government and consequently would be talking about the same thing. But they might, in another instance, agree about what constitutes a democracy and disagree about whether the United States is an instance. It would be reasonable to say that the use of certain words is *characteristically* contested, but this is often because, as in the case of "democracy," a word has historically accrued a great deal of either approbation or disapprobation on which an argument may draw.

Closely related to the issue of whether there are essentially contested concepts are variations on what social scientists often speak about as "conceptual development." What is often being discussed is actually a change from one concept to another, which are both referred to by the same word, rather than changes in some particular thing that nevertheless has retained its basic identity. It might be reasonable to claim that certain concepts, such as evolution, have changed internally or developed without transforming their basic meaning, but what is involved in studies of conceptual development is often confusion between words and concepts. Similarly, there has been considerable discussion of the manner in which concepts can, or have the potential to, be "stretched" or "travel." Although such a claim might make sense if properly unpacked, the use of words such as "stretching," "traveling," and the like often tend to constitute misplaced, or at least confusing, metaphors. In these arguments, the subject of the attributions is usually not clear, even though in most instances it seems that it is actually the scope of words or classifications that are undergoing these transformations (Satori 1970; Collier 1993; Radaelli 2000; Goertz 2005; Morgenbesser 2014). The problem with such imagery is that it may lead to odd questions such as that of how far we can stretch a concept before it breaks down or becomes another concept, although we might reasonably ask how far we can stretch the use of a word before we are talking about a different thing or class of things. Most of these discussions, however, actually revolve around the issue of how most effectively to categorize various phenomena or how certain words, because of the ways in which they have been used in the past, tend to continue to lend themselves to a particular form of usage. The heritage of use attaching to some words may suggest, or conventionally allow, greater flexibility than that of others, but there is nothing about a word itself that supports or encourages this kind of adaptation.

What might be construed as the underlying issue in an analysis such as that of Pitkin or Lukes, as well as in arguments about essential contestability, conceptual stretching, and the like, has been what a number of theorists have claimed to be the difference between the core meaning of a *concept*, such as justice, law, power, and so on, and derivative *conceptions* of these concepts (Lukes 1970; Rawls 1971; Dworkin 1972). Rawls argued that, upon reflection and analysis, it is possible to discern a common content in uses of the word "justice," which he designated as fairness, but that there are contested specifications or conceptions of what constitutes fairness—utilitarian, egalitarian, etc. Dworkin also claimed that we can isolate a general concept of fairness but that there are different "conceptions" of what it entails. These individuals were not always clear about whether they were claiming to discover a certain meaning inherent in the words "justice" and "fairness," referring to the manner in which the words had been typically used, or prescribing a particular usage. One problem with these claims is that "conception," which the dictionary also refers to "something conceived in the mind," is not easily distinguished from, or made more transparent in meaning than, "concept." But another problem often involves a failure to distinguish between different *kinds* of concepts or concept-words. It is important not to confuse these kinds or to use one kind as a paradigm for assessing another kind. Although it might be possible to construct an extended taxonomy of concept-words, there are four kinds that, I suggest, are particularly salient in political and social inquiry and which deserve special attention and an understanding of the differences between them.

Concept-Words

What I will designate as *theoretical or presentational* concept-words appear in natural science as well as in other relatively determinate linguistic communities that are bound together by assumptions and claims about what kinds of things exist and the manner of their existence and behavior. Benjamin Whorf's work has in later years been the subject of a great deal of criticism because of what was assumed to be his linguistic idealism, but what he was really claiming, somewhat like Wittgenstein, was not that the "world" is a creation of language but that ontologies are embedded in languages. Theoretical claims in natural science may appear as similar to everyday empirical claims with set standards of truth-value relating to what they represent, but theoretical claims actually represent *nothing*. They are instead, as I have already noted and will discuss more fully in a later chapter, the structure within which representation takes place and within which the facts represented gain identity. Social scientific claims and assumptions about the nature of social reality also contain theoretical concept-words, but such words are also at the core of the self-understanding of social actors and their *Weltbild*. It is this theoretical disjunction between the practice of social science and the practices that constitute its object of inquiry that gives rise to many of the epistemological, methodological, and practical problems in social inquiry. This might be referred to as the two-language or two-theory problem or condition. As I have already stressed, this is what most fundamentally distinguishes social science from natural science. Although social science is in one respect presentational in that it also involves theoretical assumptions and claims about the nature of social phenomena, it is basically a representational enterprise. No matter how social phenomena are construed by social science, they have been theoretically pre-constituted in the speech and behavior of social actors, and the task of social inquiry is to *represent* and *convey* such phenomena.

In everyday life, we are continually faced with going beyond idiographic references and attempting to find ways to represent things that possess what Wittgenstein referred to as family resemblances, that is, things that are similar but not numerically the same. In doing so, we often employ what I will refer to as *categorical* concept-words. These words may be found at all levels of discourse, but they are particularly prevalent and necessary in fields such as social science and history, which are confronted with the problem of representing, reconstructing, or interpreting historical and cultural particulars, which do not lend themselves to theoretical amalgamation but which may usefully be construed in various ways as similar. Projects designed to achieve precise definitions of social facts ultimately fail because of the variable and changing character of social phenomena, but despite the particularity of such phenomena, there is still a need for generalization. This kind of problem was what led to formulations such as Weber's ideal-types and Wittgenstein's emphasis on a philosophical method that involved the invention of fictitious "language-games" that would yield "perspicuous representations" and would reconcile particularity with the concern for generality.

In the case of social science, there is both the problem of understanding and interpreting the concept-words that are indigenous to social phenomena and the problem of formulating a language for accomplishing that task. The greatest problem in using these words is to find a language of interpretation that can adequately account for and clarify the meaning of social facts but also avoid reification or confusing the language of representation with what is represented. The latter may be the most significant problem in social inquiry, as Wittgenstein so often pointed out with respect to philosophy, and, even earlier, Max Weber had made a similar argument. The greatest danger in using categorical concept-words, as was evident in the cases of "representation" and "power," is when they are interpreted as theoretical concept-words. And there is a persistent tendency to seek representational hegemony by universalizing one mode of representation and attempting to achieve methodological unity, such as in the case of systems analysis in the 1960s or the later rise of rational choice analysis. Reification often leads to the mistake of confusing a categorical concept-word with a theoretical concept-word. For example, as I discussed earlier, for political theorists during the nineteenth century the word "State" was a theoretical concept, but by the beginning of the twentieth century it was being transformed into a categorical concept. Even today, however, the residue of that theoretical aura, as I will indicate in the next chapter, creeps into the language of state-talk.

Social scientists also typically employ a number of *analytical* concept-words. These are in many ways like categorical ones and, like the latter, easy to mistake for theoretical concept-words. But they are even more arbitrary than categories. They construct or carve out a domain that is composed, on the basis of chosen criteria, of various elements—much in the same manner that sets are constructed in formal logic. The elements of an analytical construct are not the same as parts of a whole. Any object could in principle be part of a set. David Easton claimed that what he meant by a political system was a matter of analytically factoring out particulars and constructing a whole that might have no empirical counterpart. He argued that even "a duckbilled platypus and the ace of spades" could be construed as a system, if it were, in some manner, useful as a tool of analysis (1965).

Social inquiry not only deals with values as social phenomena but often wishes to engage in evaluative and prescriptive claims about such phenomena, and this brings us to what I will refer to as *modal* concept-words on which value claims are predicated. These include "good," "beautiful," "true," "real," "rational," "probable," and so on and are involved in arguments such as those of Rawls and Dworkin, which employ words such as "justice" and "right." Unlike theoretical terms, they do not carry with them any necessary ontological commitments and are not confined to a particular practice or form of discourse. Although, as Stephen Toulmin pointed out (1958), they may, through usage, tend to acquire a certain invariant core force or meaning, their criteria of application are relative to particular practices and language-games and are what Austin spoke of as "substantive hungry." This sometimes creates the illusion of essential contestability, but it is not some universal underlying meaning that is disputed but the criteria of their use. The presence of a modal term, such as "good," in a sentence does not even necessarily indicate or dictate, despite the claims of individuals as philosophically and ideologically diverse as Leo Strauss and Charles Taylor, that it inherently involves a value or prescriptive claim, but the residual force attaching to "good" is a consequence of its past use in such sentences. This resembles what Dworkin and Rawls speak of as the difference between concept and conception, but it is a mistake to claim that there is some core meaning inherent in a word such as "justice." A problem with arguments such as those of Rawls or Dworkin is that they tend to couch their discussions in a language that suggests that they are making a discovery about justice or rights when in fact they are making an argument about what should be conceived as just or right and consequently how these words should be applied. Part of what might lead someone to assume that these are concepts that are essentially contested or stretchable is that, like theoretical concept-words, they are often used in certain claims about what is right, just, true, or beautiful, which, like theoretical claims, as I will explain further in chapter 7, cannot be compared with the world because they are constitutive of an ethical, religious, and aesthetic account of some dimension of the world. Finally, it is necessary to consider what all this means for thinking both about politics and about "politics," that is, about both the thing and the word.

The Concept of "the Political"

Any study of politics must come to grips with the problems of specifying the units and boundaries of what we take to be a political domain and of how to represent that domain. There are all sorts of ways to do this, and maybe the greatest problem is not so much determining a correct way as distinguishing between, and not confusing, these ways. But the crucial point is that the business of social science is to interpret and represent. Interpretation is not, as often construed, a particular method or approach to social inquiry but the condition of such inquiry. No matter how empiricist political science claims to be, all social inquiry is interpretive and a matter of representation, because interpretation confronts, both epistemically and practically, the conventions and actions that are the objects of interpretation. So the relevant question is that of what, exactly, is the realm of language and action we call politics?

During the twentieth century, Carl Schmitt, Arendt, Strauss, Reinhart Koselleck, Sheldon Wolin, as well as many others who have often been influenced by their work or similar arguments, tended to confer a quasi-ontological or theoretical status on politics. This led to the transformation of the adjective "political" into a noun-phrase, that is, a concept-word that named a thing that was in some way assumed to be universal despite differences and changes in its particular manifestations. For these individuals, "the political" was something transcendentally real, which manifested itself historically from time to time. But it was often viewed as less than fully realized and in danger of being effaced, as, for example, Arendt so dramatically portrayed in *The Human Condition*, and the passing of which individuals such as Wolin continued to see as a problem. This image was eventually adopted by a wide range of ideologically and epistemologically diverse strands of political theory, including poststructuralism (e.g., Mouffe 1996). Pitkin noted, accurately but approvingly, that "Wolin and Arendt are talking about what *is* political, about the meaning of 'political'; and they are trying to tell us that an important part of the meaning applies less and less well to the reality of the practice and institutions we still call, from habit, 'political'" (1972b, 213). It has, however, often been employed by others who use it in a less metaphysical but more functional manner.

The invention of "THE political" as a theoretical concept-word was originally in part the consequence of reverence for the subject matter, but it was also a strategic attempt to establish the critical authority of political theory. Politics, however, does not have a nature or essence any more than any other conventional social practice. "Politics" is not a theoretical concept. It is either a categorical or analytical concept or a designation of a particular historically and socially situated practice. There cannot, strictly speaking, be a theory of politics but only a description of such practices. There may, however, as I have already emphasized, be a theoretical account of the *kind* of phenomena of which various social practices such as politics are instances. Definitions of politics, if universalized, are almost always unsatisfactory, because, first, the problem that they seek to solve is not really definitional, that is, the problem of getting to the reality of politics and distinguishing it from other spheres of social life. Second, there are many types of definition—theoretical, functional, analytical, operational, stipulative, and so on. The questions to be asked are for what purpose a definition is constructed and what criteria of sameness are being applied.

Michael Freeden (2013) has recently advanced an important and provocative case for a more realistic but interpretive account of political inquiry. He enjoined political theorists to give political theory an "empirical grounding" by studying what takes place in the "political thinking" associated with the practices of politics rather than focusing on past political thought and advancing abstract analytical and normative claims characteristic of the work of individuals such as Rawls and Habermas. Such a redistribution of emphasis would, he suggested, ameliorate the effects of the "growing rupture" in mainstream political science between political theory and the study of comparative politics. Much of his work had been devoted to the study of political ideologies, but in 2013 his purpose was to pursue the primarily "interpretive" and "hermeneutic" endeavor of developing a "conceptual framework" for studying all forms of "political thinking" and the "cluster" of "thought-practices" that underlie what he referred to as "the political." His work prompts us once again to critically engage the problems of exactly what it means to talk about "political thinking" and about the nature of "the political." What appears to remain unresolved in Freeden's argument is both how to define "politics" and exactly what constitutes "political thinking" and an ideological "thought practice" that he claims is core of the language and activity of politics.

When we speak about something such as ideology as a form of political thinking, we are not referring to a particular thing. Typical textbooks on ideology might include subjects as diverse in many ways as liberalism, nationalism, conservatism, Marxism, feminism, ecology, etc. "Ideology" would seem to be a second-order term of art and a categorical or analytical construction for demarcating and representing syndromes of language and action that we might construe as having certain similarities. As Wittgenstein said in *On Certainty*, quoting Faust, in the beginning was the deed. The contemporary notion of "ideology" seems, however, to still reflect how the eighteenth-century French philosopher Destutt de Tracy invented the word, based it on John Locke's account of ideas as mental representations arising from experiencing the physical and social world, and spoke of language as a vehicle for expressing ideas. Ideology was conceived as a science of ideas.

What Freeden defined as "political thinking" was not something limited to what we might conventionally discriminate as politics, even though he claimed that it was particularly salient in that context. He argued that such thinking is actually "ubiquitous" and is discernible to some degree in all aspects of human intercourse and conduct and even in what is involved, for example, when one attempts to "direct a choir." What characterized it, he claimed, was a "vocabulary of finality" devoted to the search for "decontestation" and making the conditions of life constant and creating or maintaining political stability by holding linguistic meaning steady. Freeden placed special emphasis on language where, he claimed, much of political thinking becomes visible and which is the locus of a continuous endless, but ultimately futile, struggle for closure. It was in terms of this functional image of politics that Freeden wished to locate the "methodological autonomy" and universality of "the political." Although he rejected many of the past and contemporary images that have been involved in transforming the adjective "political" into a noun, he still wished to conceive of politics as a distinct but universal "form" of life that is "thicker" than simply what we have historically designated as politics and political institutions. Freeden claimed that the most important elements of political thought are concepts, which are the units of meaning and the "building blocks of political language," but he argued that many concepts are inherently fraught with indeterminacy because of the nature of language in general but especially the "essential contestability" of "super-concepts" such as democracy, which include different component "conceptions."

There is certainly no reason to question the claim that the general problems of fixing meaning are reflected in politics, but claims about the essential contestability of concepts, and particularly political concepts, is more problematical, and it is difficult to discern exactly what constitutes Freeden's concept of a concept. He also argued that "political thinking" involves much more than what is expressed in language narrowly conceived and that it is necessary to pay attention to non-verbal, "non-conceptual," and "non-rational" features such as "rhetoric" and "emotion and passion" (for a fuller discussion of Freeden's work, see Gunnell 2014a).

Although I believe that among the various recent claims to realism in political theory Freeden's stress on studying the thinking that actually takes place in politics is important, his argument still manifests the kinds of difficulties I have discussed as the mind-first attitude and the manner in which concepts have been conceived. And although the use of the phrase "the political" to discriminate an analytically and functionally distinguishable class of phenomena is always possible, and may often be useful, the origins of this phrase were in the metaphysical, essentialist, and normative modes of theorizing from which Freeden often wished to differentiate his work.

There is good reason to question the claim that because the attributes we conventionally associate with politics can be construed as generically similar to aspects of other practices, they are thereby indicative of a universal dimension of human interaction. This would seem to be an inversion of the actual relationship between what is particular and general, and it seems that there is a danger of ending up with definitions of politics that may at once be too broad and too narrow and that we may be left with odd conclusions, such as that there is much in politics that is not political and that instances of other practices may sometimes be more political than politics.

"Politics," in the first instance, refers to a specific historical, evolving, dispersed, but socially and culturally circumscribed, dimension of social life, which arguably had a beginning and might possibly have an end as a conventionally discriminated element of social organization. Other uses of the word "politics" are not in some way ultra vires, but they are necessarily derivative or metaphorical. We would not be likely to talk about such things as "academic politics" if it were not to suggest that certain general attributes we characteristically associate with historical instances of politics could be discerned in university departmental interaction. But we should not assume that we are talking about the same specific thing, even if we construed it in some way as similar. Part of the problem with the word "politics" stems from the fact that it is both a word *in* political discourse and behavior and a term for talking *about* political life, and there are always the problems of confusing and reconciling the two. Political practices do not stand still for those who wish to define politics. Observations of politics can yield claims about family resemblances among historical and cultural instances of political practice, but noting such similarities does not achieve the goal that is often being sought through these definitions, that is, the equivalent of some ur-phenomenon of which these putative instances of politics are manifestations.

There is no simple and general answer to the question of how to approach representing politics, and it is not a matter of inviting many perspectives in the hope that they will add up to a complete picture—as if we were attempting to illuminate all the characteristics of some theoretical object. But it is important not to allow slippage between, on the one hand, a figurative use of "politics" or a categorical/analytical concept of politics and, on the other hand, the use of "politics" to refer to a particular and historically situated practice. There are many well-known examples of conflating these uses, even in the case of anthropologists such as Clifford Geertz who are committed to "thick descriptions" of social phenomena but who have used Western metaphors for talking about social life in other cultures. In representing and conveying the meaning of social phenomena, we have little choice in choosing our vocabulary. We are bound either to something drawn from our familiar vernacular or to an invented formalism, but in both cases, there is the danger of reification.

It is necessary to acknowledge that there are instances of a literal attribution of theoretical status to politics, which have also contributed to the transformation of the adjective "political" into the substantive "the political" and which imply that politics has an element of essentiality that transcends its conventional forms and transformations and that gives it the status of a theoretical or natural-kind concept. Such reductionism has been a persistent theme in the history of political science and its search for scientific authority, and it is, for example, prevalent in various arguments in sociobiology and in the work of those who have turned for guidance to cognitive neuroscience (e.g., Hatemi and McDermott 2001). A political scientist, whose work I will discuss in the next chapter, has advanced what he now claims is a quantum theory of the mind, which would seem to be an attempt to achieve an ultimate fusion of mentalism and realism (Wendt 2015).

There are various complex philosophical and ideological motivations behind the emergence of essentialist notions of politics and claims about the ontology of "the political," but there is a danger of overlooking the logical type-jump that is involved in moving from specific claims about politics to a general definition. In the attempt to generalize in a manner that finds politics everywhere, we may end up finding that it is nowhere. Something that looks like politics, acts like politics, talks like politics, and about which it may in some sense be useful to speak about as if it were politics, may not, unlike the case of the proverbial duck, really be politics at all. But what constitutes political reality is, as I will discuss in the next chapter, a persistent issue.

3

The Realistic Imagination in Political Inquiry

THE CASE OF INTERNATIONAL RELATIONS

> Like everything metaphysical the harmony between thought and reality is to be found in the grammar of the language.
>
> WITTGENSTEIN

In Search of the Real

A number of contemporary political theorists have recently adopted the term "realism" as a response to the growing dominance of what they often refer to as "ideal theory." These critics pursue what some label as "non-ideal theory," but, like the term "ideal theory," this is more a category than a specific position. It involves what is claimed to be a turn away from abstract utopian images of politics and rational deliberation that are disjoined from the "real" practices of politics. According to Bernard Williams (1986, 2005), ideal theory puts moral and ethical issues first and fails to recognize the autonomy of politics and the existence of what might be called a distinctive political morality and its concerns with power, political order, and the problem of legitimacy. Mark Philp (2010, 2012) and Raymond Geuss (2008), among others, recommend a return to what they consider the realistic focus of thinkers such as Machiavelli and Max Weber, with an emphasis on institutions, leadership, and a recognition that politics is constrained by necessities created by circumstances and the need to deal with worst-case scenarios. Still others, such as Jeremy Waldron (2002), emphasize the degree to which disagreement and conflict rather than consensus are at the heart of law and political life and cannot be reduced to legal formalities and rule-based reasoning. As Freeden has pointed out, however, many of the claims to realism have remained as normative as those of the theorists that they criticize. There has seldom been a call to realism that did not reflect a normative purpose. And this was also the case with those who we may now think are classic realists such as Thucydides, Machiavelli, and Hobbes.

My concern in this chapter, however, is with a genre of realism, which has recently gained a foothold in the study of international politics. When talking about realism in this field of study, we are no longer talking only about

E. H. Carr, Hans Morgenthau, Kenneth Waltz, John Mearsheimer, and others who have rejected what they have characterized as an "idealist" approach to world politics, which they claim emerged after the First World War (see, e.g., Bell 2008, 2017). This new form of realism draws heavily on the philosophy of natural science and claims to put social science on a truly scientific foundation that would guide and ground the conduct of inquiry as well as underwrite a critical perspective and basis of normative judgment, which, the most extravagant versions suggest, would usher in a new era of human freedom. The typical arguments in this literature, however, involve less the advocacy of a specific well-defined philosophical position than the creation of an amalgam of various, and not always convincingly compatible, species of philosophical realism as well as elements of what are often considered contrary perspectives such as constructivism and hermeneutics. This agenda manifests many of the same problems that, during the middle of the twentieth century, attended the social scientific embrace of positivism and characterized the behavioral movement in political science. It exemplifies the problematic character of the relationship between philosophy and the practices of social science as well as difficulties internal to the literature of philosophical realism and its current place in the philosophy of science.

The basic conception of realism with which I am concerned here has, however, been part of the conversation of social and political theory, as well as the philosophy of social science, since at least the last quarter of the twentieth century. Although it is probably fair to say that this literature has not gained a great deal of traction in the field of political theory as a whole, it has been part of the English, European, and American conversation. Today this genre, which is often self-ascribed as "critical realism," is also an attempt to rescue realism from the anti-foundational arguments of philosophers such as Kuhn and Rorty. The roots of this literature extend back to Marx and Lenin, but in the academic world, its beginning can be located in the 1970s in England (e.g., Keat and Urry 1975; Outhwaite 1975; Hindress 1977; Layder 1990; Sayer 2000). In the United States, Peter Manicus, who had been involved with the *Journal for the Theory of Social Behavior*, was a conduit for the work of Marxist-inspired English theorists such as Roy Bhaskar as well as Anthony Giddens who were concerned with resuscitating philosophical realism but also combining it with a more qualitative or interpretive form of inquiry. Manicus (1987, 2006) advocated drawing on the philosophy of natural science in constructing a "metatheory" for the practice of social science. Some political theorists saw this as the basis of a "theory" that could correct what many had come to believe was the atheoretical methodological character of behavioral political science (Isaac 1987; Topper 2005; Shapiro 1980, 2005). Although the use of the word "theory" in the field of international relations is notoriously diverse and contested, it tends to be used generically to refer to various approaches to research, but the new realism is a less heuristic philosophical import.

Bhaskar's work in the philosophy of social science has been prominent and influential in creating a version of critical realism (e.g., 1973, 1986; Archer et al. 1998; Danermark et al. 2002). Stressing the need to take account of both the epistemological and ontological dimensions of social inquiry, Bhaskar has insisted on the independence and reality of the objects of science and on the ability to know their nature, but he has also emphasized the contingent and socially situated nature of knowledge. He has drawn upon a wide range of meta-theoretical claims ranging from the philosophy of science to hermeneutics in order to formulate a program of inquiry devoted to a general project of "human emancipation." Although he acknowledged the contribution of arguments such as Kuhn's, he criticized what he claimed were its subjectivist and idealist implications and the inability, or, more accurately, what he sees as the refusal, of this approach to advance a general explanation for transformations in science. The somewhat understated assumption in this case is that philosophy has the capacity to achieve such an explanation and to provide ontological and epistemological foundations for science. Bhaskar defends a form of "metaphysical realism" as a transcendental deduction that would both sustain particular claims to knowledge and provide a basis for critical social inquiry.

Because this literature has had a distinct effect and following, and to some extent a transformative influence, on the field of international relations, this field provides a context for concretely examining and understanding both its character and problems. The study of international relations has, from its beginnings, suffered from theoretical insecurity, uneasiness about its scientific status, and ambivalence about its relationship to the general discipline of political science. The turn to philosophical realism is the latest chapter in a search for a scientific identity. Whether social scientists have wished to emulate, or distance themselves from, the methods of natural science, they have characteristically, for at least half a century, not drawn their arguments about the nature of scientific explanation from a study of the actual practice of natural science but from the literature of the philosophy of science, which many have assumed provided not only an account of the logic of scientific explanation but a method for doing science. Very rarely in the history of political science have advocates of scientism had any significant background in the practice of science, but they also have often had limited acquaintance with the philosophical claims from which they derived their arguments. The philosophy of science has, however, hardly been a stable and uncontentious literature, and its relationship to the practice of natural science, let alone social science, is highly problematical and a matter of dispute among philosophers themselves. Because the problem of the relationship between social science and the philosophy of science is deeply rooted in political science, it is important to have a general grasp of this background and the history of these fields.

Social Science and the Philosophy of Science

During the nineteenth and early twentieth centuries, the images of explanation in natural science from which political scientists sought epistemic authority were somewhat vaguely depicted in the literature of both philosophy and social science. After the middle of the twentieth century, however, logical positivism and logical empiricism, represented by philosophers such as Rudolf Carnap, Carl Hempel, and Herbert Feigl, had been transplanted from Europe to the United States. Here this school not only contributed to the institutionalization of the philosophy of science as a subfield of philosophy but established a dominant meta-theoretical reconstruction of the logic and epistemology of natural science. This literature, which stressed the unity of scientific method, became a model for disciplines such as political science (Gunnell 1975, 1986). If political scientists, during the behavioral era, had repaired to the philosophy of science merely for rhetorical validation, it might not have been any more significant than the potted accounts of scientific method that are typically contained in introductions to textbooks in the natural sciences. Social scientists, however, often viewed the philosophy of science as not only a description of scientific practice but as the basis of what they took to be a blueprint for what was often referred to as "theory-construction." Few social scientists had either an adequate grasp of the nature and origins of the philosophies to which they subscribed or more than a tertiary acquaintance with the primary literature. These images functioned largely as the basis of a methodological ethic demanding, for example, that explanation be couched in terms of lawlike generalizations that could be tested by factual observation. Despite the rejection of empiricism by some of the social theorists who have turned to the new realism, the notion that the philosophy of science is a guide to scientific practice has persisted. One should wonder, however, why, if the philosophy of science is not part of the education of natural scientists and assumed to be the basis of scientific inquiry, it should be considered as a model for social inquiry. The irony seems apparent and requires an explanation.

It is often claimed that the decisive point in the history of natural science was its divorce from philosophy. Although there is a certain respect in which this claim is accurate, because the language of natural science did emerge from natural philosophy, it can also be misleading. The discourse of early modern science in the work of individuals such as Galileo, Descartes, Newton, and others, sought to escape the hold of religion and medieval philosophy, and entwined with their substantive scientific claims were rhetorical justificatory arguments about what today we would associate with the second-order provinces of the history and philosophy of science. These claims often involved eschewing deductive thought and speculative theory in favor of focusing on induction from material facts. This ancillary discourse was apparent as late as the work of Charles Darwin, and it was both because science had not yet evolved to the stage of being internally paradigmatic and cognitively hegemonic and because it was still challenged by rival intellectual authorities. The philosophy of science, as we know it today, was actually not initially a product of differentiation in the development of the field of philosophy but of the manner in which the practices of science, as they became internally theoretically consolidated and socially dominant, eventually sloughed off discourse that exceeded the criteria of truth and reality entailed by scientific theories. As these meta-scientific arguments became detached from the practices of science, they increasingly found a home in the field of philosophical epistemology where they became post hoc academic reconstructions of what was claimed to be the logic and epistemology that underlies scientific practices.

There has been a failure to recognize the rhetorical and ideological background and character of the philosophy of science. In the work of Francis Bacon, Auguste Comte, John Stuart Mill, and others, the rhetorical protophilosophical accounts of science were adopted and deployed as an intellectual vanguard for a variety of social programs and movements. Although today there is a tendency to view logical empiricism as an abstract account of the logic of scientific explanation, its progenitor, positivism, as articulated in the 1929 Manifesto of the Vienna Circle, was a modernist program devoted to challenging traditional intellectual and social authority and justifying what was referred to as the "scientific view of the world" (Gunnell 2009). It was also in part an attempt to re-secure the philosophical foundations of science after the decline of the assumption that Newtonian theory was a "realistic" description of the world. Nineteenth-century philosophy and science were already wary of speculative thought, and the subsequent crisis in physics, precipitated in large part by the work of Einstein, contributed to the positivist doctrine, already embraced by Ernst Mach, the intellectual father of positivism. Theories were viewed as transient instrumental mental constructs, and facts were assumed to be the foundation of knowledge and in some manner given and open to immediate perception.

Although logical empiricism stressed the nomological and deductive character of explanation, it depreciated theory in favor of the putative certainty of facts as the basis for verifying or falsifying empirical generalizations. What Hempel termed the "theoretician's dilemma" (1965), that is, the practical need for theories despite their diminished cognitive status, would be a persistent problem. The exact nature of what was taken to be the observational domain was, however, contested, elusive, and ranged from sense-data to gross physical objects. The failure to determine the character of this theoretically untainted foundation contributed to the decline of logical empiricism, which had been challenged by the work of individuals as diverse in some respects as W. V. O. Quine, Karl Popper, Kuhn, and Paul Feyerabend. Although the remnants of this philosophy remained dominant in much of the language of social science, it had, by the last part of the twentieth century, been largely discredited in philosophy, and social scientists, who had taken their cues from the philosophy of science, suffered a new identity crisis.

Although empiricism, because of its emphasis on observable facts, has sometimes been equated with realism, contemporary versions of scientific realism are defined in part by their rejection of the empiricist account of scientific theory. Realists not only question the basic assumptions behind the positivist interpretation of theory but sometimes claim that their alternate rendition of scientific explanation is not only a description of scientific practice but itself a kind of empirical hypothesis, which is supported by the practical success, and progress, of science in explaining, predicting, and controlling nature. But although this form of realism involves a rejection of traditional empiricism, its basic philosophical aspirations have been largely the same, that is, to demonstrate how scientific knowledge is possible and authoritative. Philosophical realism is opposed by versions of anti-realism which, while also unsympathetic to traditional empiricism, are skeptical of the metaphysical premises of realism as well as of the claim that the truth of scientific theories, and the doctrine of realism itself, can be demonstrated by the history and practice of science. Anti-realists, such as Michael Dummett (1978, 1991), argue that much of the conduct of natural science is based on anti-realist premises. They do not revert to the idea that theories are merely ad hoc tools for apprehending observable facts, and, like realists, they maintain that theories are often actually about unobservable entities. They claim, however, that the value of theories cannot be based on abstract criteria such as correspondence with the "world" and instead argue, like the "constructive empiricism" of Bas van Fraassen (1980), that good theories are not necessarily literally true. Both realists and anti-realists such as Larry Laudan (1977, 1990) are on the whole, however, worried about arguments such as those of

Kuhn, which they claim threaten to undermine the objectivity of science by questioning the commensurability of scientific theories.

Although logical empiricism is now philosophically obsolescent, there has, at least since the mid-1990s, been increasing difficulty in assessing exactly where the current weight of opinion resides in the philosophy of science and where the lines are to be drawn as far as parsing the arguments within and between versions of realism and anti-realism. Even some realists suggest that the only consensus in the philosophy of science is with respect to the assumption that logical positivism is dead and that there is a need to sort out the basic contemporary contending positions (Boyd, Gasper, and Trout 1991). Arthur Fine has suggested that both realism and anti-realism are basically defunct and that the best approach is to adopt what he has termed the "natural ontological attitude" (1984), which amounts to the claim that we should accept scientific claims as true, much in the same sense that we accept commonsense assertions. Realism and anti-realism both face the initial burden of demonstrating that the very questions they pose about truth and reality are, outside a particular scientific context, philosophically and practically meaningful. Despite its remaining influence in social science, the decline of logical empiricism has left many social scientists with considerable perplexity about their scientific identity, and it has also left critics of a "scientific" approach to inquiry with an anomalous target.

Realism and the Theory of International Relations

In the study of international relations, all this has prompted a search for a new rhetoric of inquiry—a new scientific ideology. This latest turn to the philosophy of science continues, however, to be somewhat ironic in view of the fact that, despite its persistent devotion to validating the activity of science, the philosophy of science has, in recent years, seldom been advanced by philosophers themselves as a foundation for scientific practice. The normative language and tone of logical empiricism, which was a residue of its historical origins, may, however, have belied the claim of individuals such as Hempel that their goal was neither to judge nor to instruct scientific practice but to reveal its logical foundations. Today, most philosophers of science, maybe with the exception of some of those, such as Imre Lakatos, who have followed Karl Popper, do not present their work as a model or methodology for informing scientific practice. To the extent that recent invocations of realism point to the deficiencies of the positivist meta-theory and its liabilities when applied to social inquiry, they are helpful. The claim, however, that the alternative is the introduction of another meta-theory is where the position most significantly goes awry. The result has been a sometimes bewildering example of philosophical promiscuity.

In the field of philosophy, there are actually several "varieties" of realism (Harré 1986). As Hilary Putnam once suggested (1987), it has displayed many "faces," and he himself, in the course of his career has exemplified some of those countenances. Although these visages are not all easily differentiated, it is possible to make some basic distinctions. Ontological or metaphysical realism involves the broad, and sometimes ambiguous, claim that there exists what is often referred to as a "mind-independent" reality, which is the basis for empirical truth-claims (e.g., Trigg 1989). Most of the individuals who subscribe to the specific label of "scientific realism" accept a version of this assumption and argue that scientific theories, including statements about unobservable entities, are true or false by virtue of the extent to which they correspond to such a putative reality. This kind of imagery, however, makes the new realism appear as a kind of Neoplatonic idealism. Some philosophers, such as Michael Devitt, stress the difference between the existence of scientific objects and the manner in which they are conceptualized, but Devitt is also a reductionist who claims that all real objects are physical in nature and ultimately explained by physical laws (1984). Although it is admitted that this "world" of objects cannot be conceptually articulated apart from the claims of science, as set forth at any particular time, it is posited as a transcendental standard which is viewed as more than merely the kind of vague image that is probably assumed by most natural scientists. Most realists embrace both semantic realism, the idea that truth is a matter of correspondence between language and reality, as well as methodological realism, or the assumption that the basic goal of science is truth rather than "saving the appearances" by simply accounting for and predicting observable phenomena.

Although the viewpoint of many natural scientists may very well appear to be similar to some version of scientific realism, many scientists, if pressed to give a meta-theoretical account of their activity, would offer something that might appear closer to some version of anti-realism or the philosophical thesis that theories are basically those propositions that science takes as justified belief in some specific context and which make sense of what is accepted at any particular point as factual data. Despite some obvious resemblances, it is also important not to confuse the meta-scientific reflections, such as the conflicting positions of scientists like Albert Einstein and Werner Heisenberg on matters such as quantum mechanics, with formal philosophical positions such as realism and anti-realism.

"Critical realism" was actually a term originally coined in the early twentieth century by the American philosopher Roy Wood Sellars. The phrase is still used to refer to a general contemporary philosophical argument (e.g., Niiniluoto 1999), but in social and political theory, "critical realism," in its various incarnations, involves the search for a meta-theory devoted to sustaining the idea of explaining and evaluating social phenomena in terms of the existence of unobservable structures, generative mechanisms, and underlying causal relations. In some instances, this approach builds on the Marxist tradition of structural explanation. Although critical realism in social inquiry often seeks support from the general literature of scientific realism, much of contemporary critical realism in social science is philosophically, to say the least, eclectic. What is involved is an attempt to reconcile various and sometimes contending post-positivist epistemologies, account for what is sometimes viewed as the problem of sorting out the relationship between agency and structure, and yet retaining a critical perspective with practical implications. It constitutes a meta-theoretical amalgam that would be unrecognizable to most of the professional philosophers from whose work it claims to derive.

Liaisons Dangereuses

The above discussion may seem as if was a long road to reach the case of the study of international politics, but it is necessary to understand the context in which the new realism emerged. Although the application of scientific and critical realism to the study of international politics is, in part, devoted to a critique of positivist-inspired accounts of theory, these realist arguments are also, somewhat ambivalently, concerned with what is often generically labeled "constructivism." This, however, like "realism," is less the name of definite philosophical position than a categorical designation. It encompasses a variety of claims to the effect that reality is less a given datum than a function of interpretive frames deployed by both social actors and social scientists, but, as used in a number of fields, including international relations, it is a very porous concept (e.g., Onuf 1989; Fierke and Jørgensen 2001). What Nicolas Onuf adapted to the field as constructionism, and much of what followed as defining this persuasion and genre, was a reprise of the kind of arguments in political theory that had begun in the 1960s as part of the critique of behavioralism. Onuf, and others such as Friedrich Kratochwil (1989), however, conceived of constructivism less as a theory than as an inclusive framework and approach for studying international politics, and this is probably an accurate description of how it has functioned. It certainly provided a perspective that could be applied to the study of international politics and statecraft, but these general claims about the manner in which human action and agency collectively, linguistically, and normatively construct the social world remained primarily the collation of a variety of philosophical voices, which did not always harmonize. The basic problem with constructivism is that it has remained significantly under-theorized.

The arguments for and against the application of scientific realism have, at times, been edifying (see, e.g., the forum in *Millennium: Journal of International Studies* 2007, 35[2]), but this has largely been in terms of an attempt to illuminate the relative merits of different meta-theories. The general issue of the relationship between philosophy and social science has seldom been directly confronted. My concern is not to do full justice, either descriptively or critically, to the arguments of particular individuals but to extract from their work an image of the basic kind of project that is represented and point to some specific problems that characterize this literature. There is reason to suggest that the current conversation in the study of international relations began with the attempt of Steve Smith and Martin Hollis (1990) to reconcile "explanation" and "understanding" (that had actually become code for positivism and post-positivism). For Smith and Hollis, however, the primary purpose was to introduce a new form of realism as the core of a scientific approach to social inquiry.

There would seem to be a general consensus, and considerable evidence, that the popularity of the realist vogue in international relations was largely attributable to the work of Alexander Wendt, who many, however, also associate with the rise of constructivism (1992). Wendt had been a colleague of Ian Shapiro, and one of Wendt's principal purposes was to attack the hold of positivism as a meta-theory in the study of international politics. He believed, much like Manicus, that this required advancing an alternative meta-theory—or combination of meta-theories, and his argument was actually a general composite or collage of philosophical claims designed to redirect the field (1999). Although he was inspired by the claims of scientific realism, constructivism and positivism were all explicitly partially incorporated by Wendt, ending in a hybrid that he dubbed "modernist constructivism." He was quite correct in noting that social scientists are less secure than natural scientists and "have turned to philosophers for methodological guidance," and this was precisely the path that he followed. One might indeed argue that some philosophical renditions of science are better than others and that we cannot adequately combat the influence of positivism in social science without confronting it on its own philosophical grounds, but it is quite another thing to assume that the way to better science is through another philosophical claim about the foundations of scientific knowledge or, particularly, through an integration and application of diverse philosophies.

Wendt claimed that realism entails putting "ontology before epistemology," and this claim, which has become something of a mantra in this literature, is defensible in the sense that the postulation of what is real must be prior to the question of how we gain knowledge of it. But what was being advocated was not primarily a social ontology but a philosophical ontology that putatively stands behind and supports all reality claims whether in natural science or social science. Wendt's statements that "theory reflects reality" and that "meaning is also regulated by a mind-independent, non-linguistic world" require a great deal of unpacking in order to identify exactly what is being claimed. Similarly, despite his emphasis on the distinction between what is "unobservable" and what is "directly observable" (1999, 47–48, 58), these terms not only have different meanings in different philosophical contexts but have no general application in the practice of science. By the point that Wendt's book was published, much of the defense of realism in the philosophy of science had given way to views that were often hardly indistinguishable from anti-realism. Most prominent in this respect was the case of Putnam, on whom Wendt relied for much of what he had to say about matters such as the existence "natural kinds," which he believed secured the idea of a reality independent of theory. The incarnation of realism on which Wendt tended to depend was advanced by Putnam in the 1970s, but by the point that Wendt's book was published, Putnam had rejected any "god's eye" view of reality and suggested that "truth" meant little more than idealized rational acceptability in the context of a particular theory.

One might ask what it means to say, as Wendt did, that in the study of politics "the state and state systems are real structures whose nature can be approximated through science" (1999, 47–48). The term "state" is a word that, in the past two centuries, has meant many different things. If Wendt was talking about the concept to which this word, as a term of art in political science, commonly refers, it designates a stipulated class of things bound together by family resemblances and certain historical connections. So surely it makes sense to speak of this class as a class of real things as opposed, for example, to a merely taxonomic concept or to the manner in which a theorist such as Easton might posit a political system as an analytical construct. But Wendt claimed that states have an underlying "nature" which is "unobservable" and that this is where political reality ultimately resides. During the nineteenth century, it had made sense, given the dominant Hegelian approach to the study of politics, to claim that the state had a "nature," which was unobservable, and that all particular states were instances of this essential nature. But it was not clear how Wendt's realism provided a comparable image.

One of the basic motives behind Wendt's project was laudable: to turn social scientific theory in the direction of fundamental claims about the nature of social reality and to move away from the typical empiricist construal of theories. The problem, however, was with his attempt to enlist philosophical realism as the vehicle for accomplishing this task as well as with attempting to conceive of terms such as "agency" and "structure" as ontological entities. The use of concepts of agency and structure involves a crucial and controversial but often inadequately explicated claim in the social scientific realists' repertoire. These concepts bear no demonstrable resemblance to the unobservable objects and reality claims that are typical of natural science. They are basically categorical or taxonomic terms, which are in many ways the ghosts of old philosophical theories such as voluntarism and determinism, the remnants of post-Marxism social theory, and the residue of nineteenth-century arguments about individualism and holism. The more recent genealogy of agency and structure involves the mid-twentieth-century arguments of individuals such as Anthony Giddens (1984). In many respects, Giddens's work is a paradigm case, as well as source, of many of the problems and contradictions manifest in the attempt of scholars in international relations to adopt realism. Giddens was among the first to argue for ontology over epistemology and to attempt to posit structure and agency as theoretical objects, and he was a leader in the movement to solve the problems of conflicting epistemologies, such as naturalism and interpretism, or action and causality, by analytically synthesizing them and then deploying the product as both a framework and method of inquiry. Little is gained, however, by resurrecting this now exhausted discussion and claiming that agency and structure can be construed as unobservable theoretical entities comparable to those often posited by natural science, such as black holes or dark energy.

One dimension of Wendt's project was the attempt to define his position by contrasting it with a characterization of certain postmodernists who, he claimed, believe that "cats and dogs" do not exist except as discursive inventions. This image of linguistic idealism was far too simplistic for a description of any seriously developed philosophical argument associated with postmodernism, but Wendt did not want his sympathy for social constructionism to stand without a realist backing. It is not, however, philosophical realism that makes it possible to conceive of states as real entities any more than it is such realism that makes it possible for natural scientists to claim that molecules exist. This is a function of first-order scientific theory, not philosophy. Although it is tempting, and common, to say, as Wendt did, that natural objects are "mind-independent," while "social kinds" are the product of ideas and beliefs and therefore "mind-dependent," this kind of distinction is meaningless if it is meant to imply more than the fact that, at any time, we are likely to draw a line between phenomena we designate as natural and those we take to be social. That line, however, has hardly been constant. The distinction is misleading if it is interpreted as the claim that natural objects are in some way given in a pre-conceptual manner that can be specified apart from scientific theories or whatever discourse we take to be authoritative. Wendt took pains to argue that despite their "mind-dependence," there are ways of approaching social kinds (in terms of causal analysis, focusing on structures, etc.) that make it possible to treat them functionally as if they were natural kinds, but this claim was also typical of the adaption of positivism to social science.

For those unfamiliar with the contemporary conversations in the philosophy of science, Wendt's work did not offer clear guidance to the average reader in international relations, who would have had little in the way of resources for evaluating these claims and the various citations to the literature of philosophical realism. Just as Wendt built his version of realism by mixing various meta-theories, he constructed an opponent composed of various elements of postmodernism and anti-realism. When he did mention a specific author such as Kuhn, he sometimes significantly misstated the argument. For example, Kuhn never said that "paradigms" create "different worlds" but only that the theoretical components of such paradigms were logically incommensurable. What Wendt referred to as the "'ultimate argument for realism,' that is, the capacity of science to 'manipulate the world,'" was, as already indicated, not only highly controversial in philosophy but so deeply assumed in certain forms of realism that it could hardly be called upon as a justification of the position. In the case of the study of international relations, it was unclear how this test could be applied to its claims, and to say that there is "some disarray in the realist camp about how to deal with this problem" was a distinct understatement (1999, 53, 56).

Wendt's work had all the hallmarks of a jury-rigged formulation, often drawn from, and confronting, material with which he seemed to be minimally familiar. But some subsequent arguments for realism displayed accentuated forms of these problems. Wendt's book was followed by Heikki Patomäki's contribution to the Bhaskar-inspired series in "studies in critical realism" (2001). One of the problems with this work was, once again, that while it subscribed to the title of "philosophical realism," no distinct philosophical argument was advanced. Patomäki's image of realism was composed from the prior ecumenical epistemological compilations of Habermas, Giddens, Paul Ricoeur, and Bhaskar—with the addition of elements of Wittgenstein, Winch, Kuhn, Jacques Derrida, Michel Foucault and with many of the major philosophers of Western civilization thrown in for good measure. Apart from Giddens and Bhaskar, most received short shrift, because the premise was that everything had led up to Bhaskar's "seminal" work and his "theory of emancipation," which transcended "both positivism and post-positivism." Unlike Wendt, Patomäki wished to add a more distinct critical dimension and stance to the theory of international relations. He provided a lucid overview of the evolution of critical realism in the philosophy of science, and from this literature, he claimed he had extracted three basic "transcendental arguments": "ontological realism" or the view that the world exists independent of our knowledge of it; "epistemological relativism" or the assumption that beliefs and knowledge claims are "socially produced"; and "judgmental rationalism" or the claim that in spite of "interpretive pluralism," we can make models of the world and determine their truth. After accessing such truth, we would, he claimed, be in a position to evaluate critically the "lay meanings" which "create social practices and relations." Patomäki identified his basic intellectual task as reconciling and synthesizing the work of Giddens and Bhaskar, both of whom, he claimed, went beyond individualistic social ontology by adding hermeneutics and the critical perspective of the Frankfurt school. The arguments of Giddens and Bhaskar were already highly syncretic, but, Patomäki claimed, while Giddens focused more on interpretation and agency, Bhaskar emphasized causal structures and relations. This, he argued, would yield an "ontology" based on "a conceptual analysis" of action, structure, power, and system. And by taking account of the "double hermeneutic" required by social inquiry and adding "iconic modeling," it would be possible to achieve "emancipatory explanation." All of this, however, required "a plurality of initial hypotheses drawn from different theories," "hermeneutic mediation between theoretical concepts," and the simultaneous embrace of a "reductive approach" (5, 7–9, 120, 123, 144). This was, indeed, meta-theoretical fantasy gone wild, and one must puzzle over what it would entail, and has entailed, for the actual study of international politics.

Although Colin Wight (2006) wished to make a stricter commitment to realism than Wendt, he presented his approach as "broadly consistent" with that of Wendt, and it was in many respects closely related to the position of Patomäki. It was certainly consistent with Wendt in that, despite all the criticisms of positions such as positivism and idealism, there was no direct examination of, or confrontation with, the argument of any specific philosopher. To a large extent, Wight focused on an indictment of positivism and its conception of theory, but positivism appeared more as the manifestations in social science of a general mood and something derived from references to secondary literature rather than from the specific claim of any particular positivist philosopher or group of philosophers. And "scientific realism" was expanded far beyond anything most philosophers would accept, as it became entangled with a particular image of "critical realism." What was offered was once more a variegated meta-theoretical scheme derived largely from the work of Bhaskar and the claims of various, and often not obviously compatible, philosophers. As in the case of Wendt, the assumption was that the practices of science rest on and can be described in terms of philosophical metaphysics, which also can be the basis of scientific reformation.

Like Patomäki, Wight embraced transcendental commitments to "a reality independent of . . . mind[s]," the assumption that "all beliefs are socially produced," and a faith that it is "possible, in principle, to choose between competing theories" (2006, 26). On their face, these claims, like some of Patomäki's generalizations, were not very contentious and could be equally attributed to positivism. Taken individually and in the abstract, it would be hard to imagine anyone disagreeing with claim that there is a "reality independent of minds," whatever exactly that phrase might actually mean. The important question would be that of what is involved in speaking about a reality that was independent of expression in language. But even more than in the case of Wendt, what Wight presented was less a distinct argument confronting another distinct argument than a series of categorical assertions about realism and its opponents, which were often supported simply by citations to a yet wider range of individual authors (Bhaskar, Mario Bunge, Ian Hacking, Peter Berger, Richard Boyd, Martin Hollis, Kuhn, Hume, Paul Feyerabend, Lakatos, Michel Foucault, Pierre Bourdieu, etc.). Re-describing Bhaskar's meta-theoretical mélange as an authority in support of this particular picture of realism deflected a confrontation with the issues involved. Anyone unfamiliar with the work of the individuals cited by Wight would have had little grasp of what they actually said or the extent to which they agreed and disagreed with one another.

As in the case of Wendt, it was very difficult to discern exactly what was meant by Wight's claims about what is and what is not "mind-dependent" and "socially produced." The bottom line in Wight's argument about realism was largely a variation of the claim, characteristic of a wide range of theorists such as Alasdair MacIntyre and Steven Lukes, that although social phenomena are the manifestation of human agents and their ideas, which must be taken into account, there are deeper underlying structural realities which can explain why people hold the ideas that they do and why they behave accordingly and which make it possible to assess the rationality of their beliefs. Wight admitted that his argument was eclectic and based on quite different sources. The problem with such eclecticism, however, was, again, not simply that of attempting to meld often quite different philosophical positions but the tendency simply to cite and subscribe to these positions as authorities, without a full elaboration and critical analysis of the arguments.

One of Wight's central concerns was, as in the case of the others, with establishing the centrality of agency and structure, but this was somewhat regressive in that it manifested many of the problems already inherent in the work of Giddens and already prominent in the work of Wendt and Patomäki. Giddens, for example, despite his rejection of positivism, actually assumed an instrumentalist conception of theory, which was the very antithesis of realism in the philosophy of science. He claimed that analytical conceptual schemes that inform inquiry are in large part what "theory" in social science is, and he included in this category functionalism and other such typical approaches, which he claimed were tacit ontologies. Giddens explicitly advanced his "theory of structuration" as an alternate framework for the "understanding of human agency and of social institutions," but one that would also serve a "critical function" (1984, xvii, xxii). This had all the characteristics of the very instrumentalist conception of theory that realism in the philosophy of science focused on criticizing. As in the case of Wendt, many of the criticisms that Wight made regarding contemporary practices and approaches in the study of international relations were relevant and persuasive, but these criticisms were not necessarily entailments of his meta-theoretical prolegomenon. For someone so committed to rejecting instrumentalism as a philosophical account of theory, Wight's "manifesto" for realism still clung to the positivist idea of observations as "theory-laden," and, like Wendt, he still cited Putnam's now long-renounced claim that without the assumptions of scientific realism, science would seem to be a "miracle."

The fascination with realism in international relations has not been without its critics, but often the criticisms are simply based on another philosophical account of science. Fred Chernoff, for example, has strongly advocated a form of anti-naturalism or conventionalism as a meta-theory, and with greater sensitivity to the actual content of the philosophical literature than many of the advocates of realism. Although Chernoff (2005), like the realists, joined in the critique of positivism, a commitment to methodological pluralism, and the embrace of causal explanation, he claimed that a meta-theory based on a "version of conventionalism," inspired in large measure by the work of the philosopher Pierre Duhem, offers the best hope and provides the basis of a predictive capacity which would be of practical aid to policymakers. Conventionalism, Chernoff argued, particularly conceived in terms of "quasi-Duhemianism," does not deny the "reality of the world beyond sense perception," but it assumes that "physical theory is inescapably conventional" and, unlike realism, does not insist that all "scientific theories refer to real entities." After describing and discussing various positions in the philosophy of science, examining challenges to a "scientific approach" such as those emanating from "critical theory, poststructuralism, and interpretive constructivism," and concluding that "conventionalism" constituted "a worthwhile alternative metatheory," Chernoff nevertheless maintained, like the realists, that meta-theory is the foundation of sound scientific practice. He stated, for example, that "the answer to the question, how do we determine the best theory does not come from IR or social science but from philosophy," and he continued to assume that precepts in the philosophy of science reflect scientific practice, "have allowed scientists to develop better theories over time," and "have led the natural sciences . . . to such great successes" (206, 54, 177). There is, however, little evidence that the progress of natural science has been a result of subscribing to the precepts of the philosophy of science, whether forms of realism or anti-realism.

Some proponents of scientific realism, such as Jonathan Joseph, specifically recognize that it "is not a theory" but a meta-theoretical formulation, which can play a critical role in examining theories and their underlying epistemological and ontological assumptions. Joseph views Marxism as a theory that particularly fits this philosophy. Like Wight, he claims to justify a realist stance by appealing to metaphysical "transcendental realism" and arguments associated with the critical realism of philosophers such as Bhaskar (Joseph and Wight 2010). And Wight has continued to press his point that social science must emulate natural science in an even more robust manner than formerly and that in order to do so it must embrace a philosophy of social science that is "parasitic" on a philosophy of natural science (2012). He has, however, later seemed to call into question some aspects of what had been his basic argument about theory.

In confronting the problem of what he claimed was the "proliferation" of theories, Wight (2013) has suggested that in the end we should conclude that there is "no such thing as theory" regarding international politics per se but only "types," such as explanatory, critical, and normative. But this prompts the question, types of what? Wight, like many other social scientists when faced with a similar kind of dilemma of reconciling such "types," recommended what he referred to as an ethic of "integrative pluralism" for solving the problem of "paradigm wars." The embrace of pluralism, however, often amounts to a regressive move that avoids making assessments and choices. Wight, however, also suggested that theories are "abstractions from a complex reality," which provide a way for making "generalizations." This is, I suggest, an apt characterization of many of the formulations that are often referred to in the literature on international relations as theories, which are various conceptual and analytical frameworks, but this seemed to be very different from Wight's previous characterization of what constitutes a theory.

Faced with the dilemma of the so-called paradigm wars, or what more accurately might be termed the meta-theoretical wars, it was almost inevitable that pluralism would surface as an answer, as it had in earlier debates in political science. Patrick Thaddeus Jackson has stressed the extent to which those who study international politics, like most political scientists, have been involved in "playing the science card" (2010), and the manner in which that card has represented diverse philosophical positions. He concluded that the answer to contending and proliferating philosophical meta-analysis is a "healthy pluralism" and the recognition that each such philosophy of science has something to offer. Jackson's argument, however, was actually not so much that we should turn to philosophy for instruction but as one aid, among others, in finding an approach to inquiry. He and Daniel Nexon (2013) view post-positivist philosophies of science as methodological "wagers," which they characterize, somewhat oddly, as "scientific ontologies." What really seems to be claimed is that we have different models and styles of representation, but whether these are suitable models is another question. It is the theoretical question.

One of the basic problems in all this literature has been a neglect of the issue of what kind of enterprise has defined the history of the philosophy of science. More specifically, there has been a lack of attention to the relationship of this field to scientific practices and particularly to social science. Little is gained in social science by importing and becoming mortgaged to philosophical debates, such as that between realism and anti-realism. What is important is less making a choice between realism and conventionalism as theories of theory than recognizing that the philosophy of science is not the key to successful science. As both William James and Wittgenstein noted, realism and idealism are primarily different "battle cries" uttered in defense of philosophical accounts of scientific knowledge, but a philosophically postulated world that exists outside that articulated by natural science is a world that no one can access. It is not that science either mirrors or constructs the world—the ontological autonomy of both the world and language are assumed—but rather that it is only in the application of language in human practices that the "world" appears. In the case of scientific practices, the space between language and the world is only opened up within the discourse of science where there are specific theoretical criteria regarding truth-values and such matters as what constitutes natural kinds, taxonomic distinctions, and so forth. The philosophies of realism and anti-realism, however, seek to state the conditions of knowledge in a manner that both transcends and underwrites specific practices of knowledge, but it has no more (or less) significance for the conduct of scientific inquiry than, for example, the philosophy of language has for speaking grammatically. The philosophy of science should be devoted, as advocated by Kuhn and others, to attempting to make sense of the practice of science, much like social science attempts to make sense of social practices, but the philosophy of science is no more the basis of science than social science is the basis of society.

At the heart of philosophical realism lies what John Dewey called the "quest for certainty" and what Wittgenstein similarly criticized as the search for the indubitable, but, as Wittgenstein stated, this urge of philosophers "satisfies a longing for the transcendent, because insofar as people think they can see the 'limit of human understanding,' they believe of course that they can see beyond it" (1998a, 22). Realism, like mentalism, has exemplified this search for what lies beyond conventions, but it is important to understand the futility of this search. And it is this that the critics of representationalism and its mentalist and realist components have attempted to demonstrate. Unless we fully understand the origins and character of this critique and how it bears on the argument for conventional realism, it makes little sense simply to cite and endorse it.

4

The Challenge to Representational Philosophy

WITTGENSTEIN, RYLE, AND AUSTIN

> "Realism," "Idealism," etc., are names which belong to metaphysics. That is, they indicate that their adherents believe they can say something specific about the essence of the world.
>
> WITTGENSTEIN

It is unlikely that we will ever fully know what the intellectual relationship was between Wittgenstein, Ryle, and Austin or exactly the extent to which their work was appropriated by later philosophers such as Sellars, but the similarities and connections between their philosophies are striking and still not sufficiently recognized, even among philosophers.

In 1929, Wittgenstein was scheduled to present a paper at the Annual Joint Session of the Aristotelian Society and the Mind Association, but although the paper was later published in the *Proceedings*, he had, by the point of the meeting, become disillusioned with what would have amounted to an extension of his argument about the logical relationships between thought, language, and the world, which had characterized his earlier work. He had decided, in light of growing reservations about that work, to deliver instead a paper on mathematics. During the following year, he would relinquish altogether his attempt to find a general logical connection between thought/language and the world, but it was at this meeting that he first met, and approached, Ryle, who, in turn, later noted that he had "for some time been a mystified admirer" of Wittgenstein. In the course of the 1930s, they developed a personal and intellectual relationship and sometimes joined each other on "walking holidays." Ryle said that he had learned a great deal from Wittgenstein, and in the early years of World War II, Wittgenstein worked with Ryle's brother at a hospital and became friendly with his family. At one point, during a dinner party, when someone asked Wittgenstein how many people actually understood his philosophy, he mentioned Ryle as one of two individuals (Monk 1990, 272–75, 436, 495). After the war, Ryle would occasionally attend Wittgenstein's lectures and appearances at Cambridge, including the lecture by Karl Popper that provoked the famous poker incident (Edmonds and Eidinow 2001). Ryle found the student adulation of Wittgenstein distasteful and was also critical of what he believed was his cryptic form of writing, but he also was critical of Popper's polemical approach. Wittgenstein and Ryle were, however, never fully at ease with each other, which may in part have been a function of the difference between the philosophical styles of Oxford and Cambridge. Their respective students were at times dismissive of the work of the others' mentor, as in the case of Elizabeth Anscombe, who was teaching at Oxford but who had studied with Wittgenstein and became his principal translator.

Whatever the exact personal relationship between Ryle and Wittgenstein might have been, they, at the very least, followed parallel intellectual journeys. These extended from Wittgenstein's lectures in English that culminated in what was later published as *The Blue and Brown Books* (1958) to the publication of Ryle's book, *The Concept of Mind* (1949). When, in that book, Ryle offered a full exposition of his position, there were, however, no footnotes and no mention of any contemporary philosopher. This manner of addressing philosophical issues without directly confronting the arguments of others was also characteristic of Wittgenstein, but by this point, the resemblance between their work was also indeed significant.

In a 1931 article, which set the tone for his later work, Ryle made a critical reference to Wittgenstein's treatment of "facts," but the remark appears to have been based on what Wittgenstein had said in the *Tractatus.* Wittgenstein's transition in the early 1930s would not be generally visible until the publication of the *Philosophical Grammar.* In the article, Ryle noted that philosophers often conceive of themselves as clarifying the concepts and judgments characteristic of both everyday life and various specialized practices by teasing out a real or underlying meaning. He claimed, however, that this was just a "gaseous way of saying" that they were attempting to determine a universal meaning for "general terms" such as "concept" and "judgment." He argued that this was "systematically misleading," because people in various contexts typically know what words mean if the words are used in some "ordinary way," and beyond this it is "fruitless to ask what the expressions really mean" (140). He claimed that the problem was that such claims about meaning are "syntactically misleading" and, like metaphysical claims about "reality," "being," and so on, appear as "quasi-ontological statements" when they do not actually refer to any particular specifiable thing (141, 143). Although terms such as "justice" are not proper names, philosophers had mistakenly come to treat them in that manner and claim that "ideas," "concepts," "thoughts," "judgments," and so forth refer to objects. Ryle did not see the basic problem as rooted in everyday speech, which had practical meaning and use, but instead in philosophical renditions of language. He noted that people typically do not really talk "nonsense—unless they are philosophizing or . . . being sententious" (168). Wittgenstein could not have said all this better and in fact soon did say it. Although the weight of scholarly opinion may be on the side of assuming that Ryle took his cues from Wittgenstein, it is very difficult to determine who might have been influencing whom—and how—but the article preceded any of Wittgenstein's work that explicitly presented similar arguments.

Wittgenstein and the Challenge to Mentalism

Between Wittgenstein's dictation of *The Blue and Brown Books* (1933–35) and his later work, through the *Investigations*, the principal concern was to disestablish the assumption that meaning is essentially a matter of correlating words and objects and to demonstrate that in general meaning is a function of how words are used. His initial reason for pursuing this theme was, however, to dispel the assumption that mental terms such as "thinking" gain meaning by reference to a thing with a particular location such as the "mind" as well as the assumption that both conferring and understanding the meaning of a word or action are mental acts or processes that take place in the head or the brain. I have argued (2014b) that his critique of mentalism is the thematic core of the *Investigations*, but this theme is actually most visible and accessible in *The Blue and Brown Books*.

He began the *Blue Book* by asking "What is the meaning of a word?" He noted that "a substantive makes us look for a thing that corresponds to it," and that this in turn has led to the assumption that there are "*certain definite* mental processes or a mental 'sense' that give life and meaning to words." He claimed that it is typically assumed that language involves the use of signs to express mental states and that people respond by the mental acts of understanding and interpreting them. He argued, however, that the problem of clarifying meaning is not a matter of determining the nature of a "queer medium" referred to as the "mind." What we might speak of the mind is actually visible and accessible in the things we say and do rather than existing in some parallel mental universe. Consequently, he claimed that thinking is not some hidden process but basically "the activity of operating with signs," whether in writing or in overt or silent speech. There is "no agent that thinks" and no particular location in which thinking takes place. To say that the thinking occurs in the mind is only a "metaphor" and a manner of speaking. The word "mind" does not refer to anything but simply designates a category of functions that human beings can learn to perform. Wittgenstein noted that what he had been trying to do was to dispel the assumption that "there '*must be*' what is called a mental process of thinking, hoping, wishing, believing, etc., independent of the process of expressing a thought, a hope, a wish, etc."

He did not deny that there may be underlying neurological and physiological processes taking place when we think and speak, but a word such as "thinking" typically does not name a thing, either material or immaterial, even though we may sometimes use it to refer to a category of things, which might include something such as making mathematical calculations without putting any marks on paper. George Orwell said that a person cannot write well if they cannot think well, but it may be equally appropriate to say that if they cannot write well they cannot think well. Even if we accept the claim that meaning something is a matter of use or what one is doing with words, rather than a mysterious mental act, one might still ask what was the intended use and still speculate about something mental attached to the words. But Wittgenstein maintained that although one might suggest, for example, that what made a painting a portrait of a particular person was the "*intention*" of the artist, he noted that such an intention is "neither a particular state of mind nor a mental process." Intention and meaning are located nowhere other than in language and action, even if the language is silent or the action is not labeled.

What he was attempting to demolish was the persistent image of meaning, sense, intention, etc., on the one hand, and of saying or doing, etc., on the other hand, as separate processes that take place separate locations. Although there may be a case in which we could imagine someone speaking aloud in one language at the same time as speaking inwardly in another, there is no such process of translating from some realm of non-linguistic thought to language, that is, there is no separate private language of thought. But because we often speak both about saying something and meaning something, we tend to hold on to the notion that we are referring to two different processes. We might say that sentences in two different languages have the same sense or meaning and believe that this is "a shadowy being" different from the sentences, But the sentences are all we have. The point of all this was simply that if we carefully analyze the actual and varied use of mental terms, it "rids us of the temptation to look for a peculiar act of thinking, independent of the act of expressing our thoughts, and stowed away in some peculiar medium." It leads us to recognize "that the experience of thinking *may* be just the experience of saying," and that it is a mistake to be captured by certain "pictures embedded in our language" and formalized in philosophical doctrines.

Because mental terms do not seem to correspond to any physical object, philosophers look for a substitute foundation of meaning and pose strange, and sometimes oxymoronic, questions such as whether there can be unconscious thoughts. The consequence, Wittgenstein stressed, is the metaphysics of realism, idealism, and solipsism. The solution is to recognize that words function as "different instruments in our language" and are characterized by their "use" in a variety of "language-games." The basic problem is that we may either confuse these types with one another or seek some fundamental common ground among them. We find, for example, that when we use the word "I" as a subject we are not naming the physical aspects of a person, but "this creates the illusion that we use this word to refer to something bodiless, which, however, has its seat in our body." And then, in opposition, one might claim that there is only a body, and thus the fruitless metaphysical contest proceeds.

In the *Brown Book*, he insisted that even in the case of emotion, there is no distinction between meaning and expression. His focus remained on dispelling the assumption that the meaning of terms such as "reading" refers to something that is happening "if not in conscious states, then in the unconscious regions" of people's "minds, or in their brains." He continued at length to focus on the "superstition" that there is a "mental act" of "thinking, wishing, expecting, believing, knowing, trying to solve a mathematical problem, mathematical induction, and so forth" that, so to speak, makes us "capable of crossing a bridge before we've got to it" and that enables us to, for example, follow a rule. It might be more like a "decision," but even that can be misleading and incline us to assume that something must be making us do what we do, some "cause." We may have "reasons," but in many cases "*we need have no reason to follow the rule as we do.* The chain of reasons has an end." While our words may be accompanied by a certain tone, gestures, forms of expression, etc., they are not accompanied by mental acts and experiences of meaning, remembering, reading, understanding, etc.

These same points were present in Wittgenstein's remarks during the 1930s in works such as the *Philosophical Grammar.* Throughout all this he pressed the point that the distinction between the "inner" and the "outer," as well as between language, thought, and action, was simply categorical rather than ontological. The same argument persisted in the *Philosophical Investigations* as well as his subsequent work on psychology. He famously began the *Investigations* with a quotation from St. Augustine in which Augustine had given an account of how, as a child, he had learned the meaning of words by correlating the "sound" that adults made with the "thing" to which they "meant" to "point." What is sometimes neglected by commentators, however, is that Wittgenstein's principal focus was on how Augustine went on to say that he understood their "intention" by observing the "bodily movements" that were a reflection of their "state of mind." By hearing words and locating them in sentences, Augustine claimed that he had not only come to "understand" the "objects the words signified" but that he had consequently learned to form those same "signs" in order to "express" the thoughts that had been heretofore imprisoned within his mind (2009, 1). For Wittgenstein, this account not only symbolized mistakes he attributed to his own earlier work but distorted both the processes involved in the acquisition of language and the manner in which words gained meaning in the contexts of usage.

He continued to insist that "meaning something is as little an experience as intending" and that intentionality is a function of a "language-game" and manifest in the conventional "forms of life" that function as "given" (2009, 9, 23, 241; *PPF*, 1, 345). He stressed that although what one "means" (*meinen*) in using words is something that takes place "only in a language," there is a tendency to fall back on the notion "that a *mental, spiritual* activity corresponds to these words" (36). He rejected the assumption that understanding, knowing, and similar terms refer to mental states in the sense of "a state of an apparatus of the mind" or "brain." Understanding is neither a matter of perceiving an "atmosphere" around a word nor an "indefinable experience." Rather than some "mental process" hidden behind the "circumstances," understanding depends on having "'mastered' a technique" (149–55) such as "how to go on" at a certain point in a calculation or how to play a game. The life of signs is in their use and expression.

He presented a yet more extended analysis of the use of the word "reading." Given all the instances in which the word "reading" is used, we might be tempted to believe that they have something essential in common, that reading "is a quite particular process" that can be explained in terms of "what goes on in the brain and the nervous system." But in fact we "use the word 'read' for a family of cases. And in different circumstances we apply different criteria for a person's reading" (156–71). What is important is to pay attention to "*how the words are used*," and "it would be quite misleading . . . to call the words a 'description of a mental state.'" It was simply that the "role of these words in our language is other than we are tempted to think," and grasping this role is what is necessary "in order to engage and solve philosophical paradoxes." He continued to stress that the connection "between the act of intending and the thing intended" is in the practice of doing something (194–97). Intention is not some mysterious mental act but rather indigenous to a game and in the rules involved in teaching and playing it. Actions and words are the same kinds of phenomena, and they both instantiate "customs" (*Gepflogenheiten*: usages, institutions), and he maintained once more that "to understand a language means to have mastered a technique." And in most instances, "when I follow the rule, I do not choose. I follow the rule *blindly*"

(199, 219). He again made it clear that it would be impossible to speak about people having intentions prior to the rules and conventions in which they participated and were "trained" to follow.

His well-known detailed analysis of the language of pain was his entry into a yet more general discussion of mental states and processes. Here he again took up his argument about the impossibility of a private language, which amounted to the claim that our thoughts are largely not only linguistic or conventional in character but comparable to, and sometimes constituting, silent versions of a public language. His basic point was that there is no phenomenal language in which the words refer "to what only the speaker can know—to his immediate private sensations" (243). A person might express a sensation such as pain in various ways, and the verbal expression of pain is an alternative to or refinement of something such as crying. He did not deny asymmetry between first- and third-person perception of pain but only maintained that first-person statements are reports and expressions rather than corrigible claims and that it made little sense for people to say literally that they "know" they are in pain. Sensations are, by definition or grammar, private, but their expression is public and can be genuine or feigned. There is no private "language which describes my inner experience and which only I myself can understand" (256).

Wittgenstein suggested that there was something fundamentally amiss with William James's attempt, much like that of Augustine, "to show that thought is possible without speech," which James attempted to do by recounting the recollections of a deaf-mute who claimed to recall "wordless" thoughts that he experienced before he had learned to write (342). There are different language-games for inner and outer, but the difference is less empirical than logical. He said that much of what we speak of as the "inner" is a delusion. "The whole complex of ideas alluded to by this word is like a painted curtain drawn in front of the scene of the actual word use." What is involved is the speech and action of a "*human being*" as a whole and the grammatical difference between two classes of concepts (1992, 63, 84). Wittgenstein recognized that his argument might sound at certain points like behaviorism and as if he were identifying pain with "*pain-behavior*," but his point was to reject the dichotomy between mind and body and stress once more "that only of a living human being and what resembles (behaves like) a living human being can one say: it has sensations; it sees; is blind; hears; is deaf; is conscious or unconscious" (2009, 281). This did not mean that these terms could not be employed to describe other creatures but only that they were intrinsic to the human conventional form of life. It is not the body, a part of the body such as the brain, or the mind (*Seele*) that experiences pain but a "human being" (283), and to be a human being is to be engaged in language-games such as those involving sensation and pain. In cases of reporting pain, it is not a matter of "justification," and persons cannot identity and describe their sensations in the way that one might describe a "room" to which one has privileged access. There is only the public language for talking about and reporting pain. Here he presented his often noted hypothetical example of persons who each claimed to have a beetle in a box to which no one else had access. They might in fact have different things, or nothing, in their box, but the word "beetle" would still have a use in the language-game even though it was not the name of a "thing" or even necessarily a "something." It is a mistake to view the "grammar of the expression of sensation on the model of 'object and name,' the object drops out of consideration as irrelevant." What might seem to be a paradox disappears once we "break with the idea that language always functions in one way, always serves the same purpose: to convey thoughts" (290–304).

The basic problem begins when "we talk of processes and states, and leave their nature undecided," which is the "decisive moment in the conjuring trick" that makes it seem that by denying the fiction one has denied the very idea of mental processes when the "aim in philosophy" was only "to show the fly the way out of the fly-bottle" (305–9). Problems arise from assuming, for example, that in order to find out what the word "think" refers to, "we watch ourselves thinking" or that there is a basic similarity between crying as "an expression of a pain" and uttering "a sentence, an expression of a thought" (316–17). There is no experience of something called "thinking," and it is a mistake to assume or that to "think in words" involves "'meanings' in my mind in addition to the verbal expressions; rather language itself is the vehicle of thought" and not "an accompaniment of speech." He maintained that "in order to want to say something, one must also have mastered a language; and yet it is clear that one can want to speak without speaking, just as one can want to dance without dancing." But "thinking is not an incorporeal process which lends life and sense to speaking, and which would be possible to detach from speaking" (339). What would constitute such an incorporeal process would be impossible to specify, and while it might serve as a metaphor for distinguishing the grammar of "think" from that of a word such as "eat," it is in the end an inappropriate expression and a source of confusion. In order to determine how a word functions, it is necessary to see how it functions rather than seek some essential meaning.

Ryle: Goodbye Mind

It would be difficult to imagine a more complete demolition of mentalism than Wittgenstein provided, and one would be forced to split hairs to find any basic disagreement between his arguments and those in Ryle's *Concept of Mind* (1949). And just as Wittgenstein had rejected any attribution of behaviorism to his work, Ryle also, despite the claims of some interpreters, was not advancing a behaviorist argument. And he made it clear that in attacking the kind of dualism he referred as "Descartes' myth," he was not implying that what he referred to as the "doctrine" or "official theory derives solely from Descartes' theories" (23). He was referring to a perspective that had a long history, in both philosophy and other academic practices as well as in everyday life. His target was the basic assumption that "body" and "mind" referred to two parallel but interacting aspects of a human being. It had been assumed that while the former is material and observable by third parties, exists in a public space, and is subject to mechanical laws, the latter is a private immaterial sphere consisting of mental states and processes only directly knowable by the subject. This "bifurcation" of the "inner" and "outer" and the relationship between them in terms of such assumptions as that the mind wills and body acts, was, however, more than a metaphor and an everyday way of speaking. It had become the basis of a "profound philosophical assumption." Mental predicates such as knowing, believing, and hoping were mistakenly assumed to refer to "special episodes" in human consciousness and the life of the mind (11–15).

Ryle emphasized the "absurdity of the official doctrine," which he referred to as the "dogma of the Ghost in the machine," and he wished to prove that it was "entirely false" and, despite its pragmatic place in everyday life, primarily a "philosopher's myth" based on what he designated as a "category mistake." This was very similar to what Wittgenstein referred to as the mistake arising from confusing different regions of language or "language-games." Despite the argument that some have attributed to Ryle, he emphatically insisted that his clarification was not a "subterfuge" concealing a denial that people have what can reasonably to called a mental life. But that life was a life of language.

He again noted that there were reasons to be careful, unlike some contemporary arguments in cognitive science, about blaming Descartes who in part had been attempting to reconcile strategically and rhetorically the conflict between faith and reason. As a consequence, Descartes sought to "press his theory of the mind" into a grammatical "mold" that was different from but parallel to how he and Galileo had formed their view of "mechanics." While the response of some later philosophers was to reduce the mind to the mechanistic model, others viewed minds as "spectral machines" that drive the bodily machine. The entire picture, however, was, he argued, misleading and philosophically "broken-backed." It assumed that the causal account that applied in mechanics must be paralleled by a comparable explanation of behavior and that it was "psychology" that accounted for such non-corporeal phenomena. Ryle intended that a result of his critical analysis would be not simply the destruction of the philosophical myth of the ghost in the machine but also, as in the case of Wittgenstein, a demonstration that metaphysical doctrines such as both "Idealism and Materialism are answers to an improper question" (16–23).

What Ryle addressed was the false assumption that what are called operations of the mind are located in "occult episodes" of which "overt acts and utterances are an effect." His point was that we are in fact referring to those acts and utterances themselves rather than to "some shadow-action covertly prefacing the overt action." References to "intelligence" were typically associated with a "special class of operations which constitute theorizing," which is considered to be the basic activity of minds and conducted silently and preceding the actions that are assumed to be their expression. In challenging this "intellectualist doctrine," he presented his well-known argument about the distinction between "knowing how and knowing that," which very closely resembled Wittgenstein's account of the different uses of the word "knowing." Ryle argued that the things that "directly display qualities of mind" are present in acts and activities themselves and do not involve prior theorizing; "intelligent practice is not the step-child of theory." Although much of what we call thinking may be "conducted in internal dialogue or silent soliloquy" and imagery, this is possible not only because we have already developed a capacity for speech, but, over time, have learned, both collectively and individually, how, as it were, to keep our words to ourselves (25–27).

Much of our thinking is not a separate activity but manifest in the techniques and conventions involved in "knowing how" to do something rather than in prior knowledge of theories, rules, or principles. In fact, as in the case of thinking silently, "efficient practice precedes the theory of it." Like Wittgenstein, he argued that to assume, for example, that doing mental arithmetic is more basic than something such as calculating on paper is to reverse the actual order, just as it is a mistake to assume that understanding what someone is doing is a form of mind reading. The notion that what is mental is a set of operations that take place "in one's head" is only a metaphor, as surely as someone stating that they "see" the point of an argument. If we say that we have a tune running in our head, someone opening our skull would not discover "a little orchestra" (28–40).

To be, for example, a "good surgeon is not the same thing as [having] knowledge of medical science," even though the two may be related in various ways. Knowing the rules of a game such as chess does not entail that one knows *how* to play it, but knowing how is not simply a matter of habit. It involves skill and technique, and although it is better conceived as a "disposition," it is not the same as one arising from physical properties and similar to subsuming something under a physical law, such as the disposition of glass to break. What is crucial here is not to approach the issue in terms of what we often construe as causes, either in the Humean sense or the idea of subsuming particulars under empirical laws, and as if a person consisted of two parts, that is, a mental part with will, purpose, and intention, and physical part that moves accordingly. It is instead a matter of a whole person's "capacities, habits, liabilities and bents." In describing the working of a person's mind we are not describing a second set of shadowy operations performed by some mental doppelganger residing in some "place" such as the head or brain. The performances are located in places such as "the chess board, the platform, the scholar's desk, the judge's bench, the lorry-driver's seat, the studio and the football field" (40–51).

Most of the remainder of Ryle's book was devoted to extended efforts to expose the actual character of concepts such as will and volition, which he argued were, in their philosophical uses as obsolete and mythical as "phlogiston" as explanations of human action (62). Like Wittgenstein, he parsed the grammar and logic of the concepts of emotion, feeling, sensation, memory, imagination, pretending, and the like, and he even rejected the claim that emotions "are internal or private experiences" or "occult inner states and processes." He claimed that "motives" are more like "reasons" than causes of actions and are instead publicly manifest in speech and action rather than known by "privileged access" to "self-knowledge" through "introspection" (83, 89, 115). He argued that "our knowledge of other people and ourselves depends on noticing how they and we behave" and particularly on what is said and reported. And, like Wittgenstein, he rejected the idea of the subject as a "self" or "I" as some kind of inner demi-being (181).

Ryle did acknowledge in the end that maybe the "deflationary tendency" of his argument and his "democratization of the offices of the old elite" and of terms such as "thinking" may have neglected the extent to which what is often considered as the "intellect" has "indeed a primacy of a certain sort." There are practices, vocations, and "products" that are designated by these terms such as "The Construction, Possession and Utilization of Theories" (280, 285–86) and the use of "didactic discourse." Such overt theorizing does involve "a lot of soliloquy and colloquy" and other such stage-setting as a preliminary. The mistake of epistemologists, however, was to analytically discriminate such an element and present it as an antecedent event. It is as if "the expression is on a lead held by a ghostly leader called a 'meaning' or a 'thought,' or that the expression is a public trace left behind by an unheard and invisible step" that functions as a cause, that is, a "shadowy" mental occurrence, which is distinguishable from a written sentence and the writing of the sentence (291–92).

Ryle finally posed the question of what the implications of his argument were for the philosophical practice of epistemology. He suggested that epistemology might be best undertaken as something such as the study of the "grammar of science" and of the "grammar of pedagogy." He argued that "the great epistemologists Locke, Hume, and Kant" were in effect doing this but that they incorrectly believed, in their "para-psychological allegories," that they were "discussing parts of the occult life-story of persons acquiring knowledge." The real reason the working of the mind was considered to be invisible was, however, simply because it was actually from the beginning "mythical" (317–18).

Ryle concluded by noting, much like Wittgenstein in the *Tractatus*, that the reason he had said little about the "science of psychology" was because the whole book was an essay in "philosophical psychology," which focused on the general meaning/use of mental concepts, including their use by psychologists. He noted again that the origins of the science of psychology were rooted in the "two-worlds" legend and that psychology was viewed as the science of the "para-Newtonian" world of mental phenomena that lay behind various visible expressions. But mental phenomena should not be understood as existing anywhere but in multifarious conventional expressions of speech and action. Although Ryle recognized that "the general trend of this book would undoubtedly, and harmlessly, be stigmatized as 'behaviouristic,'" human beings need not be considered machines simply because we can dispense with the image of the ghost in the machine. He claimed that whatever psychologists are doing or might do, it was not "the object of this book to advance the methodology of psychology" but to expose the philosophers' "two-worlds myth."

In the years following *The Concept of Mind*, Ryle clearly was not fully satisfied with what he had said about the concept of thinking and worried that he had left the impression that thought was simply a matter of talking to oneself. He argued that there are many ways in which thinking is an activity, such as what we might ascribe to *Le Penseur* or to what someone like Mozart was doing when composing music (1979). The problem was in part to answer what seemed to be the perplexing question of meaning, which went beyond the mere uttering of words. Ryle saw himself as always trying to solve "dilemmas" (1953) manifest in "either or" debates. Although he did not in any way reject his earlier arguments, he seemed to move closer to what Wittgenstein and Austin had to say about meaning, that is, as a matter of what one was doing with words and the context of what one was doing. Maybe thinking sometimes involves deciding and rehearsing what to say, maybe experimenting in the sense that one might be when engaged in a conversation, attempting to solve a problem, and so on. Also in his later years he wrote an unexpected and provocative book about Plato (1966), which might be interpreted as having some bearing on the issue of thinking. His argument was that the life of Socrates portrayed in the dialogues was really a surrogate for the intellectual life and death of Plato, and that the role of Socrates in the dialogues should be interpreted in the same way rather than as representing the historical Socrates (see Gunnell 1987).

Austin: It Is All about Words

The relationship between Wittgenstein and Austin is more complicated and hazy than that between Wittgenstein and Ryle. Austin, as some of his students have noted, was notoriously derisive about Wittgenstein's personal and literary style, but it would be difficult to ignore the similarities between their works. There is considerable textual evidence to suggest that Austin was aware of, and shared, many of Wittgenstein's arguments about linguistic meaning. He was certainly privy to the material that would be published in *The Blue and Brown Books* as well as to Wittgenstein's extended argument about how meaning is not a matter of mental states, and he endorsed the view that "word meaning" was a matter of use, which informed his argument about "how to do things with words." Although he talked about language as reflecting intentions, feelings, and thoughts, *he did not argue that these were private mental states or states of mind.* He used the word "force" for what he claimed represented a speaker's intention in the sense of what the speaker was conventionally doing with words and the conventional effect that was anticipated. It was a matter of actions and of statements in a public language in the context of a speech-act situation in which the "felicity" conditions were defined by social conventions regarding such matters as "sincerity." Although Searle was a student of Austin, it is a mistake to read back into Austin's work what Searle referred to as the mind and original mental intentionality.

Despite the lack of obvious significant personal interaction between Wittgenstein and Austin, there were at least two key similarities beyond simply a general emphasis on ordinary language. They not only both called into question mentalism but challenged what Sellars would refer to as the "myth of the given." There was a mutual recognition that words such as "real" and "mind" have many uses but no standard application. Austin's focus on how to do things with words was so similar to Wittgenstein's list of the various uses of language that it is difficult to assume that there was not some important cross-pollination. Furthermore, they both rejected the assumption that our contact with the "world" is grounded in some form of knowledge based on the immediate experience of something such as sense-data. Austin claimed that to ask about the meaning of "a concept," "ideas," an "image," and "sensa" is "spurious." This was to ask about the names of "fictitious entities" and was an example of the "fallacy of asking about nothing in particular" but acting as if one was talking about something particular. And to ask how we know other people's minds is, apart from assuming the authority of first-person reports when interpreting what people say and do, simply "barking our way up the wrong gum tree" (1961, chs. 2, 3, 4).

The reason that Austin claimed that mentalism and realism take in each other's washing is that, as he would demonstrate, their dirty laundry had much in common. In 1962, G. J. Warnock reconstructed Austin's lecture notes on the problem of perception, which had taken shape over a decade culminating in 1959. Austin argued that in the search for some irreducible foundation of knowledge, some philosophers had come to, or resurrected, the conclusion that we never directly perceive material objects but only "sense-data" and our own sense-perceptions. For Austin, the answer to this Lockean claim was not, however, to adopt the position (which, as I discuss in chapter 6, has more recently been resurrected by Searle and Taylor) that we do in fact somehow directly perceive material objects. He said that the problem resided in the "antithesis itself," because "there is no one kind of thing that we 'perceive' but many different kinds" (1962b, 2–4), which are a function of the concepts we possess. The problem with the sense-data theory was its "implication that whenever we 'perceive' there is an intermediate entity always present and informing us about something else" and that we must confront the issue of whether "we can or can't trust what it says" (11). But the notion that we can be deceived by our senses has no more general meaning than the claim that we can perceive things directly (54). The distinction between sense-data and what is perceived directly is a false dichotomy, but it appeared in Locke, Berkeley, Hume, Kant, and others, where it manifested a mutually reinforcing slippage back and forth between skepticism and certainty (61).

It is a basic mistake is to think that "reality" is a word that names a specific thing and has, any more than a term such as "good," some basic underlying a priori meaning and criteria of application (64). These are the words Austin referred to as "substantive hungry," and in support he specifically cited Wittgenstein's emphasis on the different meanings of "see" (68, 100), which suggests he was familiar with what would be the content of the *Investigations*. He noted that the history of philosophy from Plato to the present had been haunted by the "bugbears" associated with searching for the "incorrigible," that is, "the doctrine about knowledge, 'empirical' knowledge," that maintains that "it has foundations" (105). Although the uses of words are often "vague" (126), "there is no reason to say that expressions used in referring to 'material things' are (as such, intrinsically) vague" (131). The answer to the problem of foundations is not "to patch it up a bit and make it work properly; that just can't be done. The right policy is to go back to a much earlier stage, and to dismantle the whole doctrine before it gets off the ground" (142).

Whatever the connections between Wittgenstein and Austin may have been, it is difficult to ignore the affinity between their respective claims about linguistic meaning. This had been evident in a number of Austin's essays, but it was most apparent in *How to Do Things with Words* (1962a). Although I do not believe that most political theorists are aware of this fact, what has caused a great deal of difficulty in reading Austin was an essay by P. F. Strawson (1964) in which Strawson argued that what was required was to add to Austin's analysis a Gricean concept of intention, that is, intention as a mental state. Although Grice's early work did not explicitly state that he was offering a psychological account of intentionality, he later made clear (1982) that in his view language is an expression of mental states and that maybe it had evolved as a way of communicating such prior states. He argued that the use of words is to impart an intentional "non-natural" meaning, which is a matter of a speaker intending to convey to some audience that the speaker believed a certain thing. Searle's argument about original mental intentionality reinforced the tendency to interpret Austin in these terms, and this was evident, for example, in Quentin Skinner's use of Austin (Gunnell 1998). But Austin agreed with Wittgenstein's claim that "an intention is embedded in its situation, in human customs and institutions" (2009, 337).

For Austin, meaning was totally a matter of how words, and particularly sentences, are used. He framed his analysis in terms of what he referred to as locutionary, illocutionary, and perlocutionary acts. Locutionary acts incorporated phonetic acts of making sounds and signs, phatic acts of uttering sentences in accordance with the grammatical and syntactical rules, and rhetic acts of following conventions of sense and reference. Any fully meaningful sentence included all these dimensions or else it was "infelicitous" and likely to "misfire," because the conventions embraced and conveyed by a speaker might be different from those of a listener. Various types of illocutionary acts were specified by their *force*, which was a conventional intention reflected in what a person was doing with words and thus the key element in the overall meaning of a sentence. Whatever the *content* of a sentence might be, its meaning was a function of its *force*. Finally, he distinguished perlocutionary acts that might be the intended and unintended conventional and practical consequences or effects of uttering a sentence. Austin's long list of illocutionary verbs illustrated some of the many linguistic actions that could be performed with words in ordinary language.

By the end of this work, his earlier focus on explicit performative speech acts, such as "I promise," as distinguished from "constative" or descriptive speech acts, receded, and all speech acts or locutions were conceived as, "*ipso facto*," having an illocutionary dimension. The use of words was to perform actions, and in effect Austin was offering a model of actions, which can be viewed as having the same meaning structure as his analysis of speech. His scheme provides a basis for the analysis of both speech and action (Gunnell 1998, ch. 2). As noted previously, Austin did speak of the necessity for the speaker to have the appropriate "thoughts, feelings, or intentions," and to be sincere, but there is no indication that he was talking about mental states that gave meaning to words and that were separate from language. In order to have these thoughts and feelings, it was necessary to know the conventions that made them possible. Austin was using everyday words to indicate the conventional disposition of a speaker in the context of a speech-act situation, which was necessary for the act to be effective. It was in the context of this situation that the appropriateness or inappropriateness of conventional invocations would be decided. For Austin the conventional effect of a speech act would be a successful and intelligible action and not, as in the case of a possible perlocutionary act, a consequence or result causing a change in some state of affairs or course of events. For example, he noted that the consequence of the conventional act of naming a ship would be "felicitous" if accepted and agreed on by participants, but the implications could be highly variable.

Austin's analysis has distinct practical implications. For example, in matters of law, the criminality of an action or statement is often assessed in terms of "intent," but if it is assumed that intent is an antecedent causal mental state or act located in the someplace called the "mind," we are immediately off on the wrong foot and seeking something that cannot be found. The problem is similar to that of "originalism" in interpreting the United States Constitution, when the question posed is what was in the mind of the founders. Their words were, however, not clues to what was in their "mind" but instead exactly what was, so to speak, in their minds. In order to understand the meaning of what has been done in words or actions, we are inevitably driven back to the circumstances in which the action or statement took place as well as to a consideration of whether in speaking about intent we are talking about the liability attaching to the locution itself or to its purpose in the sense of the perlocutionary effects it was designed to produce or inadvertently produced.

Evidence of intent is always in the end discursive and not a matter of divining mental phenomena.

Despite disagreements between Searle and Derrida, they were both among those who believe that Austin excluded non-serious cases of speech, but this was simply incorrect. Although, much like Wittgenstein, Austin considered these cases, such as the act of pretending, to be "parasitic," he said nothing that would rule out non-serious or even deceptive speech acts as something that could be done with words. But, once again, the distinction between serious and non-serious was not a mental matter but one of what in the context could be concluded about what one said or did. This was the site of meaning, which, however, is so often neglected in the search for some deeper foundation in the mind or the world.

The Invention of the Mind

It is significant that the typical dictionary still defines the "mind" as a "place" in human beings where thinking, judging, reasoning, willing, perceiving, feeling, and remembering take place. This stance is not, however, a naïve formulation that requires replacement as a practical attitude. Like Prometheus, we often do think prior to speaking and acting, and, like Rodin's *Penseur*, we can engage in thinking as an activity. Much of what we associate with the mind and thinking is, however, simply manifest in our abilities, capacities, and what we do and say without a silent formal rehearsal, but a problem begins when the image of language and action as expressions of thought becomes the paradigm and is transformed into a philosophical doctrine about the primacy of thought and a theoretical premise of social theory and research. We begin to assume that there is something like a language of thought that is translated into various natural languages. We then seek a place where that language of thought resides and conclude that it is in a place we call the mind, which is located in the head, whether the brain or some emergent inorganic entity.

We might very well ask how human beings came to invent the traditional concept of the mind, and there are a number of possible "just-so" stories that might serve, such as Sellars's account discussed in the next chapter. It might be suggested, for example, that the origin was in part the propensity to seek causes for the actions we observe and, failing to see material causes, we posited invisible ones. But, as Wittgenstein would stress, it is a fundamental mistake to attribute to a mind what a person as a whole is capable of doing and treat the mind as a kind of shadow person or homunculus. As a formal philosophical claim, the mind-first thesis might be considered as old as Plato, but he spoke about thought as the mind holding a conversation with itself, which implied that thought was linguistic. Aristotle, however, claimed (*De interpretatione* 16a 3–8) that "spoken words are the symbols of mental experience and written words are the symbols of spoken words. Just as all men have not the same writing, so all men have not the same speech sounds, but the mental experiences, which these directly symbolize, are the same for all, as also are those things of which our experience are the images." He pictured a soul, which consisted of three parts (nutritive, sensitive, and rational). Christians such as St. Augustine conceived the rational soul as a non-natural counterpart of the body, but it was Descartes who took Aristotle's nutritive and sensitive souls and attributed them to the body and its physical mechanisms, while conceiving of the rational soul as the substance of mind and source of volition, will, and reason. Descartes was, however, in a strange way correct when he denied that animals possessed thought and reason because they did not possess speech, which he believed was the visible sign of these faculties. Rationalist dualism persisted in both Lockean empiricism and Kantian philosophical idealism, and it lived on in the field of psychology, which made the mysterious mind its province of study. The so-called cognitive revolution that began in the 1950s was in part a response to the challenge of behaviorism and an attempt to rescue the concept of mind as a real but theoretically posited object, which could be represented functionally by computational models. The computational theory of reasoning is, however, as in the case of Fodor, often combined with a neo-Lockean representational theory of mind, which conceives the content of mental states as a relationship between a thinker and symbolic representations that constitute a language of thought.

In both philosophy and social theory, much has been made of the manner in which mind-body dualism has ostensibly been challenged by arguments derived from neuroscience and its philosophical derivations, which reject folk psychology and claim not only to remedy "Descartes's error" by demonstrating that the "mind" is actually the brain but that large elements of thought and judgment are subconscious brain processes (e.g., Damasio 1994). What has happened is that *the brain has become the last refuge of the occult mind.* The content and functions once attributed to the Cartesian mind, such as representation and introspection, emotion, and so on, have simply been attributed to the brain, which is viewed as the repository of concepts and other mental objects. But these objects are no more in the brain than they were in mind. All that has changed is that the inorganic mind has been replaced by the organic brain. The brain-as-mind argument has, however, within the last few years, become widely embraced among social scientists who argue that it offers a solution not only to the conundrum of the mind but to how emotions, and affect in general, play a role in social life and can be studied on a naturalistic basis (Gunnell 2007, 2012). This proposition, however, largely restructures and projects the same basic dualistic image. Scientists image the brain in attempt to show that these "mind-things" are happening, but what these images reveal are not mental states such as belief that function as causes of what we say and do but only the biological conditions of speech and action as well as the neural traces of the activities in which people are engaged. My argument is not intended to disparage the functions of the brain, but the brain reacts to inputs from language that created signals in the brain, which technology seems to suggest can be transmitted back as language, but the brain has no language of its own.

The proper challenge to varieties of mind-first dualism is neither some form of materialist monism nor a reversion to either methodological or theoretical behaviorism. We have good uses, both literally and figuratively, for the word "mind" as well as "belief," "intention," "motive," and various other mental predicates, but it is necessary to examine carefully the assumptions that have been extracted from both folk psychology and its philosophical perpetuation and elaboration. Studies of social behavior almost always assume that such behavior is the manifestation of intentions, beliefs, ideologies, values, preferences, and various other vaguely specified and described mental states and processes. What is ironic is that when these ideational phenomena are articulated, they seem indistinguishable from their verbal expression, which is a fact that should raise suspicion about the existence of a fundamental difference between language and human thought, that is, the assumption that the content of thought is something different from language but not overtly expressed. Although mental phenomena are often deemed to be only secondarily accessible and are operationally defined in terms of the language and behavior of which they are assumed to be an expression, the basic premise is that of mental causation. Even though rational choice analysis in social science is not typically based on a psychological theory, it models the mind-first account, and while some philosophers speak of "propositional attitudes," that is, believing, desiring, and so on, as explanations of action, these attitudes are also modeled on language.

The response to dualism should not be to assume either that the "inner" is not capable of being studied empirically or that it is only the "outer" that actually exists. Although there is what we can reasonably speak of as episodes of thought, these are primarily manifestations of the human capacity to perform silently or in imagination what can be done overtly—such as singing a song or making mathematical calculations. Human beings did not acquire language in order to express either innate or acquired thoughts but, quite the opposite, learned to perform conventional tasks without overt expression. Whether viewed from the perspective of ontogeny, phylogeny, or anthropology, the doing actually preceded the thinking. There is a fundamental difference between first- and third-person reports of what a person is feeling and thinking, but there is no special language of thought, which is expressed in a natural language such as English in a manner that parallels how, for example, we translate from English to German and in terms of which we introspectively examine and monitor our mental states and thought processes. It would, for example, be misleading to say that an English speaker might have a thought that could not be adequately expressed in English but could be expressed in German. The fact of the matter is that it would only be in German that one could have the thought. The concept of the mind as the seat of agency, the self, or the "I" where thinking, deciding, judging, and the like take place and which uses the body and language as a means of expression is a myth. The assumption that there are mental episodes that are in some way fundamentally hidden is true only in the sense that people can speak without moving their lips or making a sound—or speak without the company of others. There is not some place in which beliefs, values, emotions, and the like exist and are swirling around but occasionally escape or are intentionally released into the public domain. This claim is not a rejection of the commonsense intentional image that characterizes everyday life, where we quite reasonably assume that when someone acts or speaks that there is a belief, reason, purpose, judgment, or the like that is being expressed. The mistake is to assume that the expressions are just symptoms of primitive mental acts and that the meaning of the act or utterance is somewhere other than in those performances themselves.

It is necessary to look closely at some of the more recent challenges to representational philosophy and the manner in which they give support to an argument for conventional realism. These later challenges are diverse, but while most reinforce the critique of mentalism, some of the answers to the problem of realism are more problematical.

5

Contemporary Anti-representationalism

SELLARS, DAVIDSON, PUTNAM, MCDOWELL, AND DENNETT

Language is not something that is first given a structure and then fitted on to reality.

WITTGENSTEIN

Sellars and the Myth of the Given

Austin's arguments, about both mentalism and foundationalism, in some ways anticipated the more developed and systematic treatment by the American scholar Wilfrid Sellars in his 1956 lectures in London titled "Empiricism and the Philosophy of Mind." Sellars admired both the *Tractatus* and the *Investigations* and argued that although there were some major differences between these works, there was also considerable continuity. His interest in Wittgenstein was evident in his own "reflections on language games," and he once said that "the influence of the later Wittgenstein has done increasing justice to the manifest image [our everyday vision of the world]" and "has made clear the folly of attempting to replace it *piecemeal* by fragments of the scientific image" (1963, 15)—or by some philosophical construction. He was pointing to the incommensurability of first-order discourses, but his primary goal was to undermine the claim, common to realism, including most forms of empiricism, that there is some kind of access to an epistemological "given" or form of non-inferential pre-conceptual knowledge of particulars or "knowledge by acquaintance." The assumption of such a "given" had been the crux of the nature/convention distinction, and Sellars claimed that hardly any major philosopher had been free of some form of this "myth" and the general "framework of givenness" (127–31). In both political science and political theory, it had been presumed that knowledge was based on immediate experience or non-epistemic facts that constituted the foundation of knowledge and the core of human consciousness, whether these facts were construed as sense-data, material objects, universals, and so on.

Like Austin, Sellars was demonstrating the manner in which formulations of empiricist realism were inflected with a kind of idealism and the assumption that all we really know are our own ideas. Much of his essay was consequently devoted to refuting the assumption that there are primitive private perceptual "inner episodes" such as the sensation of seeing a color or colored object, which constitute the very "paradigm of empirical knowledge" to which people have privileged access and that provide the basis of more complex forms of knowing (134). Sellars did not wish to deny, any more than Wittgenstein or Ryle, that there are what we might refer to as "inner episodes," but the content of those episodes was linguistic and conceptual. He insisted that, for example, the "ability to recognize that something *looks green*, presupposes possession of the concept of being green," and that a person could only have the concept of being green in the context of other concepts of color and some holistic general image of how things are in the world (146–48).

Drawing on early passages of Wittgenstein's *Investigations*, Sellars noted that one source of what he called the "Myth of the Given" derives from a tendency, when we picture "'a child—or a carrier of slabs' [as Wittgenstein depicted a primitive language user in the *Investigations*] learning their first language," to "locate the language learner in a structured logical space in which *we* are at home." This is what Sellars dubbed a "space of reasons" or what we might call the space of conventions. This is a first-order "world of physical objects, colored, producing sounds, existing in Space and Time." But it is a mistake to assume that "the process of teaching a child to use language is that of teaching it to discriminate elements within a logical space of particulars, universals, facts, etc., of which it is already undiscriminatingly aware, and to associate these discriminated elements with verbal symbols" (161–62). Sellars denied that there is "any awareness of logical space prior to, or independent of, the acquisition of language." Although he declined simply to "*equate* concepts with words, and thinking, in so far as it is episodic, with verbal episodes," he noted that his argument was in "a relatively Pickwickian sense an equation of thinking with the use of language" (162).

He argued that there are no "self-authenticating episodes" that are "the unmoved movers of empirical knowledge, 'knowings in presence' which are presupposed by all other knowledge," and which would support the assumption that a "perceptually given is the foundation of empirical knowledge" (169–70). And he claimed that it is possible to "distinguish between observations and thoughts, on the one hand, and their verbal expression on the other, without making the mistakes of traditional dualism." He maintained that in rejecting traditional empiricism, he was not saying that "empirical knowledge has *no* foundation" but only that the term "foundation" could be a misleading metaphor and that "*above all*, the picture is misleading because of its static character. One seems forced to choose between the picture of an elephant which rests on a tortoise (What supports the tortoise?) and the picture of a great Hegelian serpent of knowledge with its tail in its mouth (Where does it begin?). Neither will do. For empirical knowledge, like its sophisticated extension, science, is rational, not because it has a *foundation* but because it is a self-correcting enterprise which can put *any* claim in jeopardy, though not *all* at once" (170).

Sellars argued that the language of science was an emergent discourse rooted in the "pre-scientific stage" of "ordinary usage." Consequently, there is a sense in which the scientific image of the world "*replaces* the commonsense picture; a sense in which the scientific account of 'what there is' *supersedes* the descriptive ontology of everyday life" and "that in the dimension of describing and explaining the world, science is the measure of all things, of what is that it is, and of what is not that it is not" (171–73). But nevertheless the scientific image of the world neither should nor could be substituted for what he referred to as the "manifest image," which governed the language characteristic of practical everyday activities. These were different, and sometimes competing, first-order discourses. What should be relinquished, however, was the general positivist view that commonsense language, or some more basic phenomenal language, reflects and discriminates given facts of the world and that scientific theories are mental instruments for organizing and explaining those facts. We must

> give up the idea that we begin our sojourn in this world with any—even a vague, fragmentary, and undiscriminating—awareness of the logical space of particulars, kinds, facts, and resemblances, and of a long process of publicly reinforced responses to public objects (including verbal performances) in public situations. . . . *For we now recognize that instead of coming to have a concept of something because we have noticed that sort of thing, to have the ability to notice a sort of thing is already to have the concept of that sort of thing, and cannot account for it.* (175–76)

Sellars's focus on the problem of the "given" also involved the question of how there can be inner episodes that are at once private and to which a person has privileged access but that can also be knowable by others and constitute the basis of intersubjectivity. He argued that there "not only are inner episodes" but that they are quite "effable" in intersubjective discourse because they are linguistic (176). He believed that he disagreed with Ryle, but Ryle had not actually denied the existence of mental episodes in the sense that Sellars appeared to specify and define them. For both philosophers, the basic content of these episodes was linguistic. But one problem with the classical empiricist tradition was that it assimilated thoughts to the same category as sensations and viewed them as private objects of introspection. Sellars argued that if we purge ourselves of this assumption, we can say that there are episodes of thinking to which we have a kind of first-person access that others cannot have but that it is a mistake to characterize this access as a form of internal perception. His task was to demonstrate in what sense there are inner experiences that are linguistic, and he once again wanted "to add that it will turn out that the view I am about to expound could, with equal appropriateness, be represented as a modified form of the view that thoughts are *linguistic* episodes." He explained this by inventing what he described as a piece of "anthropological science fiction" (178). Rorty had begun his book with a history of the concept of mind that traced its philosophical evolution, but Sellars constructed a story of what might have been its ethnological origins and development.

This fable involved postulating an early history of humans that began at the stage in which they spoke only something resembling what Sellars characterized as a language referring to public objects (or a language similar to that Wittgenstein had attributed to his "builders" and their "slab" talk). Humans eventually, however, under the tutelage of a person named "Jones, a prophetic genius," learned to internalize this language, but this led them to imagine themselves as having a private language of thought. This second stage of our hypothetical ancestors' development involved Jones explaining why people appeared to behave intelligently even when they did not say what they were doing. Jones's theory was "perfectly compatible with the idea that the ability to have thoughts is acquired in the process of acquiring overt speech and that only after such speech is well established, can 'inner speech' occur without its overt culmination." Once Jones had advanced the view that observable verbal expressions could be understood as expressions of thoughts, this provided not only a way of interpreting others but a mode of "self-description." Sellars claimed that "this story helps us understand that concepts pertaining to such inner episodes as thoughts are primarily and essentially *intersubjective*, as intersubjective as the concept of a positron, and that the reporting role of these concepts—and the fact that each of us has a privileged access to his thoughts—constitutes a dimension of the use of these concepts which is *built on* and *presupposes* this intersubjective status. My myth has shown the fact that language is essentially an *intersubjective* achievement, and is learned in intersubjective contexts." He noted that this point had been stressed by philosophers such as Wittgenstein and that it made clear that although mental episodes are, in one sense, private, they are not absolutely private, because they take place in a public language (188–89).

Sellars continued his story by suggesting that our ancestors would have still lacked references to such things as sensations, feelings, and emotions which had typically been included among "immediate experiences." What Jones finally needed was the introduction of other hypothetical entities, which he called "impressions" and which originated in parts of the body such as the eye. Just as in the case of "thoughts," Jones taught people a theory of perception that allowed them to use "the language of impressions" to draw conclusions about the existence of other inner episodes that were "essentially *intersubjective*" but could also play "a reporting role" and sustain the idea of individual "privileged access" (189, 194). Just as in the case of thoughts, overt behavior was taken as evidence of these episodes, but what was acquired was actually a dimension of language that relied on the linguistic resources that also functioned as mental discourse.

Sellars concluded by saying that he had "used a myth to kill a myth—the Myth of the Given. But is my myth really a myth" (195–96) or is it actually a plausible account of the invention of the mind and the origin of folk psychology? What constituted the given was the notion of a language of thought coupled with an image of a reality that provided the foundations of knowledge. Ryle, Wittgenstein, Austin, and Sellars were all making the same basic claim. Although there are many respects in which we can view thought and speech as distinct but related, they have the same basic content. Consequently, most variations of thought/language dualism are not tenable. Second, there are no philosophical foundations of knowledge in terms of which to either underwrite or disqualify actual practices of knowledge.

Sellars pointedly rejected what I have referred to as mentalism and realism, but after Sellars the conversation in some respects began to go adrift. While the unity of language and thought continued to be reinforced, the issue of how language and "mind" connected with the "world" seemed to reassert itself.

Clarifying Davidson

Davidson was an interesting individual who became a sort of philosopher's philosopher and did not receive the general attention of someone such as Rorty. He entered the vocation of philosophy at Harvard after an undergraduate major in comparative literature and later serving in the Navy. He was also a gifted pianist, attended Harvard Business School, and later worked as a television scriptwriter in Hollywood. He came to philosophy relatively late in life, and although he taught at various institutions, he spent much of his later career at Berkeley. His work consists of a long series of essays in which his arguments evolved or were at least increasingly clarified. The logical positivist

Otto Neurath once metaphorically compared scientific knowledge to a ship that sailors continually rebuild at sea. Davidson's Harvard mentor, W. V. O. Quine, applied this metaphor to the enterprise of philosophy, and, in turn, Davidson applied it to Quine's work. But it also could be applied to Davidson. It is important to recognize that various interpretations of Davidson have depended a great deal on where the interpreter entered the stream of his essays and for what reason.

His early work, in the 1960s, was related to decision theory and distinguished by bucking the trend in post-positivist philosophy by reconstituting the argument that reasons are causes of action (1963). There is much that might be criticized in this formulation (see Gunnell 1998), but his account of causality was, as he later said, "probabilistic" (2004, 219), that is, reasons are causes and rationalizations of action in that they are typically construed as the expression of acquired propositional attitudes. And these, he later made clear, require the possession of language. In this early work (1980, 1984), he had stressed the physio-neurological basis of mental phenomena and maintained that each object that can be identified as mental is, in principle, identical to one identified in physical terms. At the same time, however, he recognized that the "mind" and subjective states are "anomalous" with respect to the laws that govern natural phenomena, and this, as he would later maintain, was because they are linguistic.

Davidson was initially somewhat circumspect about his relationship to Wittgenstein's philosophy, but in his later work he explicitly moved closer to Wittgenstein with respect to arguing that there is no way to speak of human thought apart from language and that language is a social phenomenon. There may be some reason to believe that his increasing affinity with Wittgenstein had something to do with his third marriage, which was to the daughter of Stanley Cavell. Marcia Cavell, who edited Davidson's posthumously published essays, argued that Wittgenstein and Davidson were at one in adopting a social theory of language and claiming that there is no human thought without language (Cavell 1993). Like Wittgenstein, his basic concern was not with judging social phenomena but with understanding and interpreting them. According to Davidson, what constitutes mental episodes of thought, or what he referred to as the "propositional attitudes" of belief, intention, desire, hope, and the like, have the same content as language, and he claimed that the possession of language is a condition of thought.

Although the residue of Quine's philosophy is apparent in Davidson's work, he departed from some of the most distinctive of Quine's arguments, such as the latter's claim about how to naturalize epistemology by grounding it in physiological responses to the external world. But despite his positivist background, Quine famously attacked two central "dogmas" of the positivist/logical empiricist theory of meaning: the analytic/synthetic distinction, which supported the theory/fact dichotomy, and the verificationist theory of meaning, which was based on the assumption of a given factual observation language. And he complemented this critique with claims about the underdetermination of theories by evidence and the indeterminacy of translation. Central to Quine's philosophy was a holistic view, which might suggest that truth and reality are internal to theories, but he still retained a remnant of the dualistic perspective and argued that a theoretical structure contains, and is grounded by, sensory-based observation sentences and corresponding beliefs. Epistemology, he claimed, could, from this perspective, be made scientific by investigating how language is acquired and how an intersubjective image of the world arises from immediate experience. This was related to his account of "radical translation" whereby interpretation was based on the behavior of speakers and the assumption of a basic commonality of experience, which allowed an interpreter some initial access to any conceptual scheme and which was a position that Davidson, in his own way, would embrace.

While Davidson retained certain aspects of Quine's account of interpretation, he took aim at what he construed as a "third-dogma of empiricism" in Quine's residual "scheme/content," or theory/fact, dualism and what Davidson claimed were its relativistic implications. He argued that this dualism had stretched from at least Kant to Quine. He also attributed this to Kuhn, but incorrectly, because Kuhn definitely did not view theories as conceptual schemes imposed on facts. Davidson also incorrectly claimed that Kuhn embraced a consensus or communal view of truth. Davidson implied that this criticism might also apply to Wittgenstein, but Davidson was referring less to Wittgenstein himself than to those whom Davidson described as his "translators." Despite the arguments of philosophers such as Saul Kripke, this view of truth was not the argument advanced by Wittgenstein and Kuhn. Davidson's answer was that the elimination of scheme/content dualism allows direct contact with the objects in the world in terms of which we judge the truth and falsity of opinions and gain access to reality without intermediate representations. This claim of immediate contact would remain problematical in Davidson's work. The questions here are what concept is the referent of the word "world" and what are these "objects" that in some way are given to immediate and universal experience.

Despite early definitions of his position as a form of philosophical realism and a coherence theory of truth, Davidson later specifically rejected both labels. He did, however, subscribe to a kind of general model of truth, based on Alfred Tarski's formal abstract construction of a correspondence theory. Davidson, however, designed this as a framework and "passing theory" for interpreting truth-claims in various natural languages, and it might be construed in a Wittgensteinian sense as a kind of "perspicuous representation" for interpreting, and pointing to "family resemblances" between diverse instances of truth-claims in a variety of linguistic domains. What is most important to note is that he rejected the assumption that "philosophers are in charge of a special sort of truth" that provides a basis for assessing claims to truth in various social practices (1994, 44). According to Davidson, "the methodological problem of interpretation" is to determine, given the sentences that speakers assume to be true, what their beliefs are and consequently what their words mean. He argued that it is not ultimately a sharing of conventions through common participation in a linguistic practice that makes communication and interpretation possible but rather the sharing of beliefs about certain elements of a common world. Although he allowed that there may be some residual indeterminacy in interpretation, he claimed that the assumption of "massive agreement" in beliefs and truth-conditions, coupled with the application of a principle of "charity" with respect to the possibility of common beliefs, maximizes the possibility of interpretive success. He claimed that the idea of "massive error" about the world is simply not intelligible, and the very fact that communication can take place between individuals and cultures and that there is the possibility of successful translation and interpretation proves the existence of an objective and shared view of the world. The exact locus of this "massive agreement" seemed nebulous, but although he rejected Quine's version of naturalism, he still considered himself, in his own way, a "naturalized epistemologist" (2001, 194).

The problem here is what constitutes this generic "world" that all language users hold in common, but for Davidson once we have rejected the scheme/content division, there is no room for the claim that there are incommensurable differences between communities of speakers. But he seemed to take "incommensurable" to mean untranslatable and uncommunicable. He insisted that there is always a bedrock of shared beliefs and truths which assures us of a common sense of rationality and that "the basis of objectivity is intersubjectivity" (1994, 50). He argued that although each person has a private perspective on the world, this does not lead to conceptual relativism.

Davidson's version of a social theory of language was based on the argument that both a person's initial acquisition of language, as well as the development of more complex forms, requires the "triangulation" of at least two speakers and a world of commonly perceived objects. This picture might seem to fit well with Wittgenstein's account of the primitive language of the "builders," but although this would seem to be the case in the acquisition of language, it is more difficult to see how it applies to the later development of language and the specification and discrimination of objects. Davidson never made clear exactly what composed the world of objects that people supposedly held in common, despite the different names they might ascribe to them. He seemed to have assumed something like an at least rudimentary logical space that everyone shared. This may be the case today with some closely connected societies, but it seems more dubious historically and in the case vastly different cultures.

Davidson, however, was unequivocal in claiming that thought is grounded in language and participation in a community of speakers. Like Sellars, he claimed that although there is a sort of first-person authority about, and privileged access to, knowledge of our "own mind" and "of what happens inside ourselves," this is not a matter of introspection and the existence of a Cartesian theater and a private language of thought representing mental objects that thoughts are about. Although he claimed that we sometimes come to be conscious of what we believe by reflecting on what we say and do, we normally know what we think before acting or speaking. He continued, however, to maintain that thinking and propositional attitudes such as belief and intention are already linguistic. We largely know what we believe because we know what we hold to be true. Interpretation, however, assumes asymmetry between an interpreter and who or what is interpreted (2001, 12–14). He wanted to dispense with the whole tradition that assumed the existence of representations or "objects before the mind" from which we putatively gain access to the external world and which are the content of subjectivity. He argued that we must dispense with "the myth of the subjective, the idea that thoughts require mental objects" (38).

Like Wittgenstein, Ryle, and Sellars, Davidson argued that the "subjective," conceived as a private domain of sense-data is a "myth," because intersubjectivity is rooted in language and in the manner in which a person's own thoughts are used to make sense of the thoughts of others (1994, 51). What are "present to the mind" are propositional attitudes, that is, language. Although he accepted that these attitudes are identified in terms of the social and historical context in which they were learned, he still maintained that they are caused by objects "that anchor language to the world" and thereby make communication and shared standards of truth and objectivity possible and rule out global skepticism. Traditional assumptions about the dualism of objectivity and subjectivity are rooted in "a concept of the mind with its private states and objects." He maintained that it was necessary "to be rid of representations and with them the correspondence theory of truth." "Empiricism with its view of subjective ('experience') as the foundation of objective empirical knowledge" is mistaken, because "empirical knowledge has no epistemological foundation, and needs none." He stressed that although "subjective states" may in some way be "supervenient in the state of the brain or nervous system," they are not "psychic" objects of thought and "ghostly entities" located in the "mind" or things that can be treated as subjects of natural science, even though they are as "real" and as objective as physical states and partly identified in terms of their "causes and effects" and the objects that they are about (2001, 52, 61–62, 72).

Like Wittgenstein and Ryle, he was wary of the concept of the "self," and he claimed that despite the various ways this term is used in philosophy and psychology, it "doesn't play any clear role in ordinary speech" (2001, 85). But he suggested nevertheless that there is a certain "irreducibility" that attaches to the concept of the self, because it is ultimately individuals who share language. What creatures, and things, can actually be said to think, and have propositional attitudes, was somewhat of an open question for Davidson, but, on the whole, because of the interdependence of thought and language, he equated "rational creatures" with those who have language and who possess a significant network of beliefs and concepts. This, he claimed, is why dogs cannot have beliefs, even though they might be able to discriminate between objects that we would designate as cats and cows. To have the concept of a cat would require being able to recognize a mistake in applying the concept as well as the capacity to locate the concept in a web of concepts, or what Davidson referred to as the "*holism of the mental*," which reflected the holism of language. Although language is "an instrument for the expression of propositional contents," propositional attitudes presuppose the possession of language (123, 126, 127, 130).

For Davidson, then, language and thought are largely only episodically different. The basic content is the same. Consequently, he claimed that "neither an infant 1 week old nor a snail is a rational creature." The crucial difference is the possession of propositional attitudes which depend on the "gift of tongues" (95–96). Although thinking cannot be simply "reduced to linguistic activity," it cannot be correlated with "physical or neurological" phenomena. The point is simply that "a creature cannot have a thought unless it has a language" and the ability "to interpret the speech and thoughts of others." He claimed that "to have a belief, it is necessary to have the concept of belief," and to have the concept requires the possession of language and that because "rationality is a social trait, only language-users have it" (102, 105). Although Davidson maintained, like Wittgenstein, that "language is necessarily a social affair" (117), it cannot be reduced to following rules and conventional routines and practices (as some have taken Wittgenstein to have said). He continued to stress that there is no requirement for a "community" but only, at the most basic level, interaction between two speakers—such as a teacher and a child—and the world, which is the basis of both the "emergence of language" and a concept of objective truth.

Davidson argued that various attempts to come up with a general theory of truth had failed because of the mistaken assumption that truth was an object, when it is only a concept that is applicable to certain claims in various contexts of language use. Nevertheless he was concerned that what he characterized as the "deflationary" arguments of philosophers such as Nietzsche, Dewey, and Rorty had gone too far by debunking the concept itself and failing to recognize how truth-conditions are tied to meaning and thought. He wanted to "rehabilitate" the concept of truth without making the mistakes of the past (2005, ch. 1). Although he explicitly agreed with Wittgenstein's social account of language, he continued to worry that certain interpreters of Wittgenstein had claimed that this is a matter of sharing specific rules when the basic problem is that of what makes communication possible, which for Davidson was grounded in triangulation. Like Wittgenstein, however, he wanted to stress that language does not obscure the world from us but opens it to us. Language is not a "mirror" of reality but an advanced mode of perception that provides criteria of objectivity and truth. "Neither thought nor language can come first, for each requires the other." If we want to say that we perceive the world though language it must be in the sense of "having language" rather than as a medium of apprehension (141).

It seems in the end what remained most problematical in Davidson's work was his continuing commitment to a form of "external epistemology" and to a common world composed of basic objects that can be specified outside any theory. It may be difficult to construe this as other than a remnant of the "given." We can throw some additional light on this issue by examining how Hilary Putnam, after a long career of transitions from one form of realism to another, finally, by the late 1990s, arrived a vision of what he referred to as a form of realism that dispensed with the assumptions of representational philosophy.

Pinning Down Putnam

By the end of the twentieth century, Putnam had rejected dominant forms of scientific and metaphysical realism, including several to which he had once subscribed. He adopted a formulation that he explicitly equated with Wittgenstein and Austin (but which he claimed was foreshadowed in Aristotle as well as in the work of pragmatists such as William James and John Dewey).

As in the case of Davidson, an interpretation of Putnam depends to a large extent on the stage in his work that a reader happens to engage his arguments. All his work had, however, involved a search for an answer to what he called "the great question of realism" or the problem of how language attaches to the world. As in the case of Davidson, however, there was a problem with what it means to speak about attaching to the world if the "world" is not defined.

Putnam had begun in the 1950s as a logical empiricist but by the 1960s had embraced semantic externalism and a causal theory of reference similar to that of Kripke as well as a functionalist theory of mind, that is, the claim that the mind and mental states are analogous to the software of a computer. By the end of the 1970s, however, he had rejected the assumption that knowledge is based on the existence of a mind/language independent world. He instead subscribed to what he referred to as "internal realism," which was an idealized image of epistemic justification that rejected the idea of a correspondence theory of truth. By the 1990s, however, he renounced this position as simply an alternative to or negation of metaphysical realism and as yet another fruitless attempt to specify some trans-contextual account of truth.

His final position was actually a challenge to the whole debate about such things as realism and anti-realism and to any claim about an absolute conception of the world. He recognized that it was a mistake to interpret Wittgenstein as an anti-realist, because Wittgenstein had rejected the assumptions that supported claims about both realism and anti-realism. Like Austin, Putnam argued that realism and anti-realism simply "mirror" one another. He claimed that it was the very failure of empiricism that had long ago driven philosophers toward idealism as a solution, but he nevertheless maintained that "there is a way to do justice to our sense that knowledge claims are responsible to reality without recoiling into metaphysical fantasy" (1999, 4). The phrase "responsible to reality" still seemed, however, to imply a lingering representationalist problematic, but, at the same time, he rejected the assumption "that there must be an interface between our cognitive powers and the external world" (10). As an alternative, he advanced what he referred to as "direct," "natural," or "pragmatic" realism. Somewhat like Davidson, he presented this new form of realism as a disposal of the issue how we access the "world" and the recognition, as a philosophical claim, of its needlessness and unintelligibility. But speaking about this disposal as direct realism might still seem to imply that there is a universal that stands behind all reality claims. But on the other hand he also seemed to say that "reality" is indigenous to particular language-games.

Putnam claimed that if we examine something such as Wittgenstein's treatment of the duck/rabbit figure, it is clear that the visual experience is not a mental version or representation of the drawing on which we impose an interpretation. The sense that we attribute to the drawing is in the drawing itself and in the use of language as a whole. There is no need to philosophically underwrite our language-games and our various uses of the word "true." Mathematical necessity, for example, is neither, as the realist might claim, something that is deeper than our calculations but neither is it, as the anti-realist might claim, simply a heuristic. Mathematical necessity is a function of the language-game of mathematics. The criteria of truth are in the language-game. This might seem like a return to internal realism, but Putnam wished to find space between his argument and what he considered to be Rorty's relativism. He still wanted to hold on to an element of traditional realism, but he insisted that the world does not interpret our words for us or provide them with meaning. He claimed that the objects that we experience and perceive are "external," but we see them in terms of our theoretical and conceptual resources. This, however, still seemed to presume a gap between reality and our claims about it.

Putnam denied any ontological foundation of ethical judgment and criticized the "inflationary metaphysics" that had characterized the search for such foundations. He utterly rejected "the idea that there is a set of substantive necessary truths that it is the task of philosophy to discover," and he defended what he referred to as "pragmatic pluralism," that is, the claim that there are simply many language-games and uses of the words "reality" and "truth" (2005, 16–17, 21). He accepted what he referred to as "conceptual relativity" or "conceptual pluralism," which assumed different and incommensurable "optional languages" and "conventions" with different ontologies (43). He argued that the "whole idea that the *world* dictates a unique 'true' way of dividing up the world . . . is a piece of philosophical parochialism. But that parochialism is and always has been behind the subject called Ontology" and the assumption that objects are the ground of objectivity. He argued that there is "objectivity without objects" (51–52). He also spurned claims about a "bottomless regress of interpretations" which he attributed to individuals such as Foucault and Derrida and which he characterized as actually a form of "cultural imperialism." He included Rorty in this category, whom he characterized as embracing an "explicit" and "cultural relativism" (121), but Rorty refused the attribution of relativism if it meant anything more than the rejection of traditional realism.

As in the case of Davidson, Putnam, in the end, seemed ambivalent and to have some difficulty in articulating what constituted "direct realism." At times he seemed to be suggesting an identity between language and the "world" but at other times suggesting that language is something that attaches to a separate "world." But this problem was even more pronounced in the work of John McDowell.

Ambivalence in McDowell

McDowell's book *Mind and World* (1996) must be counted among the ranks of the anti-representationalist literature, but the title itself seems to imply the problem that occasioned representationalism. McDowell, in this respect, found it necessary to engage with philosophers such as Rorty and Davidson. Davidson noted that one of the differences between them is that "Rorty and I think that the interface between our bodies and the world is causal and nothing more, while McDowell holds that the world directly presents us with propositional contents" (2005, 321). For Rorty, what is given as the facts of the world are what is most immediately a matter of a tradition within a culture, but he seems to have assumed a deeper empirical connection. The proposition of causal connections between language and the "world" seems, however, to still be haunted by representationalism.

McDowell's book began with references to "mind," "thought," "world," "concepts," and other abstract terms that he seemed to assume are intelligible objects but to which he did not ascribe theoretical content. This failure plagued his whole discussion. He claimed, however, that his basic goal was the therapeutic one, in a somewhat Wittgensteinian sense, of less trying to solve the problem of the "relation of mind to world" than "exorcizing" the philosophical "anxieties" that gave rise to the appearance of the problem and to "unmask that appearance as illusion." He particularly wanted to challenge naturalized epistemologies, which he attributed to Davidson, and to advocate what he considered to be a kind of "minimal empiricism," which would be an alternative to "bald naturalism" and the "Given." He claimed that this required putting thought and mental episodes in a "normative context" of judgment and belief regarding how things are in the empirical world, but these, he argued, would at the same time be "answerable to the world" and qualify as knowledge. He suggested that "experience" of the world could be conceived as belonging to what Sellars called the "logical space of reasons" rather than as just "impressions" and that it is possible to rescue experience and empiricism by conceiving what is empirical or "natural" as conceptual. Nature, he maintained, includes our human "second nature," which is defined by our "conceptual capacities" (1996, xi–xxiv).

If his goal was to set aside the problem of how mind relates to the world, his argument still seemed to turn on this problem. He claimed that "concepts mediate the relation between minds and the world" or thought and reality (4). This image of concepts interfacing between mind and world is difficult to bring into focus as other than a return to the assumption that there is some "world" that stands outside our first-order claims. McDowell drew heavily on Kant's claim that "thoughts without content are empty and that intuitions without concepts are blind," which he took to mean that although we possess conceptual "freedom" and "spontaneity," it must be "constrained from outside" by experience and not become a self-contained game of coherence. He claimed, however, that "experiences already have conceptual content," and even though experience is "passive," it involves what is conceptual and spontaneous and therefore open to change (10, 13). He maintained that "if we reject the given, we are not thereby abolishing the outer reality" (21), but at the same time we must recognize the "unboundedness of the conceptual." "Although reality is independent of our thinking," it should not be viewed as "outside an outer boundary that encloses the conceptual sphere" (24–26).

I believe that this is ultimately an incoherent argument, which was an attempt to both reject and accept elements of the representational image. In making the case for a direct access to the world (27), he called upon Wittgenstein's remark in the *Investigations* that "When we say, and *mean*, that such-and-such is the case, we—and our meaning—do not stop anywhere short of the fact; but we mean: *this is so*" (2009, 95). This seems to be an odd reference, because the context of the remark was Wittgenstein's critique of his former Tractarian claim about the connection between language and the world, but McDowell's point was that "there is no ontological gap between the sort of thing one can mean, or generally the sort of thing one can think, and the sort of thing that can be the case," that is, "between thought, as such, and the world," even if thoughts can be false. He claimed that if we are to accept the independence of reality, we must accept a constraint on thinking and judging, but this constraint does not need to come from outside "*thinkable contents*" or "what is *thinkable*" (28). He wanted to avoid both idealism and realism, but there remained a question about exactly what he was saying that went beyond what, for example, Putnam had formerly espoused as "internal realism."

McDowell claimed that "experiences are impressions made by the world on our senses, products of receptivity," but because "those impressions themselves already have conceptual content," humans, unlike "mere animals," have "perceptual sensitivity to features of our environment" that takes a "special form" (47, 64). He claimed that "our second nature is the way it is not only because of the potentialities we are born with, but also because of upbringing, our *Bildung*" (87). "In mere animals, sentience is in the service of a mode of life that is structured exclusively by immediate biological imperatives," but when we "acquire conceptual powers," we have a second nature (115). He argued that the problem with something such as Thomas Nagel's question of what it is like to be a bat makes the mistake of treating what is at best "only a proto-subjectivity as if it were a full-fledged subjectivity" but one beyond our ken. Like Davidson, he claimed that "human infants are mere animals, distinctive only in their potential" (123).

It seems that despite McDowell's emphasis on such things as the primacy of concepts, he was struggling to articulate and reconcile at least two contending philosophical positions—direct realism and representational mediationalism. Austin once said that when facing this kind of dilemma the best solution is to jettison both and seek a new position. What was also still left hanging in McDowell's argument was exactly what constituted thinking and concepts as well as what role was played by references to the "world" and "reality." He finally noted something that had been glaringly absent from his discussion. He stated that "so far I have scarcely mentioned language" (124), but all along it seems that it was actually the possession of language that put us in the space of reasons and allowed a platform of "tradition" that is modified as humans develop. Although he wanted to exorcize the problems of representationalism, he seems to have found it difficult to extricate himself from the representational vocabulary and from treating such terms as "mind," "world," and "reality" as objects that we could trace the relationship between.

The answer to the issue in which McDowell was entangled is, first of all, to recognize that when we ask about something such as the relationship between the "mind" and the "world," it is not like talking about the relationship between two objects that have already been endowed with content. And it is not that our concepts mediate between our "mind" and the "world" or that our concepts are constrained by the "world." The world is what is presented *in* our concepts, that is, in our language. It is a mistake to talk about mind and world as if we were confronting an empirical problem, but there is in some respects a way of conceiving this issue as an empirical problem, which might have some bearing on philosophical matters. In this respect, it is worth looking at the work of Daniel Dennett.

Dennett: Making Wittgenstein and Ryle Empirical

Dennett had been a student of Ryle at Oxford, and he remained in contact with him. Shortly before Ryle's death, Dennett received a letter from Ryle responding to Dennett's forthcoming long critical review (1977) of Fodor's 1975 book in which Fodor had criticized Ryle's concept of mind. Ryle said that he was not sure that the book was "*about* anything" and expressed his grave doubts that Fodor's talk of mental representations and "mentalese" referred in any way to what Ryle considered was involved in "thinking," which was largely a matter of using words silently. He suggested that Fodor's cognitive psychology sounded "like the latter days of phlogiston-theory."

Ryle's influence on Dennett's analysis of mind and consciousness is apparent, and Dennett said that his "debt" to Wittgenstein was "large and long-standing." He initially conceived his arguments as a "radical" approach to a "redoing of Wittgenstein's attack on the 'objects' of conscious experience" (1991). The basic projects of Wittgenstein and Dennett are significantly different, but they are in many respects complementary. Dennett's aim, like that of Ryle, was to undermine the Cartesian image of the mind, but he also wanted to present a biological explanation of an alternative vision. Commentators often make a mistake when they reference the work of Dennett, and the work of Richard Dawkins on whom Dennett relied, for the purpose of either supporting or criticizing claims about biological reductionism. The attempt to explain social phenomena naturalistically is dubious, if for no other reason than the fact that what we take to be natural is hardly stable, and the explanation of social phenomena is, as Wittgenstein insisted, an explanation of meaning. It might, however, be interesting to speculate about how to explain the *existence* of social phenomena, and this was Dennett's ultimate concern. Although Dawkins and Dennett sought to explain the evolutionary biological foundations of human language and the characteristics we often associate with the word "consciousness," they argued that language and social phenomena in general are emergent and autonomous.

When Dawkins spoke about the "selfish gene" (1976), he was employing what Dennett would designate as the "intentional stance." Hume had claimed that animals think and reason because of what seemed to be behavioral and functional similarities between human and animal behavior, and Dennett noted that we can, and typically do, take this stance and apply our folk psychology to animals, and even physical objects, in order to predict and make sense of their behavior. We might say, for example, that it looks as if it wants to rain or that the dog intended to catch a rabbit. But he argued that literally to attribute thought to a creature requires the presence of linguistic capabilities that animals do not possess. Because, for example, animals are incapable of saying what mental state they are in, they are incapable of what we typically speak of as human thought.

Dennett's approach is only materialistic and reductionist in the sense that he argued that the properties that we typically attribute to the human mind and consciousness can be explained in terms of Darwinian evolutionary biology and the functioning of the brain. But he did not claim that these are the same as the brain. He could even be interpreted as an "eliminativist" with respect to the concept of the mind and has to some extent invited this ascription, but what he wished to eliminate is the myth of the mind as a Cartesian theater rather than the concept of the mind as a synonym for human linguistic and conceptual capacities. Many dualists, such as David Chalmers, claim that the actual content of the mind and consciousness is the persistent "hard problem" in philosophy and maybe in the end ineffable and mysterious, but Dennett was intent on revealing this content and how it operates rather than accepting the behaviorists' conclusion that it does not exist or cannot be accessed. Dennett has repeated his basic argument in a series of publications, the latest of which and most accessible and comprehensive is *From Bacteria to Bach and Back: The Evolution of Minds* (2017).

Dennett is not, despite what many critics, including Stanley Cavell, have claimed, a "consciousness denier" but a consciousness explainer. He argued that, both methodologically and in principle, the content of what we often refer to as consciousness could be discovered by what he referred to as "heterophenomenology," which would be a third-person "neutral portrayal of exactly *what it is like to be* that subject—in the subject's own terms, given the best interpretation we can muster" (1991, 98). This would amount to an empirical account of what we tend to speak of as the "mind" and "the maximally inclusive science of consciousness" (2005, 91). This fictional or at least notational product of first-person reports of what a person is thinking, feeling, or such, at a particular moment in a continuing Joycean mental narrative, would in turn produce multiple "drafts" of what we mean by the "self." All of this, however, might differ massively between cultures, but what biologically supports this narrative as well as most of what we designate as elements of mental capacity is, Dennett argued, a "virtual machine," that is, the complex parallel processing structure of the brain. However one may judge Dennett's particular method of accessing and explaining consciousness, it is clear that his project is not to explain *away* the concepts of mind and consciousness but to explain the existence of the characteristics that are typically attributed to them. And he is as much opposed to simply identifying the mind with the brain as he is with any form of traditional dualism. What his analysis entails is that whatever we might consider consciousness in a variety of creatures, what we mean by speaking of human consciousness is inseparable from language. It makes no sense to ask a bat what it is like to be a bat, but we can ask a human what it is like to be a human.

Dennett's long Darwinian story of the evolution of what we might think of as human consciousness (1995) culminated in an account of the transition to what surpassed human biology. What was ultimately crucial for Dennett was his reading of Dawkins's book. Although Dawkins is sometimes categorized as a sociobiologist, he presented an extended argument about the manner in which human evolution had led to the emergence of "units of cultural transmission analogous to the genes," which he and Dennett dubbed "memes." Dennett argued that "an impersonal, unreflective, robotic, mindless little scrap of molecular machinery is the ultimate basis of all the agency, and hence, meaning, and hence consciousness, in the universe," but this latter dimension of human life is sui generis. Although a person is made up of robots, a human being as a whole is not a robot. But Dennett claimed that characteristics of the human dimension such as "intentionality doesn't come from on high; it percolates up from below, from the initially mindless and pointless algorithmic processes that gradually acquire meaning and intelligence as they develop" (205). What distinguishes the human species is "reliance on cultural transmission of information, and hence on cultural evolution" of which language and its artifacts are the primary medium and of which memes and their vehicles such as books and pictures are the units (331, 338). For Dennett, the mind, thinking, and consciousness are simply names for the classes of things that humans distinctively can do, and these are really all functions of language and convention.

The term "meme" has now been incorporated into the language of popular culture, where its use is not always entirely clear, but even for Dawkins and Dennett, it is less a specific thing than a semantic classification. Although they argue that the human genotype has remained constant, the phenotype has been radically transformed by cultural evolution. This has taken place through the invasion of memes which, via the recursive Baldwin effect, have changed the hardware and architecture of the brain and added "systems of representation" (Dennett 1991, 191), which mediate between us and the environment and enhance the capabilities of the hardware. For both Dawkins and Dennett, the operation of memes is analogous to genes, that is, replicators seeking their own good, and the effects are by no means necessarily beneficial for biological fitness and survival. Consequently, there is constant tension between the biological imperatives of the genes and the cultural impact of memes, but in the end, only humans can "rise above the imperatives of our genes" (Dennett 1995, 365). Memes are an evolutionary "crane" that is an integral part of the development of our phenotype, and our human intelligence should not be considered diminished because it is the result of millions of years of biological evolution rather than some mysterious or metaphysical element of human nature.

Even though most philosophers seem to agree that traditional dualism is false, there are still those such as Chomsky and Nagel who believe that something is left out of an account such as that of Dennett, that is, what are often referred to as "qualia" and other subjective feelings or what philosophers such as Searle take to be ontological subjectivity. Dennett sees this as simply the residue of dualism and what he was the first to label as "folk psychology," which he believes is a useful heuristic but theoretically false. One of his principal concerns is the residual attachment to what he refers to as the "Zombie Hunch" embraced by philosophers such as Chalmers, that is, the belief that there could be a creature (or computer) that could do everything that a human could do but still lack qualia, understanding, consciousness, and subjectivity. Dennett argues that this idea is incoherent. There is no traditional subject in charge, and, what we might refer to in shorthand as the "mind" is in fact a "meme machine" that other animals lack, because they lack language as something more than a form of communication (2005, 172). Dawkins and Dennett did not initially provide a highly developed theory of memes, but, among others, Susan Blackmore (1999), with a long forward by Dawkins, has attempted to present a more complete picture of the "meme machine." The characteristics that are attributed to consciousness really depend on the capacity for convention or what the anthropologist Terrence Deacon speaks of as symbolization and how this capacity "emerged from matter" (2012, 1997).

For several years I have followed the debate between the field linguist Daniel Everett and Chomsky (and the latter's various mind-first followers). The debate has recently been clearly but polemically summarized in Tom Wolfe's *The Kingdom of Speech* (2016). Although we may never know exactly when or how human language emerged, Everett argued, after many years of intensive study of the Pirahã people of the Amazon, that language, as the Sapir-Whorf hypothesis had suggested, is a cultural artifact rather than, as Pinker claims, an "instinct" rooted in a mysterious genetic mutation that resulted in a universal language of thought expressed through the medium of culturally diverse natural languages. I suggest that Everett's thesis complements both Wittgenstein's philosophical account and Dennett's evolutionary addendum.

Although the more recent critics of representationalism have often taken their cues from Wittgenstein, there is, as we have seen, sometimes a question of whether they have fully exorcized the problems or whether they have attempted to solve them by suggesting that we have some sort of pragmatic, direct, causal, or unmediated access to the world. They emphasized that it is impossible to separate what we speak about as human thought from the possession of language, but the metaphor of direct realism is problematical. It implies two specified objects that are connected without intermediary links, but although this might apply in the case of normal science where a particular accepted object is assigned a name, the "world," as such, is not such an object. For Wittgenstein, the relationship between language and the world was a unity. To talk about a world that stands apart from language or about a language that does not embody a world is meaningless. Such a world without content is the world that is "well lost." If there is a world that somehow impinges on us causally to reveal its contents or if we have some kind of direct access to the world, it seems as if it would be necessary to ask why, over time, there have been so many incommensurable accounts of the "world" within science, between science, religion, politics, and common sense, and between different cultures. The point is not that the "world" is a figment of linguistic imagination but that it is only to be found in the presentations of first-order discourses. And it is necessary to explore more fully the nature of first-order practices and the distinction between representation and presentation.

First-order practices can be described as primordial, ontological, given, theoretical, foundational, and presentational in that they are the source of the "facts of nature" and tell us what exists and the manner of its existence. In searching for "reality," we cannot go beyond these, because they are what give content to the concept of the "world," are the "rock bottom" of conventionality, and are the basic object of interpretive representative second-order philosophical and social inquiry. In order to explain more fully the character of first-order and second-order practices, and the difference between presentation and representation, as well as the relationship between them, I will, in the next chapter, trace the emergence of this distinction in the *Tractatus* and in its later manifestations in Wittgenstein's work. Along the way, I want to dispel the common assumption that the *Tractatus* is an impenetrable and mysterious work as well as the belief that, given his repudiation of his earlier approach to philosophy, that it is not really relevant to understanding his philosophy. My reading, however, must be placed in the context of current scholarship.

Beginning in the 1990s, a significant number of scholars have joined Cora Diamond in some form of what has been variously called the "resolute," "austere," "new," and "therapeutic" reading of the *Tractatus.* Wittgenstein had claimed that the sentences of the work were nonsense but that they nevertheless were elucidatory. For some interpreters this had meant that the book was intended to convey somewhat ineffable truths, but for Diamond and others it signified that Wittgenstein intended to demonstrate that the kind of philosophical project in which he seemed to be engaged was fruitless and literally nonsense and misconceived and that by implication this meant that he had never been committed to the endeavor. To read the book in any other way Diamond argued (1991) was to "chicken out."

It would be a mistake to assume that this argument is one-dimensional. It has taken some quite interesting forms and raised some provocative questions, but, on the whole, this deconstructionist reading is often, I believe, a case of over-interpretation that flies in the face of biographical, autobiographical, and textual evidence, which all indicate that despite some significant continuities between his earlier and later work, there were some very important and decisive shifts in his philosophy. I suggest that if the book is approached without preconceptions and various prior agendas, it contains, despite some difficult portions, a relatively straightforward argument. What I wish to accomplish in discussing this book is at least threefold. First, my distinction between representation and presentation is a further part of my defense of conventional realism. Second, I want to make clear both how Wittgenstein's philosophy significantly changed between the *Tractatus* and the *Investigations* but also the continuities between the earlier and later work and particularly *On Certainty*. And third, as I noted in the introduction, although Wittgenstein's name often comes up in political theory, there are very few theorists who are familiar with the actual content of the *Tractatus*, and so it is important to offer a clear interpretation of this complex work.

6

Presentation and Representation in Social Inquiry

> I take it that Michelangelo was as good as anyone can be and did his best, and here is the picture of the Deity creating Adam. . . . If we ever saw this, we certainly wouldn't think this the Deity. The picture has to be used in an entirely different way if we are to call the man in that queer blanket, God.
>
> The way you use the word "God" does not show *whom* you mean, but what you mean.
>
> WITTGENSTEIN

A Critical Distinction

In the English language, there is considerable variation in the uses of the terms "present" and "represent," just as there is in German in the case of *Darstellung* and *Vorstellung*. One can, of course, like Humpty-Dumpty and James Joyce, use these terms to mean whatever one wants, but, both etymologically and grammatically, an important conceptual distinction is often implied. In this respect, *only what has already been presented can be re-presented.* Michelangelo might be interpreted as attempting to represent a biblical presentation of God, but I suggest that even in terms of that construal, he was not *representing* God but *presenting* a conception of God.

As I have already pointed out, it can be misleading to speak about something such as how the everyday practice of natural science represents natural facts, because what is involved is an internal relationship. These fields are engaged at the theoretical level in the "presentation" of these facts, which then becomes the subject of their investigations. Although social inquiry either must assume or present a theoretical account of social phenomena, its basic practice is one of investigating and representing an autonomous presentational domain of conceptually pre-constituted facticity to which such inquiry has no internal logical relationship. The purpose of an interpretation is to clarify and convey the meaning that is endemic in the objects of inquiry, which is composed of what social actors say and do. We may claim that a particular interpretation is right or wrong, but our assessment does not determine the constitution of what is interpreted.

If someone maintains that theories in natural science represent prior facts of nature, it would be in the same sense that we might refer to what we see when we look in a mirror as a representation. It is, of course, a reflection and not, strictly speaking, a representation any more than, for example, an echo is a representation of a sound wave or smoke is a representation of fire. These are internally related. The representations advanced by social science are, however, depictions, which can be compared with the objects that they depict and in terms of which their verisimilitude can be debated. In the case of art, what is usually classified as "representative," "figurative," and "realistic" all refer to the *depiction* of certain objects or events, even if the depictions are considered romantic, impressionist, or abstract. Representations are constructed and stand in for and refer to objects that have been presented and "show" themselves in word and deed. There are, however, also purely presentational mediums, which do not refer to anything outside the symbolic universe that they project. This is the case with certain forms of art, but in the theater there are both representational and presentational mediums. In representational performances, the audience is assumed to be something of a voyeur, largely ignored, and left to interpret what is going on, but in presentational theater the audience is expressly acknowledged and drawn into the action such as in the case of Thornton Wilder's *Our Town* in which the "stage manager" speaks to the audience.

Some of the complexities of the relationship between the concepts of presentation and representation can be fruitfully sorted out and explored through a close examination of Wittgenstein's *Tractatus.* Four aspects of this work that I emphasize are, first, how Wittgenstein at this point still assumed a basic disjunction between thought and language. Second, what he referred to as representation was fundamentally different than how he would conceive it in the *Investigations.* Third, despite differences between the *Tractatus* and his later work, there were important similarities, one of which was the recognition, so evident in *On Certainty*, that scientific representations of the "world" presuppose theoretical presentations. And fourth, his intention was not to elevate empirical propositions as the paradigm of meaning but to distinguish them as a particular form of meaning.

Presentation and Representation in the *Tractatus Logico-Philosophicus*

It is at least a matter of historical interest that the main title of the book was not actually Wittgenstein's original formulation, which became his subtitle and translated as "A Logical Philosophical Treatise." The Latin title was the suggestion of G. E. Moore, but it may also have alluded to Spinoza, whom Bertrand Russell considered the "noblest" of philosophers. One might speculate that Wittgenstein believed, and reasonably, that there was a parallel between his "Logical Philosophical" and Spinoza's "Theological Political." In each case, the first term was considered to be the essence of the second.

In the preface, Wittgenstein claimed that the "problems of philosophy" are manifestations of the fact that "the logic of our language is misunderstood," but that once that logic is clarified, "what can be said at all can be said clearly, and what we cannot speak about we must pass over in silence." What he referred to as what can be "said" was, however, even on his terms, actually a very specific and narrow sense of *sagen*. It is a mistake to interpret him as claiming that only a small number of statements are meaningful. What he was arguing was that only a small class of statements could be said in a way that was characteristic of factual statements in natural science, and he would also make clear that such statements did not exhaust the scope of natural science. He maintained that there are many *thoughts* that are *not* assessable in terms of truth and falsity by comparison with the world. He said that "the aim of the book is to draw a limit . . . to the *expression* [*Ausdrückt*] of thoughts [*Gedanken*]; for in order to be able to draw a limit to thought, we should have to find both sides of the limit thinkable (i.e. we would have to be able to think what cannot be thought)" (emphasis added). Therefore he claimed that it is only "in language that a limit can be drawn" and that "what lies on the other side will be simply nonsense [*Unsinn*]," that is, attempting to say what cannot be thought. But here we confront a major and persistently contentious issue in the interpretation of the *Tractatus.*

When he spoke about various statements as "nonsense," did this word, as typically used in German, mean something totally meaningless, untrue, and just plain baloney, or did it signify only what lacked what is often translated as "propositional" sense, that is, what is empirically perceivable and demonstrable. It seems that the answer is the latter, because the claim was advanced in the context of making a general distinction between those thoughts that can be stated as empirical claims and those that cannot. And he would go on to specify a number of forms of language that were meaningful but not statements of empirical fact. When he used *Unsinn* in the *Tractatus*, he was usually referring to grammatical confusions, while he often used *unsinnig*, a less pejorative term, to indicate a variety of sentences that were in some respect meaningful but could not be compared to the "world." For example, he designated some statements that took the *form* of empirical propositions as actually "pseudo-propositions" (*Scheinsätze*), but this did not necessarily entail that they lacked intelligible meaning.

He claimed that the basic value of his work was in the "thoughts expressed," which, as he would make clear, included expressions that were not themselves empirical propositions. They were, he claimed, "shown" or presented. And "the better the thoughts—the more the nail has been hit on the head—the greater will be the value." He also claimed that "the *truth* of the thoughts that are here communicated seems to me unassailable and definitive" and that his book provided the "final solution of the problems" of philosophy, by which he presumably meant the problems associated with how to represent the world, which had been at the heart of traditional philosophy. He noted, nevertheless, "*how little has been achieved when these problems are solved*" (emphasis added), which again implied that there were realms of meaning that exceeded the limits of empirical propositions.

Wittgenstein continually stressed that the basic perspective from which the book was written was the problem of how to represent the "facts" that compose the physical "world," which, in effect, was to ask how the everyday practice of natural science is possible. *But what he referred to as representation was actually a matter of logical identity*, and this was decisively different from what in his later work he would mean by "representation." A "fact" consisted of a "state of affairs," which, in turn, was a combination of autonomous, nameable, "unalterable" "objects," which were independent of each other but nevertheless parts of a "structure" in which they "stand in a determinate relation to one another." The "world" or "reality" was simply conceived as the "totality of existing states of affairs," and the fundamental question posed was how language could *represent* this world (1–2.061). His answer was logical identity.

He wanted to construct a one-to-one "picture" or "model of reality" in which the "elements of the picture are the representatives of objects." He claimed that the "pictorial form is the possibility that things are related to one another in the same way as the elements of a picture," which is "how a picture is attached to reality," "reaches out to it," and can be "laid against reality as a measure." The correct relationship is achieved when there is "something identical in a picture and what it depicts." This "something identical" was what he claimed was a *logic* that permeated both language and the world and which thereby internally connected them. Since he was, from the outset, forced to deal with the problem of how to define representation, this required confronting the issue of what was *not* representation and could not be empirically stated. This included the nature of the connection between a signifier and what was signified, which could only be "shown," because a picture cannot "place itself outside its representative form" and "depict its pictorial form." Nevertheless, it "displays" (*weist*) that form. What the picture and what it represents have, or do not have, in common, is this "logical form, i.e., the form of reality," and agreement or lack of agreement with "reality" was the criterion of determining if a picture had meaning or "sense" (*Sinn*) and could be judged as either true or false (2.12–2.23).

In the *Tractatus*, then, a "logical picture of reality" began as a pre-linguistic thought, and the "totality of true thoughts," that is, thoughts that could be expressed as empirical propositions and verified, was "a picture of the world." He claimed that there are, however, no a priori correct thoughts of this kind, and it is only through the verbal expression or "projection" of a thought, or what he referred to as a "propositional sign" or statement of fact, that it "can be perceived by the senses" and compared with the world. However, much like his later equation of meaning and use, he insisted again that "what signs fail to express, their application 'shows' [*zeigt*]." The most "simple" or "primitive" signs were "names," which could be "explained by means of 'elucidations' [*Erläuterungen*], which consisted of 'propositions' [*Sätze*] that contain the primitive signs," and "only in the nexus of a propositional sentence does a name have meaning." So truth and meaning required both correspondence and coherence. The "totality of propositions is a language," and "definitions are rules for translating from one language to another" (3–4.001).

He claimed that although humans have a capacity "to construct languages capable of expressing every sense," our "everyday language is part of the human organism and is no less complicated," and "the tacit conventions on which the understanding of everyday language depends are enormously complicated." Consequently, it is not "possible to gather immediately from it what the logic of language is." Because "language disguises thought," and like "the outward form of the clothing" that "is not designed to reveal the form of the body," a person cannot easily "infer the form of thought beneath it." He would cling to a similar argument in the *Investigations*, but it would not be thought that was often disguised but rather the way in which language was being used. Although he maintained that "all philosophy is a critique of language," and the task of philosophy should be to clarify the logic of language, he claimed that "most of the propositions and questions of philosophers" have arisen from a failure to understand that logic, and many of what are considered "the deepest problems are in fact *not* problems at all." Thus he claimed that most of the propositions (*Sätze*) and questions to be found in philosophical works are not false but *unsinnig* in that they lack empirical meaning (4.002–4.0031). This was, however, as he would go on to make clear, also the case with the *Tractatus* itself.

It is important to note that he did not conceive of an empirical claim as necessarily taking the form of a written sentence in a natural language. It was a picture or model of reality and could even consist of signs such as musical notes. These were all forms of "saying." His point, however, was to demonstrate how the logical structure of a symbolic form could mirror the logical structure of the world and how this connection was a mode of "internal relationship." He illustrated this by noting how "a gramophone record, the musical idea, the written notes, and the sound-waves all stand for one another in the same internal relation of depicting that holds between language and the world," that is, they were all in one respect the same and each could be derived from another. He argued that in this respect "a proposition shows [*zeigt*] its sense" and how it "constructs a world with the help of logical scaffolding" and gains meaning. This logic had meaning (*Sinn*) that was independent of the facts. Even though it could not, itself, be represented and judged true or false, it was "shown" in the application or use of a sentence (4.01–4.061). Again, his construal of representation was logical identity.

He emphasized once more that "the totality of true propositions is the whole of natural science." This entailed, however, that "philosophy is not one of the natural sciences," and that, like the *Tractatus* itself, it was a discourse that was, in his words, either "above" or "below" science. Again, he claimed that "philosophy aims at the logical clarification of thoughts" and is not a "body of doctrine but an activity" consisting of "elucidations" and the "clarification of propositions" rather than creating "'philosophical' propositions" of the kind that he had defined as empirical propositions. The purpose was to make "thoughts" less "cloudy and indistinct" and to give them "sharp boundaries," such as that between sentences representing the world and those that performed other functions such as "presenting" or "showing." What he was saying about thoughts was, however, what he would later say about language use.

This focus on thoughts was not, he claimed, the same as that of psychology and its study of mental processes, any more than of "any other natural science," but he did suggest, as Ryle later would, that in effect epistemology or the "theory of knowledge is the philosophy of psychology." He argued that "philosophy sets limits to the much disputed sphere of natural science" and to "what can be thought; and in doing so to what cannot be thought" about the world. *His principal concern was not to debase claims that were not factual but instead to demonstrate the difference.* Philosophy could "signify what cannot be said, by *presenting* clearly what can be said" in empirical propositions (emphasis added). And he reiterated that "everything that can be thought at all can be thought clearly" and that "all that can be put into words can be put clearly," even if, in practice, it often is not put clearly. But he repeated that although, in principle, "propositions can represent [*darstellen*] the whole of reality, they cannot represent what they must have in common with reality in order to be able to represent it." The logical internal relation between language and the world was outside the world but nevertheless "mirrored" (*spiegelt*) or manifest in propositions about the world. "What finds its reflection in language, language cannot represent," and "what expresses *itself* in language, *we* cannot represent in language." He reiterated that a proposition "shows" (*zeigt*) or "presents" (*weist*) the logical form of reality, and "what *can* be shown, *cannot* be said," that is, what is involved in showing cannot be stated in a manner whose truth or falsity can be evaluated by comparison with the world (4.11–4.122).

All of this implicitly raised the question of, among other things, the status of what he referred to as a "formal concept," which he stressed should not be conceived "as a proper concept-word [*Begriffswort*]," that is, a word that referred to an object. Such concepts were "senseless" or nonsensical (*unsinnige*) but not the kind of complete nonsense that might arise from something such as mixing up the phrase "there are objects," which was *Unsinn*, with a phrase such as "there are books." While true elementary propositions consisting of names are capable of completely describing the world and, in the process "showing" what they say, tautologies, contradictions, and other such concepts that belong to the "symbolism" of logic, show what they say by actually saying nothing, in that they do not represent anything. They are *sinnlos* but not meaningless (4.461–4.611).

After an extended critical discussion of certain problems in formal logic, truth-functions, and probability theory, he turned to questions about propositions in psychology, such as talking about what someone believes or thinks. He concluded that his analysis "shows [*zeigt*] that there is no such thing as the soul [mind, *Seele*]—the subject, etc.—as it is conceived in the superficial psychology of the present day." He stressed, and would continue to maintain in his later work, that "there is no such thing as the subject that thinks or entertains ideas," that is, the "metaphysical subject" as an object that is part of the world. It is simply "a limit of the world in the same way that the eye is a limit to the visual field but not a part of it." He suggested that in this sense solipsism was a kind of "pure realism." It was in this context that he claimed that "*the limits of my language mean the limits of my world.*" He concluded that since "logic pervades the world: the limits of the world are also its limits," and that once we understand the underlying logic of our language, we can see that "all the propositions of our everyday language, just as they stand, are in perfect logical order," even if that order is not always apparent. This suggested that "what the solipsist *means* is quite correct" even though that meaning "cannot be said, but makes itself manifest [*zeigt*]," in that "the world is *my* world" and the "limits of language (of the language which I alone understand) mean the limits of my world." As in the preface, he reiterated that since "we cannot think what we cannot think . . . what we cannot think we cannot say either" (5.5421–5.64).

An important, but often overlooked, point in the *Tractatus*, which is crucial for my argument, was the recognition that although the practice of science was in the business of stating facts, these facts were defined within, and internally related to, theories. He noted that "Darwin's theory," like, for example, "Newtonian mechanics, imposes a unified form on the description of the world" (4.1122). Such a description is "'a priori' and tells us nothing about the world" but instead presents a framework for describing the world, which itself cannot be compared with the world and judged true or false. But in this way, claims such as "the laws of physics, with all their logical apparatus, still speak, however indirectly, about the objects of the world." He argued that "the whole modern conception of the world is founded on the illusion that the so-called laws of nature are the explanation of natural phenomena" and are causal in the manner that fate or god may have functioned in former times. These laws do not directly represent the world in the manner of empirical generalizations but instead indicate the meaning or "sense [*Sinn*] of the world," which itself is "outside the world" and provides the context of explanation (6.13–6.41). As he would again stress in *On Certainty*, they "show" or present the world. Although in his later work he would strongly reject what he sometimes referred to as theoretical explanations in favor of description and clarification, what he was referring to as "theories" at this point reflected a very narrow image of theory, which included such things as metaphysics. If we think of theory in a broader sense, consistent with what he specified in the *Tractatus* as scientific theories as well as with what we today would usually classify as theories in natural science (evolution, plate tectonics, relativity, etc.), we can ascribe a theory to the *Investigations*, that is, a theory or presentational claim about the nature of conventional phenomena as well as an entailed methodology regarding what is involved in representing such phenomena.

It might seem ironic that so much of what he talked about in the book included things that were *not* representable in the manner he specified. Among the many things that were only manifest in presentation were not only scientific theories but logic. Logic was not a body of doctrine, but a reflection or mirror-image of the world. Logic, he claimed, is "transcendental" and not itself empirical. It was, like mathematics, a symbolism consisting of "pseudo-propositions" and not something "experimental" or something that "expresses a thought." The various things that he claimed stood outside the world of fact were not all identically the same thing, but they belonged to the same general category. Among these things were logic, formal concepts, scientific theories, values, ethics, aesthetics, and philosophy. So, again, it is important to recognize that the *Tractatus* was not holding up empirical propositions as the essence of meaning but showing how they constituted a very limited realm of meaning.

He maintained, for example, that in the world, there is no "value" that has the status of a fact. Consequently, "it is impossible for there to be propositions of ethics," because, like logic, "ethics is transcendental" and cannot be expressed in empirical propositions. This was also the case with "aesthetics" and with what might be considered "mystical," such as the manner in which "it is not *how* things are in the world that is mystical but *that* it exists." But although "there are things that cannot be put into words" and are mystical, "*they make themselves manifest* [*zeigt*]" in various ways. These ways were, nevertheless, as he had already indicated, not necessarily lacking meaning and even verbal expression, but they were not assertoric in the manner that he had defined empirical propositions.

He suggested that, in principle, it might seem that "the correct method in philosophy would really be . . . to say nothing except what can be said" as propositions of natural science, but, as he had already noted, philosophy consisted of "elucidations" that stood outside the facts of the world. He claimed that "my propositions [*Sätze*] [and here he meant "sentences" or at least *Scheinsätze*] serve as elucidations in the following way: anyone who understands me eventually recognizes them as nonsensical" in that they were senseless (*unsinnig*). When a reader has "used them—as steps to climb beyond them—he must, so to speak, throw away the ladder after he has climbed up it. He must transcend these propositions and then he will see the world aright." And, as he said in the preface, "what we cannot speak about [empirically] we must pass over in silence" and discern them in terms of what is manifest or shows/presents itself in its application (6.53–6.54). In a letter to Russell (McGuinness and von Wright 1997, 124–25), he repeated basically what he had said in the preface: "the main point of the *theory* [emphasis added] is that what can be said [*gesagt*] by proposition [*Satz*]—i.e. by language (and what comes to the same, what can be *thought*) and what is not expressed by proposition, but only shown [*gezeigt*]; which, I believe, is the cardinal problem of philosophy." This is what I have referred to as the difference between representation and presentation.

If we read the *Tractatus* as simply a defense of empirical science, we miss a large dimension of what he was arguing. There was, he maintained, an ethical point to the *Tractatus*. Although there has been considerable controversy about what that point may have been, it was at least in part to distinguish between empirical judgments and value judgments. Although positivists read the work as depreciating the cognitive status of values, Wittgenstein actually insisted on the autonomy of values and ethical judgment as presentational claims. He could be construed as a moral realist in the sense of a theoretical or presentational realist.

While the *Tractatus* struggled with the issue of how thought and language could represent the world, *the "world" (Welt) is barely mentioned* in the *Investigations* and then primarily in the context of expressly rejecting what might seem to be the basic project defined in the *Tractatus*. Wittgenstein had early on, even before the publication of the *Tractatus*, noted that "the difficulty of my theory of logical portrayal was that of finding a connexion between the signs on paper and a situation outside in the world" (2012, 19), but he finally concluded that there was no such logical connection. The question of how a sentence could represent the world was answered by saying that nothing mysterious is involved and that it is apparent in the use of the sentence (2009, 435). Language was related to the "world" by being applied to objects in the world, but it was in the course of such application that the objects were discriminated and given an identity. The relationship was one of unity.

This image of philosophy as clarification and elucidation would persist in Wittgenstein's work despite fundamental changes in his philosophical position. In later years, he said that "anything that can be reached with a ladder does not interest me," which might imply that he rejected the ladder metaphor as characterizing the role of philosophy. But what at that point he was rejecting was not the idea of philosophy as elucidation but the notion of philosophy as attempting to answer the kinds of questions that had preoccupied metaphysics and representational philosophy.

The *Investigations*: Some Key Transitions

Although there are some important similarities between the *Tractatus* and Wittgenstein's later work, there can be little doubt that he fundamentally changed his view of such things as the nature of logic and the relationships both between language and thought and between language and the world. The distinction between representation and presentation persisted, but in a more radical manner—*because representations were no longer conceived as grounded in an internal logical identity between signifier and signified*. They belonged to a different order of discourse, and one of the greatest problems was to distinguish representations from what was represented. And although he was still concerned with what constituted nonsense, he developed a broader view of the matter.

In the *Investigations*, he noted that if some combination of words is deemed to lack sense or meaning, this renders it nonsense (*Unsinn*) and "excludes it from the sphere of language, and thereby bounds the domain of language," but he claimed that the act of drawing such a boundary "is not yet to say what I am drawing it for," which could be for "various kinds of reasons" (2009, 499–500). When he used *Unsinn* in the *Investigations*, he was not doing so for any single specific reason. It did not, however, usually connote what he at one point talked about as "plain nonsense" or what simply lacked any intelligible meaning, that is, what was *sinnlos*, or maybe, because it was something such as a truism, simply *unsinnig* (39–40, 119, 247, 252, 511–13; *PPF* 19). It might, however, include what was peculiarly "philosophers' nonsense," such as taking literally the claim that "I know what I want" (524; *PPF* 309), but in examining such a case, the concern was to move from "unobvious to obvious nonsense" (464). He emphasized that using a word without a fixed meaning did not necessarily make the word nonsense or impair its use (79), and nonsense was not without meaning when used, for example, in a nonsense poem or fairy tale (282). And he famously said "Don't *for heaven's sake*, be afraid of talking nonsense! Only don't fail to pay attention to your nonsense" (1998, 64).

By the 1930s, he had moved steadily in the direction of conceiving of philosophy as a form of social inquiry, that is, understanding, interpreting, and representing language-games and forms of life. He was no longer concerned with how philosophy could underwrite or judge claims about the natural world but instead with the question of how the conventions that defined social phenomena could be understood and represented or interpreted. Two themes emerged as central. The first was that the subject of representation is not thoughts, that is, the mental states and processes of social actors, and the second was that although representation requires a language of representation, this should not be confused with what is represented. Interpretations or representations did not determine meaning, which are intrinsic to the language or practice that is being represented. Although when Wittgenstein wrote the *Tractatus*, he clearly believed that language was a vehicle for expressing thoughts, even if he could not specify exactly what constituted thought. "'Does a Gedanke consist of words?' No! But of psychical constituents that have the same sort of relation to reality as words. What those constituents are I don't know" (1998b, 131). By the point of his lectures in English that were published as *The Blue and Brown Books*, he had, as I have already discussed, concluded that it was meaningless to talk about the content of thought as other than something linguistic and manifest in social practices and conventions.

His argument assumed that a representation and what was represented belonged to two different levels of concepts, which were not internally related. Although much of the *Investigations* was devoted to the issues of what kind of thing is represented and how to represent it, he noted that "the concept of representation of what is seen, like that of a copy, is very elastic, and so *together with it* is the concept of what is seen" (2009; *PPF* 147). In the *Tractatus*, he had already noted that a geometric cube could be seen as two different facts, but although he no longer believed that the vehicle of representation and the object of representation shared a common logical form, he still wanted to solve the problem of how to achieve interpretive "clarity" about meaning. He noted, however, that "there is not a single philosophical method, though there are indeed methods, different therapies, as it were." These had to be adapted to a particular subject matter, which "consisted of language and the activities into which it is woven" (7) and which constituted various "forms of life." But it was also necessary to *invent* language-games, which served as ideal-types and modes of investigation and representation.

A central problem, as in all representation and interpretation, was how to avoid what he now saw as the mistake (which he had made in the *Tractatus*) of confusing the "mode" or "means of representation" with the thing that is represented (50), that is, where "one predicates of the thing what lies in the mode of representation" (50, 104, 397). The problem was to gain an adequate "*overview*" (*übersehen*) by "finding and inventing *intermediate links*," which would yield a synoptic, surveyable, summary (*übersichtliche*) and produce understanding by grasping "connections" between particulars and serve as *objects of comparison*, which through similarities and dissimilarities, are meant to throw light on features of our language. He claimed that such a "representation is of fundamental importance" and characterizes "the way we represent things, how we look at matters" (122, 130). He posed the question of whether this was a "*Weltanschauung*," but he later decided it was not because, unlike Spengler's use of the term, it did not assume that there was some underlying essence that was manifest in, and allowed one to speak in general about, the particular phenomena under investigation. Family resemblances were in the eye of the "representer." Wittgenstein often used anthropological examples to illustrate philosophical investigation. He once noted that philosophy was not ethnology—the purposes and modes of inquiry were peculiar to each, but he said that we must approach the subject matter of philosophy from an ethnological perspective, that is, an interpretive perspective.

In his later work, he set himself against the "dogmas" of traditional metaphysics as well as the attempt of philosophy to perform as if it were a natural science. His concern was no longer with a logical "*super*-order" that "the world and thinking must have in common." The "world" was not a "*super*-concept" but only a word with various "humble" uses (96–97). There was, however, the question of how to perform interpreting and representing. Despite sometimes heated debates about the proper method, this is a pragmatic matter, depending on the interpretive purpose and the particular objects of investigation. As Wittgenstein stressed, there are many potential forms of "perspicuous representation," and, as Max Weber argued, there are many ideal-types that might be employed. The great dangers in social inquiry, as both individuals emphasized, are fossilizing a mode of representation, reifying the form of representation, confusing one form with another, and assuming that one form is paradigmatic.

What Wittgenstein had to say in the *Tractatus*, and later in his "Lecture on Ethics," about values and ethical judgment squares with what was implicit in the *Investigations* but clearly enunciated in *On Certainty*. Values may seem indeterminate, but they are no more or less indeterminate than facts. Both gain their status in terms of their presentational foundations, either inherited or acquired. The image of the arbitrariness and fragility, and even relativity, of values is more a legend than anything convincingly demonstrated. Both fact and value are conventional, that is, grounded in conventions. When conventions are weakened, whether in the manner in which Kuhn characterized paradigms and theories in natural science, or in the manner of upheavals in social and cultural practices, what is factual becomes as contested as what is right and just. But as both Wittgenstein and Kuhn pointed out, it is in these situations that new presentational claims and innovations emerge. There is no general explanation for why and how this happens, such as someone such as Bhaskar claimed, but it is possible to suggest, as Kuhn did, a syndrome by noting family resemblances among instances of transformation. When things change, either in science or politics, some people, however, will attempt, as Wittgenstein noted in *On Certainty*, to stay in the "saddle" no matter how much the facts or values may "buck," while others embrace new concepts and change the criteria for applying words such as "good," "true," and "real." This is why Wittgenstein put ethics, aesthetics, and scientific theories in the same general category. Just as claims about what things populate the world, values tell us what is right and wrong—and, as I will argue in the next chapter, both are ungrounded apart from the presentational conventions that support them.

There is an important sense in which Bishop Berkeley was on the right track. He was attacking the representational arguments of Descartes and Locke, but his problem was the retention of the concept of a mind populated by ideas. Once we dispense with "mind" and "idea" as anything more than useful words that can be applied in a number of ways, we can gain some traction, but what still retains a hold on much of our everyday way of speaking and on philosophy is the two-worlds, or appearance and reality, metaphor.

This may apply when we talk about something such as the story of the Wizard of Oz, but not when we talk about a "world" that exceeds the content of our concepts but which itself cannot be specified and described. It is this ghost that requires busting. As I have stressed, natural scientists are not actually subscribers to the two-worlds myth, because they assume that they are like explorers opening up new frontiers and often do not realize, as Kuhn pointed out in the case of Max Planck, that they have re-conceptualized some dimension of the "world" that they have been investigating rather than finding new information about it. It is the remnants of the two-worlds myth that motivates philosophers to seek a "world" that is pre-conceptual and pre-conventional, and political theorists follow suit in this search for epistemic privilege.

7

Conventional Realism

Not empiricism and yet realism in philosophy, that is the hardest thing. (Against Ramsey.)
WITTGENSTEIN

Seeking a "Mind" and "World" beyond Conventions: Searle and Taylor

Although John Searle and Charles Taylor have acknowledged and confronted some of the problems raised by critics of representationalism, they have remained captured by the perspective from which those problems emanated. They deserve particular attention, because their claims are in some respects remarkably similar as well as closely tied to the practices of social inquiry.

Although no contemporary philosopher has done more than Searle to develop a theory of what he conceives as the conventional and socially constructed character of social facts, his image of conventionality was severely constrained both by his account of the ideational ground of the meaning of speech and action and by an attachment to empiricist/metaphysical foundationalism. Searle was a student of Austin and devoted a great deal of effort to elaborating Austin's account of speech acts, but Searle assumed something that Austin had not. This was that speech acts are expressions of ontologically prior mental states and processes signified by terms such as "purpose" and "intention" and that conventional acts are ultimately based on what Searle referred to as non-conventional "brute facts." Although Searle stressed the reality of conventional and social facts and the "constitutive rules" that are the basis of collective intentionality, and which transcend individual intentionality and form a holistic system of institutions and social relations, this was, in his view, a derivative form of reality. He emphasized what he referred to as the "construction of social reality," which he did not want confused with the claims of those who talk about the "social construction of reality," which for him amounted to the "social destruction of reality."

It is difficult to separate Searle's philosophical arguments from his quite evident ideological concerns about what he viewed as the problems of modern culture, which he believed were informed and exacerbated by certain philosophical trends such as that associated with deconstructionism and the work of individuals such as Jacques Derrida who, Searle believed, undermined confidence in the very idea of truth. He noted that "one of the most fascinating—and terrifying—features of the era in which I write is the steady erosion of acceptance of large institutional structures around the world" as well as an erosion of belief in objective truth, in both philosophy and social life. He argued that we must begin with the "transcendental" assumption there is a "reality totally independent of us" and of "all social constructions" and that true statements "correspond to facts" composing that reality (1995, 117, 119–20). This, he claimed, was necessary in order to make sense of the very possibility of human communication and understanding and of judging the validity of various social beliefs.

It is, however, difficult to understand what is meant by a "reality independent of us." If it means an unrepresentable reality independent of language and concepts, it would seem to be more a matter of faith than philosophy. The creative literary figure, philosopher, and lawyer, Owen Barfield (1898–1997), whose arguments about the evolution of human "consciousness" in some ways foreshadowed the arguments of Kuhn and others, nevertheless accounted for this evolution as stages of "collective representations" and forms of "participation" in an ultimately "unrepresented" reality, which he spoke of metaphorically as "the particles" (Barfield 1957, 1963). But what is behind our representations is not some mysterious unknowable realm of reality but what has been *presented* in first-order discourses.

It is perfectly reasonable to say that natural science presents us with a world independent of "us," even if we see ourselves as part of that natural world, and it would be difficult to name anyone who said otherwise. It is, however, something else to suggest that this world is independent of language and convention, because it is in language and convention that we confront it. For Searle, the answer to the "world" question was to assume both an unrepresented metaphysical reality and a factual reality rooted in both natural science and common sense. Searle has often referred to mountains and various things of "sheer physical possession" that are somehow just there and directly accessible to everyone, and he claimed that if you do not believe in external reality, falling off a cliff will make you a believer. Much of what counts for Searle as reality is similar to what Wittgenstein attributed to G. E. Moore in *On Certainty*—a recitation of what someone already believes, whether in everyday life, natural science, or religion, that is, what happens to stand fast for them at a particular time and place. Although for Wittgenstein, realism, as well as idealism, was basically only what he referred to as a rhetorical metaphysical "battle cry," Searle specifically argued that these are not simply "battle cries" but a faith that is required today at a point when "irrationalism" abounds. Although Searle rejected certain physical causal explanations of social facts, he posited a general "background" universe of pre-discursive "abilities, dispositions, and tendencies" that function as "causal structures" and that are prior to and "enable" perception, semantics, and the existence of truth-conditions. These included what he considered to be the neurobiological system that underlies the "mind" as an emergent autonomous entity that is the repository of subjective experience expressed in language.

More recently, Searle has attempted to make an argument for what he refers to as "direct realism," which he sees as similar to "naïve realism" and that would bypass the problems of representationalism and overcome what might seem to be the ambiguities in the work of Davidson, Putnam, and McDowell. His most focused exposition of this matter was his *Seeing Things as They Are* (2015). Here he argued that we can avoid the skepticism inherent in representationalism, because we perceive the "world" directly, and that we need not worry about thought experiments such as the "brain in the vat" or films such as the *Matrix* that might shake our faith in what we see.

Searle joined the critics of representationalism in taking a firm stand against what he referred to as the "bad argument" of "conceptual dualism," that is, the residue of the claim that we never directly encounter external objects but only reflections and representations such as sense-data. This position, in one form or another, had, he agreed, dominated philosophy from ancient times but had become particularly prominent after Descartes and had, at least through Kant, informed both realism and idealism and made epistemology the core of philosophical endeavor. Searle claimed, however, that you can dispense with epistemological intermediaries and be assured that you "are *directly* seeing objects and states of affairs, and these have an existence totally *independent* of your perception of them" (11). He claimed that these are also independent of the subjective experiences that take place in our "heads." He argued that there is, so to speak, immaculate perception or perception before conception and that there is a causal connection between objects in the world and our perceptions of them. He dealt with the classic problem of things such as "hallucinations" by arguing, as opposed to "disjunctivists," that the difference between such illusions and veridical perceptions is simply that in the case of the former there is no actual intentional object, that is, what many philosophers speak of as an object toward which thought and language are directed, but he claimed that they are both perceptions (ch. 6). While our thoughts of something are "representations," what we see is the thing itself.

In response to the classic problem of how the subjective visual field reflects features of the objective visual field, Searle claimed that the answer is "intentional causation," by which he meant that the objects cause the perception (126–28). Searle referred to this as "raw phenomenology," that is, that "perceptual experience is just a raw piece of brute phenomenological data" (135). He argued, however, that although we start with perceptions of "basic features" of the world, we move up from these basic veridical visual impressions and appearances to more qualitative and refined descriptions of what a thing is. He claimed that it is also necessary to take into account the "particularity" of recognition, which depends on personal phenomenology and is determined by an individual's past experience. Searle's argument, then, was that we see the "world" face-to-face rather than through a glass darkly, but the obvious question here is what "world" is being specified. Scientists have always claimed to see the world directly, as have theologians, but these worlds, both within and between science and religion, have often been worlds apart.

With respect to his analysis of human action as based on "intrinsic" mental intentionality, Searle was providing what amounted to a philosophical version of "folk psychology," and his analysis of perception is like a philosophical counterpart of "folk epistemology." Searle's account works for a situation in which a person has acquired a language, a space of reasons, and a capacity for conceptual designation and discrimination of objects. This is what Austin referred to as "linguistic phenomenology," which is not "raw" at all. Searle's position is actually not so far from sense-data theory as he might claim or from the brand of logical positivism characteristic of someone such as May Brodbeck, who argued that "some features of the world—like pencil, clock, clouds, thunder, clouds, and dog—have direct references we can see and touch; they stand out almost begging for names" (1968, 4).

Charles Taylor's arguments are more complex, but he also opted for a similar phenomenological solution. Taylor had been a major voice in the mid-twentieth-century challenge to empiricist behaviorist psychology (1964) and to the attempt by social scientists to emulate what they believed to be the logic of explanation in the natural sciences. He argued for the autonomy of social phenomena and of social inquiry (1970), and some of his early work (1967) focused on the case of behavioralism in political science. Taylor's principal argument (to which I among other critics of behavioralism subscribed in the 1960s) was that the type of explanation that applied to the study of human action was teleological in character and properly approached in terms of mental factors such as purposes, reasons, intentions, and motives, which were internal to the description of an action rather than things that could be construed as antecedent events conforming to a model of causal explanation.

By the point of his influential article "Interpretation and the Sciences of Man" (1971), two things were quite evident. First, there was a lack of any specific account of exactly what kind of phenomena were referred to by terms such as "purpose" and "intention." But the assumption still seemed to be that these were mental phenomena, which were expressed in language and thereby, in a derivative manner, objective and accessible through interpretation. Second, although Taylor challenged the applicability to social inquiry of the positivist/empiricist model of explanation, with its account of "verification" in terms of what, like Searle, he referred to as "brute data," he believed that it was a formulation that fitted the conduct of natural science, and to which the "progress of natural science has lent great credibility" as a universal benchmark of "certainty" (9). For Taylor, interpretation always entailed critical judgment and an aspiration to find something that in its own way resembled and paralleled the certainty of science. Despite the publication of a considerable body of literature in the philosophy of science that had called into question the logical empiricist model as a description of science, Taylor continued, and still continues, to accept that model and the image of facts as "given" to immediate experience.

In constructing an account of interpretation, Taylor drew on a large and diverse body of Continental literature, such as the work of Paul Ricoeur, H.-G. Gadamer, and Jürgen Habermas, but such inquiry, he argued, is ultimately a matter of "intuition" and "insight" even if constrained by the inevitable limitations of the "hermeneutic circle." He criticized how in positivism "epistemology dictates ontology," but he offered little in the way of an ontology of "social reality" and the "human subject" that he claimed was the bearer of thought and the author of "social action" within a "background" of intersubjectively shared meanings. What became most evident in the article was the degree to which Taylor's concern was what he believed to be the critical function and possibilities of the "interpretive turn." Interpretation, as he conceived it, was a somewhat elitist activity and "not something in which anyone can engage, regardless of their level of thought." It required both a unique "sensibility and understanding" and reaching a position of cognitive "superiority" where one could both "understand one's own position and that of one's opponents, but not the other way around." He claimed that such a gap of "intuitions" necessarily involves a conflict "between different fundamental options," and thereby interpretation was not simply a matter of theory but practice and a matter of achieving a basis for exposing "error" in the practices addressed. He claimed that "inauthenticity, bad faith, and self-delusion" are inevitable in the self-interpretation of social actors, and the goal of interpretive inquiry must be "to replace this confused, incomplete, and partly erroneous self-interpretation by a correct one" that produces greater "clarity" than the "lived interpretation." Interpretation, he argued, should not be conducted by adherents of some ideology, because it required "freedom from illusions in the sense of error which is rooted and expressed in one's way of life" (46–48). He did not specify any particular person who exemplified these exceptional qualities, but if he was not referring to himself, it was certainly to philosophers and political theorists (1983) as a class who, through their access to the foundations of knowledge, or at least their marginal position in society, could achieve a more objective stance and be qualified as social critics.

What Taylor (1984) believed disqualified someone such as Michel Foucault from this role was what he claimed to be Foucault's destruction of "*the* subject" as the source of meaning and thereby the "conscious action" that was the object of interpretation, his "Nietzschean refusal of the notion of truth as having any meaning outside a given order of power," and his failure to recognize what Taylor believed to be the self-evident progress of both science and liberal pluralism at the heart of Western civilization. For Taylor, political theory was conceived as the thoughtful and reflective dimension of political life that "transforms its own object" just as an individual's reflective thinking can transform their behavior (1983, 74). He recognized, however, that if the interpreter was to sit in judgment of the actions and beliefs of social actors and institutions, the "validation," as well as "invalidation," of such judgments required more than simply their assertion. Taylor claimed that in the case of the natural sciences such validation was much less "controversial," because it depended on our access to "brute" facts, while social theory necessarily involved more in the way of persuasion. But he was optimistic about the historical possibility of social enlightenment through science. It is somewhat paradoxical that after devoting so much attention to defending the autonomy of social phenomena rooted in subjective meaning and contrasting social inquiry as an interpretive enterprise with the brute-factual image of natural science, he turned to natural science as a standard of truth in support of critical social theorizing. He argued that "the advance of our civilization of a scientific understanding of the natural world" is what "we have every reason to believe is a significant gain of truth" (1984, 179). He maintained that this "theoretical understanding" and "theoretical culture" as well as the technological control associated with Western society and science have no "counterpart" in primitive cultures (1982), and his implication was that contemporary Western culture produces those qualified to engage in critical interpretive inquiry. The question that remained, as in the case of Searle, was what assured the success of natural science's access to the "world" and qualified it as the ultimate repository of "brute facts" and the criterion of what is real and what made it possible for social theorists to sort out true from erroneous belief in human practices.

In 2015, Taylor collaborated with Hubert Dreyfus in a project they referred to as *Retrieving Realism.* "Retrieval" was an appropriate word, because what they wanted to recover was an image of realism that had been severely endangered. This book was the result of a long collaboration between the authors, and much of it contained material written in previous contexts as well as portions of a manuscript that Taylor would publish the subsequent year. Like Searle, Dreyfus and Taylor wanted to overcome what they referred to as "mediational philosophy" and demonstrate how the mind had immediate access to the "world" and "reality."

In calling representationalism into question and arguing for what they, like Searle, referred to as "direct realism," they claimed that neither the "linguistic turn" nor the "materialist turn" in philosophy had been successful in overcoming and dispensing with problems such as skepticism. Their alternative was what they referred to as "contact theory," which viewed knowledge as based on "unmediated contact with the reality known," and which at its core resembled "naïve realism" (17). They focused on developing a position that they claimed was, in various respects, characteristic of the work of Wittgenstein, Merleau-Ponty, and Heidegger, and in which "truth is self-authenticating" (4).

Dreyfus and Taylor stressed that while someone such as Rorty is a "minimalist," who simply wanted to set aside such questions as how mind makes contact with reality, they were "maximalists" who wanted to confront these issues head on and provide answers (41). But what they offered as an unmediated access to the "world" was a kind of revelatory philosophy in which epistemological popes and priests were not needed to stand between reality seekers and their object. Although at various points they relied selectively on references to Wittgenstein, there was little to suggest that his work lent authority to their arguments. Their claims were largely based on phenomenology and particularly on their reading of the work of Heidegger and Merleau-Ponty as an explanation of how we gain contact with the world by our everyday holistic transactional "coping," which leads to an "unproblematic realism" that is not haunted by Cartesian problems. This, they claimed, would avoid what they characterized (incorrectly) as the coherence theories of Rorty and Davidson, which, they claimed, would leave us forever trapped in our beliefs and encourage relativism and anti-realism. They claimed that Heidegger and Merleau-Ponty showed how our human capacities to deal with the world lead to the formation of new beliefs, which can, in turn, be "checked" against "facts" we directly perceive. Whether or not this was a convincing account of someone such as Heidegger is open to question, but this was not what Taylor would ultimately claim as his principal inspiration.

What is important to note in these arguments is, as in the case of some of the other philosophers who have been critical of representational philosophy, "mind" and "world" remained undefined. One might ask, what conception of mind and what conception of world was assumed. These objects continued to be ghostly concepts.

In addition to their disagreements with Rorty, they also differed from other anti-representationalists, such as McDowell, who argued that our contact with the world is always conceptual. Dreyfus and Taylor maintained that we must go beyond concepts and language and assume a "primordial" relation to the world that is "non-propositional and in part even preconceptual" and which is the foundation of our "conceptual beliefs" (18, 51). They agreed with McDowell's view that although our coping with the world involves creativity and "free spontaneity," it is nevertheless bounded by the world's causal external "constraint." But unlike McDowell, they claimed that spontaneity and perceptional experience happen with "epistemic skills" that human animals possess in a "protoconceptual" form and that operates "at a level below the conceptual" (18, 51, 75). What the addition of a "linguistic dimension" achieves, they maintained, is a platform for bringing latent concepts, propositional thinking, and belief to the surface, where we primarily operate after infancy. It is not surprising that Wittgenstein did not appear at this point in their argument, because they *explicitly rejected what they acknowledged as the "growing conviction that language is essential to thought"* (90).

Their vision was that of a "me" as an "agent embedded in society, and at grips with the world," a world that is a "co-production of me and the world." Although they suggested that it may turn out, if we follow the proper "scientific method," that a particular production may be wrong, we can try again to get it right. Like Searle, they argued that worries about the existence of a real world associated with hypothetical arguments such as that about a brain in a vat or a film like the *Matrix* can be discounted as simply a hangover induced by the skeptical worries that characteristically accompanied mediationalism. One of the problems they saw with the mediational stance was its "monological" perspective. In its place, they wanted to emphasize the "primacy of conversation in the human linguistic life." There is not just one "me" but many who are directly in contact with the "real world" (99). This sounded a bit like Davidson, but one might ask how it is possible to be a co-producer with what is produced. The metaphor seems suspect, but they called upon Gadamer's image of "fusing horizons," both the horizons of the interpreters and those of what is interpreted, but for Gadamer these were discursive realms. They recognized that there are, or may be, "alternate takes on and construals of reality" (107), but they did not want this to lead into a slide toward anti-realism and relativism. They disagreed with what they believed to be Davidson's epistemic solution to achieving commonality and opted instead for what they saw as Gadamer's more ontological claim that everyone in their own way is in touch with reality. They claimed that "total unintelligibility of another culture is not an option" (112), but who, we might ask, ever made such a claim?

Dreyfus and Taylor maintained that in the end they had succeeded in "retrieving realism," but that is exactly the point. They retrieved a realism that is deeply in question, a realism that assumes a world that is the object of knowledge but ultimately never fully knowable and representable. It is once again philosophy as theology. They recognized that their picture of embedded coping might still be interpreted as a form of mediationalism and seem to "block all access to the universe as it is in itself," which they took to be the implication of Rorty's position. But, "standing on the shoulders of Merleau-Ponty and Samuel Todes," they fell back on Taylor's long-standing argument in favor of the "robust realism" of scientific practitioners. They argued that this is supported by the fact that supersession of worldviews in the history of science does not indicate a lack of ultimate access to an independent universe. In addition to the confirmation provided by its practical utility, science demonstrates the progress of knowledge and the correctness of the correspondence theory of truth, which we must come to acknowledge as transcending everyday efforts to cope (131–33). Here again Wittgenstein had, not surprisingly, faded from view. They drew upon Saul Kripke's theory of "natural kinds" and "rigid designation" as transcending, and persisting through, changing scientific theories. They did not, however, mention the extent to which these arguments had been called into question, even by some former adherents such as Putnam.

In 2016, Taylor published *The Language Animal.* Since the late 1980s, he had been studying the romantic theory of language in the late eighteenth-century work of individuals such as Johann Herder, Johann Hamann, and Wilhelm von Humboldt, which had led him to take up a study of post-romantic poetics. *The Language Animal* was undertaken as something of an aside inspired by his reading of these philosophers and his collaboration with Dreyfus. It was from this romantic literature that Taylor principally attempted to support his argument.

He argued that this literature could be construed as a challenge to what he referred to as the "enframing" and "designative" argument of representational philosophy, whereby language was viewed primarily as an instrument for expressing ideas and naming objects. He focused on how the romantics had stressed instead the "constitutive," "expressive," and "figuring" capacity of language and the manner in which words only have meaning within a lexicon and a context of language practices similar to what Wittgenstein referred to as a form of life. He noted Wittgenstein's argument against the impossibility of a private language, which reflected the basic thesis that "we could never have the silent, monological, inner language if we hadn't first acquired the language capacity in its expressed-enacted form" (34). Although Taylor claimed that Wittgenstein was the most "celebrated" modern proponent of this position (30), he did not examine in any detail what Wittgenstein had said about the relationship between language and thought. Taylor claimed, however, that his basic "inspiration" was the work of Herder.

Herder and the romantics viewed language as basically a vehicle of a primordial mode of thought, even though they conceived of language as a creative device through which much of the later progress of thought and concepts was made possible. Herder's central concerns were with the human "soul" and the distinction between the respective "languages" of humans and animals. He claimed that while animals are confined to instinct, humans have a capacity for representation, which is at the core of what he referred to as the human "circle" or "sphere." This was the sphere of human freedom and reflective awareness and the source of spoken language, but prior to this stage of development was an inner language that was the original source of later sociability, *Bildung*, and human progress. On the whole, Herder's work seems like a poor candidate for a refutation of mediational philosophy.

In the end, Taylor seems not to have actually challenged the assumption that language is a vehicle for the expression of thought but only to have distinguished between linguistic thought and what, like Herder, he claimed to be a more basic mode of thought. Although he agreed that we could not have an "inner language" without having first acquired a natural language and that in this sense "speech is the expression of thought," this was what he referred to as "reflective" thought, "of thought which deals with objects in the linguistic dimension." He argued that there was in fact a kind of human thought that preceded the linguistic form and from which "we can detach our thinking over some of its extent from public expression, and even from natural language" and that "our language straddles the boundary between 'mind' and body" (333).

My answer to the problem of "directness" requires recognizing that the criterion of what is real resides in the presentations of first-order discourses rather than in the postulation of a connection to some abstract extra-conventional "world." A natural response to this claim might be that it is still mediational in character, that first-order discourses mediate between us and the world, but this is no more the case than the claim that locating the world in first-order discourses amounts to linguistic idealism. With the acquisition of a language, we acquire a world, but the content of the "world," whether in science, common sense, politics, religion, and so forth, changes, and our language accordingly, among both individuals and collectivities. The image of a world beyond conventions is necessarily devoid of content. There is no phantom world hovering behind or above what is available in first-order discourses. This is not to say that language creates the world, whatever that could mean, but it is meaningless to talk about a world that stands outside the conventions in which it is presented. It would be like asking about the nature of motion that exists outside all the past and present commonsense and scientific accounts of motion. Would we want to say that such a question just reduces motion to language? Well, it would be to say that there is nowhere else to find it. Wittgenstein once said that "no language is conceivable which does not represent this world" (1975, 47), but it is equally the case that there is no identifiable world that is not presented in language.

Our Conventional World

What is most distinctively unique about human beings and what makes it possible for them to understand one another is not that they all encounter the same primordial world. What Wittgenstein spoke of as the common, and distinctive, behavior of humankind was our conventional life. While some, like McDowell, refer to this as our "second nature," it is actually our primary nature. What is classified as conventional often refers to what is typical, ordinary, or accepted, but also to what is invented, constructed, or in some manner artificial and a matter of decision and choice, as opposed to what is somehow natural and given. But this characterization is a far too narrow view. Conventions are actually the vehicles of the "world" and the medium in which we live. Given, however, the historical depth, philosophical pervasiveness, and discursive tensile strength of the network of arguments that have sustained the nature/convention distinction, it is not surprising how difficult it is to escape it.

This distinction is at least as old as ancient Greek philosophy. Aristotle, for example, classified both money and names as conventional but claimed that justice is natural. But the whole notion of what is natural has been based on the assumption that certain things are somehow simply "there" and accessible without linguistic specification, but what is categorized as natural is always conventional. *The proper distinction is not between nature and convention but rather between various conventions of linguistic usage and the character of the propositions involved.* Despite the fact that the natural/conventional distinction has dominated the history of philosophy, there were early on some indications of an alternative perspective.

If we look carefully at the first book of Plato's *Republic*, and what is often characterized as the debate about whether justice is conventional or natural, it was not actually a debate about whether or not practices of justice were a matter of human agreement. No one could deny that they were based on agreement. The actual issue was the criterion of agreement, that is, whether or not the criterion was in some manner necessary and given. What became apparent in the dialogue was that the social forms of justice are always conventional even if the criterion of what is just is assumed to be some fact of either a transcendental or physical kind. In the course of the dialogue, it also became obvious that what was ultimately considered just was inevitably a matter of persuasion. In this drama, not only were Adeimantus and Glaucon finally convinced by Socrates's argument but even Thrasymachus eventually threw in the towel.

When Galileo wrote to the Grand Duchess Christina in defense of an empirical study of the universe, he claimed that "this great book of the world was not written by nature to be read" only by philosophers such as Aristotle. In this case, he probably was re-invoking a claim that had often been voiced in Christian theology since as early as the third century. This Neoplatonist image of the possibility of approaching the natural world hermeneutically had been adapted by the church father Origen as a way of understanding the meaning of God's creation. By the twelfth century, Christian theologians had embraced the assumption that God had written two complementary books, the Scriptures and the "book" of nature. By the sixteenth century, however, questions of priority began to emerge. Galileo, however, did not actually speak about a book written by God but by *nature*, which had been rendered in the language of mathematics and therefore constituted an object of interpretation. Wittgenstein might be interpreted as agreeing with Galileo in that he claimed that nature is only manifest in discursive presentations, in this case the language of mathematics. Rousseau's image of the natural state of human beings was actually a thought experiment in which human beings were paradoxically stripped of all the characteristics that made them distinctly human, that is, their capacity for convention. And the states of nature conceived by Locke and Hobbes were actually not pre-conventional at all but simply in various ways inconvenient. There is simply no way to extricate ourselves from conventions—and no reason to attempt to do so. Certainty is not a matter of escaping from convention, because conventions are where certainty resides.

The question that must be posed, however, is that of where in language does the "world" and "nature" appear. Wittgenstein's answer to this question was basically what I have referred to as *first-order* discourses and practices. These contain the kind of propositions on which he focused in *On Certainty* (*Gewissheit*) and which I designate as presentational. Although *On Certainty* was written in his aphoristic style, the argument is actually quite linear. Here, as in the *Tractatus*, he confronted the issue of the relationship between language and the "world" but now embracing the position that had characterized the *Investigations* and particularly the emphasis on how language-games change. A careful reading of this book neutralizes the charges and worries, even, as I will point out in the next chapter, among some Wittgensteinian scholars, that his later work creates a picture of people trapped in static language-games, which inhibit, if not totally prevent, genuine communication and which are impervious to rational external criticism.

The argument of *On Certainty* is that the ultimate basis of judgment is not a *representation* of anything. It is a *presentational* framework within which representation and judgment take place, whether in science, morals, or some other sphere of discourse. He returned to the distinction he had adumbrated in the *Tractatus* and maintained that the practices of life contain within themselves and "show" the foundational assumptions on which they are grounded (7, 285, 426–27, 431) even if not explicitly formulated, as they might be in the case of a scientific theory. It is only within language-games that certainty and doubt are meaningful concepts. At the foundation of any language-game and form of life is a class of propositions that are empirical in the sense that they are claims about what elements compose the world but nevertheless cannot be compared to the world and spoken about as representing the "world." These propositions constitute the structure in which the components of the world are represented. The consequence, he argued, is that we must dispense with the quest for some version of transcendental certainty and recognize that what we mean by the words designating the facts of the "world" often change along with our concepts. These basic propositions function as a foundation of what we hold to be true and free from doubt. These might change, but unlike testing a hypothesis, it would involve a conversion experience whereby the manner in which the constitution of some dimension of the world is conceived undergoes a transformation. It would be as if some typical empirical propositions were transformed into basic assumptions about the "world," but these too in time might lose this status and be replaced by others. What

Wittgenstein continually stressed was that this confluence of foundational and hypothetical propositions constituted a system within which judgments are made and into which people are initiated when they first acquire language as well as when they appropriate new forms of language and belief that, at least temporarily, become authoritative and excluded from doubt. He noted, however, that it is very difficult to come to grips with the idea that there is nothing outside the system that serves as a ground of our beliefs and the certainty that attaches to the descriptions of the "world" and what we take to be real and the difference between truth and falsity.

He emphasized still once again that, despite what might seem to be the solidity of various systems of belief, the system and its language-games do change, but the vehicle of that change is ultimately persuasion rather some yet deeper ground of reality and objectivity. Such persuasion provides the only resolution for debate such as in the case of those who believe the creation story in the Bible and those who believe that the story has been proven false by science. What is involved in such instances is often not actually a contradiction, which requires some common ground of dispute, but a conflict between different ultimately incommensurable forms of life that may, under particular circumstances, be construed by the parties, or an outside observer, as coming into conflict. He made clear that there is no philosophical basis for, either practically or theoretically, resolving such an issue. He asked if this ultimately entailed that what we take as knowledge is a matter of decision and indicates that our view of the world and our social and moral values are simply arbitrary and matters of choice. His answer was that these are less a matter of decision, in the typical use of that term, than the fact that there is an absence of doubt in a context of certainty. What he was arguing against was what he had referred to in the *Investigations* as the dogmatism of metaphysics that professed to possess transcendental philosophical grounds of certainty and judgment. Such seductive claims, however, underlie whole academic enterprises in both philosophy and social theory.

General doubting or skepticism as a basic stance of inquiry would simply lead to a kind of infinite regress, where one would need to investigate the investigation and so on. But no substantive practice is actually based on such a skeptical stance. And he emphasized that focusing on putative mental states and psychological terms such as "belief" is simply a diversion from understanding the practices and forms of action and language on which justification is based. He pointed out that neither philosophical realism nor mentalism provides answers. What Wittgenstein was advancing was not the position that there are no reasons for claiming one *Weltbild* to be better than another, but only that philosophy does not hold any special key, either theoretically or practically, to settling such a dispute. The foundations of knowledge are internal to the practices of life. Some have suggested that this makes Wittgenstein a foundationalist after all, but although he might be called an internal foundationalist, this only serves to obscure his critique of metaphysics as an external basis of authority. As he pointed out, a foundation cannot be separated from the whole house.

On Certainty was the culmination of Wittgenstein's career, and although it has sometimes been interpreted as constituting a fundamental shift in his work, it was in fact an explicit statement of what had been implicit. Although, as I will discuss in chapter 8, a common worry about his view of certainty has been that it amounts to a coherence theory of truth, which confines us to existing language-games, the point of his remarks was, first, that there cannot be any theory of truth because truth is not an object. It is only a word that is applied with various criteria in a variety of contexts. More important still was the fact that those who play the games of philosophy and social inquiry are not the arbiters of language-games but interpreters, representers, and commentators. It is a mistake to assume that when talking about different views of the "world" or different worldviews that we are talking about different perspectives on the same thing, but instead, as Ryle pointed out, about two different concepts, which, as in the case of the world, might be referred to by the same word. The world is an empty concept until filled with the content of a first-order discourse.

We should not, however, slip into the idiom of saying that the "world" is socially or linguistically constructed, because, first of all, there is no such thing as "THE" world. "World" is simply a word attached to various, and often competing, conceptions of what exists. And, second, although we might reasonably talk about constructing a model of what we take to be the world, we do not construct worlds but conceive and present them. And we do not want to say that language mediates between "mind" and "world," that we see the world through language, or that it is a key by which we gain entrance to the world. To mediate or be a key would presuppose that we could specify the world that was a party to the mediation or specify what the key unlocked. It is not that language cloaks or uncloaks the world but rather that it is in language and conventions that a concept of the "world" becomes an object. The question that remains, however, is that of exactly what we are talking about when we talk about conventions. Despite the prolific use of "convention" among philosophers and social scientists, little has been accomplished as far as clarifying the concept of convention. The first step in disambiguation should be to point out that "convention" is not the type of concept that refers to a particular thing but to a class or kind of things that have similar characteristics. Conventions emerge and exist by agreement, as Hume said, "betwixt us," but, again, to say that everything is conventional is not to say that conventions create the objects on which agreement is based. If, however, Wittgenstein was what I have referred to as conventional realist, it is necessary to look more closely at the image of realism he rejected.

There are many ways in which Wittgenstein's often noted remark about realism and empiricism, and "against Ramsey," can be, and have been, interpreted. Frank Ramsey, a brilliant, but prematurely deceased (age twenty-six) mathematician and philosopher was influential in Wittgenstein's return to philosophy at Cambridge after his unsuccessful sojourn teaching elementary school in Austria. Ramsey became his nominal dissertation supervisor as well as interlocutor, and they both taught courses in the foundations of mathematics at the same time. Ramsey was a defender of Wittgenstein's work and learned German in order to make an early translation of the *Tractatus.* And Wittgenstein acknowledged Ramsey's role in his subsequent philosophical development. But they differed on some important issues.

Both Ramsey and Wittgenstein flirted with American pragmatism, but Wittgenstein's relationship to pragmatism is a complex question, and the details are outside the scope of this book (see, e.g., Chauviré and Plaud 2012; Moyal-Sharrock 2003). He definitely saw certain affinities between his work and pragmatism, but he worried (1969, 422) that pragmatism might imply a "*Weltanschauung*," which he wanted to resist. What he shared included Pierce's rejection of the assumption that philosophy begins with doubt, and although he did not agree with James's psychology, he read his *Varieties of Religious Experience* with interest. He sympathized with the pragmatist identification of belief with forms of action and with its rejection of a search for ultimate certainty, but he did not subscribe to testing his propositions in terms of their utility. Where Ramsey and Wittgenstein appeared to differ most was with regard to Ramsey's pragmatic claim that logic was experimental. This was not compatible with either the *Tractatus* or how Wittgenstein later conceived logic as immanent in human practices. In was in this respect that he insisted that it is necessary to recognize "*the limits of empiricism*" (1978, pt. 3, 71). Wittgenstein believed that Ramsey was in some respect a material reductionist, because he claimed that there was no ontological difference between universals and particulars and that scientific theories were in principle eliminable once they had performed their task of organizing and explaining facts. But Ramsey's argument might also be interpreted as a precursor of the post-empiricist claim that facts are entailments of theories. But if realism was not empiricism, what was it? For Wittgenstein, it was the recognition that "the limit of the empirical—is *concept-formation*" (1978, pt. 4, 29).

The distinction between what is natural and conventional continues, however, to persist among a wide range of philosophers and social theorists, despite intellectual and ideological differences, because it is viewed as supporting an external critical perspective, which allows what is natural to stand as a firm ground of judgment. This is what Searle claimed to exist "beyond *all* representations." What exists beyond all representations is, however, presentations. Searle, like so many others, was looking in the wrong place for the foundations of knowledge. These foundations are not located in a metaphysical realm but instead within those practices. And there is not one presentation, and its entailed representations, such as the theories and facts of natural science, that stands beyond persuasion as authoritative. The anxiety about not finding some universal foundation does not typically arise from within first-order practices but in the second-order discourses of philosophy, social theory, and other pretenders to epistemic and practical superiority over their subject matter. The vestiges of the nature/convention distinction are, however, very difficult to dislodge and have appeared even in what might seem to be unlikely places.

Despite the fact that Peter Winch has often been interpreted as epitomizing a commitment to the relativity of values and rationality, he followed his *Idea of a Social Science* (1958) with an argument justifying the difference between "nature and convention" (1959). He stated explicitly that he wished "to argue against the idea that there need be no fixed points in all this change and variety, that there are no norms of human behaviour that could not be different from what they are, and that everything in human morality is therefore ultimately conventional in character." He claimed, on the contrary, that there are "certain moral conceptions which, in one form or another, must be recognized in any human society" and which must be "presupposed by any possible conventions." These, he argued, "arise out of any common life between men" and are grounded in "the social conditions of language and rationality" (1959, 238–41). He expressed his sympathy with Vico's conception of a "natural law of the peoples" and Vico's claim, much like that of Aristotle, that despite the existence of diverse forms of linguistic expression, "there must in the nature of human things be a mental language common to all nations," which allows for sharing the "same meanings" and that could support the concept of natural "justice" (251).

Similarly, in his essay "Understanding a Primitive Society," which so many have also criticized as a defense of relativism, as well as in the preface to the second edition of *The Idea of a Social Science* (1972), Winch defended the idea that the very nature of human society imposes a variety of "limiting conditions," which constrain judgment. He noted a certain affinity between his argument and Jürgen Habermas's claim that there are norms of rationality inherent in language and social interaction. Winch's argument did not, however, solve the problem but only demonstrated that in fact there are no limits to conventionality that are not in themselves conventional. How we conceive and perceive nature is not prior to convention. Although there are few philosophers who have better perceived the implications of Wittgenstein's work for thinking about social inquiry, Winch's courage, after so much criticism of him as a relativist, seemed to fail him when it came to the problem of nature and convention. *It is easy to forget that when we talk about such natural limiting conditions, we are really adopting a particular convention regarding what is natural. We can paraphrase Protagoras and say that of "all things, conventions are the measure."* The difficulty, however, is still that of pinning down even more exactly what various conventions have in common.

One of the most extensive and influential treatments has been that of the philosopher David Lewis (1969), but, like a number of others, he less addressed the issue of what conventions are than how they function. He claimed, presupposing an individualist social ontology, that they are the product of individual agreement and serve as a response to coordination problems arising from conflicts between diverse interests and preferences. Stanley Cavell, drawing on the work of Wittgenstein and Austin, has had a great deal to say about conventions and how they operate, but despite his identifying many of what might be described as the characteristics of conventions, we still often seem at a loss in specifying precisely what we are talking about. So the question is what it is we "come down" to when we reach the "rock bottom" of conventions.

There is no one place in the corpus of Wittgenstein's work where he fully discussed this issue, but interpreters have also not systematically examined what he had to say about the matter. The simple answer, which had been there all along and actually noted by nearly everyone, was that for Wittgenstein, the rock bottom was "agreement." The two words in the *Investigations* (41, 355), as well as in the *Tractatus*, that are typically translated as "convention" are *Abmachung* and *Übereinkunft*, which both basically allude to "agreement" (*Zustimmung, Übereinstimmung*), in either an explicit or tacit consensual manner. But, we might ask, agreement in what? It was primarily agreement in language, but he claimed that "to imagine a language means to imagine a form of life." He said that "the term 'language-*game*' is meant to bring into prominence the fact that the *speaking* of language is part of an activity, or of a form of life." It is not that "human agreement decides what is true and what is false" but that "human beings" "agree in the *language* they use," which "is not agreement in opinions but in a form of life," which must be accepted as "given" (2009, 19, 23, 241, 345). So it is crucial to confront what is meant by a "form of life."

Some have argued that this was some natural datum, but such a proposition cannot be sustained by a careful examination of Wittgenstein's work. A form of life did not simply involve an agreement on how to use language but, we might say, an agreement about the way things are or how they should be (2009, 1, 345), which for Wittgenstein was a matter of "grammar." This is where "*essence* is expressed" and that which tells us what kind of object anything is, "since the only correlate in language to an objective necessity is an arbitrary [*willkürlich*] rule" (371–73). Because such a rule or convention is autonomous and not hostage to some independent reality, essence is to be found in the conventions that are constitutive of language and meaning.

Despite all the, sometimes exaggerated, scholarly attention that has been devoted to what Wittgenstein referred to as a form of life and the various and loose ways in which the phrase has been employed, it was in his view, as in the case of convention, not a particular thing, and this in part explains his actual limited discussion, and even mention, of it. The terms *Lebensform* and *Form des Lebens* had a long history and various uses in a number of fields during the nineteenth and early twentieth centuries. These included the arguments of Oswald Spengler, but although Wittgenstein found the term useful, he took strong issue with Spengler's claim that he had discovered something immanent and substantively universal in the history of civilizations. For Wittgenstein, the term was employed as a means of representation, that is, an example of his "method" of "perspicuous representation," and functioned as an "ideal type." His limited and diverse uses of the phrase did, however, get close to his basic point about conventionality and the manner in which language and the activities and practices in which it is employed imply the regularities manifest in instances of custom and habit (*Gepflogenheit*).

As early as 1930, Wittgenstein had begun to emphasize the identity of language and thought. He noted that he no longer had a "phenomenological language, or 'primary language' as I used to call it, in mind as my goal. I no longer hold it to be necessary. All that is possible and necessary is to separate what is essential from what is inessential in *our* language" (1975, pt. 1, 1). He said that "a child learning a language only learns it by beginning to think in it . . . there is no preliminary stage in which a child already uses a language, uses it, so to speak for communication but does not yet think in it." It is important, however, that Wittgenstein did not define language narrowly and recognized that "thought processes" involve "a medley of symbols," of which those that might be narrowly defined as linguistic "perhaps form only a small part." But beyond the identity of thought and language, his essential claim was that one "*cannot use language to get outside language*" (emphasis added), that is, to find what is non-conventionally "real." He stressed that "grammatical conventions cannot be justified by describing what is represented: any such description already presupposes the grammatical rules" (2009, 5–7), which was in effect to say that reality is presented in conventions. He noted that "the limit of language manifests itself in the impossibility of describing the fact that corresponds to (is the translation of) a sentence without simply repeating the sentence" (1998, 3). Although "time and again the attempt is made to use language to limit the world and set it in relief," (which had included what he had attempted in the *Tractatus*), this is impossible, because what we take to be the "self-evidence of the world expresses itself in language" (1975, pt. 4, 47).

He had, from the point of his earliest writings, consistently linked meaning with the conventions governing the "use" and "application" (*Gebrauch, Anwendung*) of language. Although in the *Tractatus* he had claimed that we can use certain forms of language to grasp the logical form of the world, he had, at least by the 1930s, concluded that the properties of the world do not determine or make necessary certain conventions or explain and justify what they represent. "If I could describe the point of grammatical conventions by saying they are made necessary by certain properties of the colours (say), then that would make the conventions superfluous, since in that case I would be able to say precisely that which the conventions exclude my saying." Consequently, "an explanation of meaning is not an empirical proposition and not a causal explanation, but a rule, a convention" (1974, pt. 2, 32). He claimed that "the connection between 'language and reality' is made by definitions of words" and is neither psychological nor causal. It belongs to "grammar" and "consists of conventions," such as "pointing to a building stone and saying 'that is a pillar'" or "saying the word 'red' means this colour" (1974, pt. 2, 19, 55–56; pt. 9, 138).

The objects composing the "world" are not untainted by concepts, that is, what is identified and discriminated as an object. Although he suggested that this can be achieved, even in the case of animals, by training, he argued that "genuine" conventions require the application of language and understanding the "game" that is being played. The meaning of language is a matter of the "conventions" governing "*use.*" He claimed that "if you talk about *essence*—, you are merely noting a convention. But here one would like to retort: there is no greater difference than that between a proposition about the depth of the essence and one about—a mere convention. But what if I reply: to the *depth* that we see in the essence there corresponds the *deep* need for the convention" (1978, pt. 1, 74). His concern was "not with improving grammatical conventions" but with understanding and interpreting them. And he stressed that in the case, for example, of using the word "think," it is not the kind of concept that refers to a particular "phenomenon" but simply means that "we can all play the language-game with the word 'think'" (1980, 550).

One might find it strange that by the point that he composed the *Investigations*, "convention" was hardly mentioned. In an important respect, however, that is because conventions, and the issue of how to interpret and represent them, is the subject of the whole book and its focus on grammar, language-games, and the like. His use of "rules," for example, was largely an exemplar and a surrogate for conventions as a whole and should not be construed narrowly in the way that people sometimes think of rules as restrictive and unchanging—which he specifically argued against. Although he sometimes spoke of conventions as arbitrary, this was a response to the common assumption that facts of nature verified the definition of things such as colors. He maintained that in the case of a claim about what is real, an objection is actually a matter of objecting to a convention specifying the criteria for using the word "real."

> This finds expression in questions as to the essence of language, of propositions, of thought.—For if we too in these investigations are trying to understand the essence of language—its function, its structure,—yet *this* is not what those questions have in view. For they see in the essence, not something that already lies open to view and that becomes surveyable by a rearrangement, but something that lies *beneath* the surface. Something that lies within, which we see when we look *into* the thing, and which an analysis digs out. "*The essence is hidden from us*": this is the form our problem now assumes. We ask: "*What is* language?" "*What* is a proposition?" And the answer to these questions is to be given once for all; and independently of any future experience. (2009, 92)

But he said that even what we might think of as the language of our sense impressions "like any other is founded on convention" (2009, 355). There is no private language in which we register our sense impressions or from which we translate them into a public language.

It is important at this point to engage more fully the problem of what Wittgenstein was talking about when he spoke about the "facts of nature." He noted that "what we have to mention in order to explain the significance, I mean the importance, of a concept, are often extremely general facts of nature: such facts as are hardly ever mentioned because of their great generality" (2009, 142). And he went on to say that "if the formation of concepts can be explained by facts of nature, should we not be interested, not in grammar, but rather in that nature which is the basis of grammar?" But he immediately rejected such a claim and said that "our interest certainly includes the correspondence between concepts and very general facts of nature. . . . But our interest does not fall back upon these possible causes of the formation of concepts; we are not doing natural science; nor yet natural history—since we can also invent fictitious natural history for our purposes" (365). It is interesting that he never mentions any specific facts as examples, but this is because the facts of nature are the product of the first-order discourses that he would discuss in *On Certainty*, facts that are open to change and are matters of convention. He noted that "I am not saying: if such-and-such facts of nature were different people would have different concepts (in the sense of a hypothesis). But: if anyone believes that certain concepts are absolutely the correct ones, and that having different ones would mean not realizing [perceiving] something that we realize [perceive]—then let him imagine certain very general facts of nature to be different from what we are used to, and the formation of concepts different from the usual ones will become intelligible to him" (2009; *PPF* 366). It is "easy to give a ground in facts of nature for this structure of concepts," because it is in our concepts that the facts of nature appear (1980, vol. 1, 45). It may be "hard to imagine concepts other than our own, because we never become aware of certain very general facts of nature. It doesn't occur to us to imagine them differently from what they are. But if we do then even concepts which are different from the ones we're used to no longer seem unnatural to us" (1992, vol. 1, 209). Many of our conventions reflect what *we take to be* the facts of nature, and Wittgenstein was not disputing that point. And he continued to emphasize how what we take those facts to be undergoes change.

The theory of conventional realism solves some of the most persistent issues in philosophy and social science, such as how thought relates to speech and action and how language relates to the "world." Speech, action, and thought are all modes of convention; they are all discursive phenomena. One mode can be the explanation of the other, as in saying that a thought might be the source of an action, but only in some circumstantial manner—such as how water might be considered an explanation of steam, when each is a mode of H_2O. And an instance of a mode might, as Austin suggested in demonstrating "how to do things with words," be analyzable into component conventions. What can be the bearer of conventions is actually an empirical question, and though it might be going too far to have a bumper sticker saying that "only humans do it conventionally," humans are the paradigm case. We might train certain animals to act according to conventions, but this would not necessarily mean that they are really living a life of convention. It is, however, illusory, as Wittgenstein pointed out, to seek the proverbial "subject" or ultimate source of agency as well as its location. And whether we are referring to agency or structure as explanatory factors, we are really referring to forms or classes of conventionality. The theory of conventional realism also dissolves such dilemmas as whether intentionality is located in individuals or collectivities. It is located in conventions to which either individuals or collectivities may subscribe or to which conventions may be attributed.

The persistent question, however, which is at the root of concerns about conventionality, is whether or not social inquiry has some special capacity to judge the presentational premises that are internally constitutive of a social *Weltbild*, and particularly the values that are attached to it. The contingency of the relationship between a practice and an interpretation of a practice has led social theorists to seek a transcendental basis of authority for interpreting and judging their subject matter, some standard of what is universally real, true, and objective. The source of this putative authority has often been a claim about employing the methods of natural science, but increasingly social theorists have turned to a variety of philosophical sources. What is being sought in these cases is what amounts to an epistemic or theoretical answer to the practical problem of the relationship between inquiry and its object. Although this may have been endemic in the history of philosophy and the history of political thought, there is a significant difference between, for example, the practical rhetorical context of authors from Plato to Marx and the dislocated rarified claims of academic practitioners who claim to be the last remnant of that classic canon.

The principal task of social inquiry is to interpret, clarify, and convey meaning. But this performance, as Wittgenstein said, "leaves everything as it is." Whether there is a practical consequence to such performance is a contingent matter, which cannot be settled by claims to transcendental grounds of judgment. In modern society, most of academic social inquiry may not even have an effect or consequence as inevitable as that of an anthropologist studying a remote aboriginal tribe, but it is certainly free to criticize and attempt to make inquiry a practical manner. What is not legitimate is to believe that social inquiry has access to some ground of critical judgment that exceeds the presentational claims and assumptions of its subject matter. Yet, as I will argue in the next chapter, philosophers continue to offer the hope of such foundations, and social scientists and social theorists continue to be enticed by various forms of these visions of truth and reality.

8

The Quest for the Real and the Fear of Relativism

This method consists essentially in leaving the question of *truth* and asking about *sense* instead.

WITTGENSTEIN

Social scientists have typically, and appropriately, been intent on providing an account of what is "really" going on in various forms of social interaction. Many social theorists, however, as we have seen in the case of Taylor, have attempted to ground these accounts on a universal sense of what is real and true, which would, they claim, both allow objective epistemic access to social practices and establish a privileged basis for rational critical judgment. Those who are not professional philosophers have often turned to philosophy in a search of such authority, but here they have encountered what many philosophers have designated as their archenemy. And social theorists have felt a special sense of urgency in joining the battle. The exact identity of the foe is difficult to specify, but it is typically ascribed to those such as Wittgenstein, Winch, and Kuhn whom they classify as relativists. The work of the social theorist Steven Lukes is a paradigm case of the many attempts, in his words, to "put relativism in its place" by finding a form of realism that would validate the efforts of theorists to interpret and judge such objects of inquiry as the exercise of power.

Lukes's (1970) response to what he took to be the relativistic implications of Winch's (1964) essay "Understanding a Primitive Society" was to claim, like many others at that time, such as Alasdair MacIntyre, that the transcendental assumption of universally applicable logical criteria of rationality is necessary for both understanding and evaluating social beliefs. More than a decade later, Lukes was still intent on joining what he pejoratively characterized as the debate between "rationality and relativism" (1982) and resisting what he believed to be Wittgenstein's and Winch's challenges to critical reason and even to the possibility of communication between cultures. At this point, however, he claimed to have found philosophical validation in the philosophy of Davidson. What Lukes extrapolated from Davidson's work was the conclusion that both interpreting and judging alien cultures are possible because of the existence of a "bridgehead" of beliefs, which are common to all rational human beings, and which would enable both an understanding of such cultures and a basis for sorting out truth and error in their practices and their conception of the world. Lukes, however eventually recognized that this was a dubious application of Davidson's arguments.

In a symposium on Winch (2000), Lukes analyzed a controversy in anthropology about how to explain why the Hawaiians killed Captain James Cook (whether they became disillusioned after deciding he was not a god or whether they simply became irritated by his presence and took the next instrumentally rational step). Lukes did not relinquish his basic claim that "assessing the rationality of the beliefs and practices of other cultures is always both possible and necessary," but he concluded that he had been wrong in attempting to derive from Davidson's work "methodological prescriptions for success in anthropology" (16). Although he was now wary of assuming that "philosopher's precepts should guide anthropological practice," he remained convinced that he had, from the beginning, been on the "right track." He claimed that "all cultures . . . engage in the cognitive enterprise of reasoning and face the common human predicament of trying to get the world right: of understanding, predicting and controlling their environment, natural and social." Consequently, he argued, we can always ask whether they have performed effectively and well, and we can do so on the basis of "criteria that must be independent of any particular culture" (15–16). What exactly constituted such criteria was, however, still blowing in the wind.

After the turn of the century, Lukes saw new challenges emerging in the growing sensitivity to social diversity and multiculturalism, which he believed tended to create skepticism about rational "universalism" and the possibility of authoritative external judgment. He returned to his general claim that there is a "common human nature," a sense of "*universal reason*," and a "cosmopolitan vision of humanity" that function as a "bridgehead" and allow "mutual interpretation" across cultures as well as a basis of external judgment (2003, 13–14). He offered his former colleague Martin Hollis's aphorism of "liberalism for the liberals and cannibalism for the cannibals" as a warning against the "slide into relativism" inherent in what he claimed was Wittgenstein's image of forms of life as constituting "unbridgeable differences" (27, 104).

Lukes's search for a realist foundation for a critical social science resurfaced again in a symposium he edited on the relevance for anthropology of John Searle's philosophy. In the symposium, Searle (2006b) reiterated his basic account of institutional facts, but his claims about their foundation in brute facts raised questions among anthropologists about how this could be reconciled with the manner in which the criteria for specifying what is real and true may differ among various cultures. Searle (2006a) nevertheless insisted that "one massive constraint on truth cuts through all forms of life" and that it is necessary to assume the "background assumption" of "external realism." He contended that "truths about the real world," which were "absolute and universal across all cultures," had been discovered by science and become "public property," whether or not they were acknowledged by all cultures. He noted that although people might act on the basis of "massive falsehoods," which have "status functions" in some society, there are, for example, "no witches and there never have been any" (113, 115). This, however, would be about as meaningful as saying that there is no divine right of kings and never was. Extrapolating our current beliefs backward in time does little to help us to understand either the past or the present. Lukes, however, found new solace in Searle's realism, which he saw as a basis for exposing the manner in which the "brute realities of social life" and the existence of "brute interests" and "brute power" distort social life (Lukes 2006, 8).

Although Lukes was eventually willing to countenance a certain degree of cognitive relativism, he remained concerned about how a "journey down the road to moral relativism begins from the observation of the fact of diversity" in society. He asked "how in a postmetaphysical and foundationless world, can one justify subscribing to universal norms and values" (2008, 129, 133). His assumption was that philosophical anti-foundationalism would entail the loss of standards in practices such as science, but, as I have stressed, such fear arises from looking in the wrong place for foundations. The foundations of human practices are in the practices themselves. Lukes also worried that assuming the existence of fundamental differences in belief and moral norms would entail the assumption that there is no "right" to criticize another person or culture. He claimed, however, that there was still a way forward "without accepting a notion of cultures so sealed off from one another that we have to accept *abstention*-denial of 'our right' to judge the beliefs and practices of others" (151). The claim that Wittgenstein, Kuhn, or Winch ever argued, or even implied, that cultures were necessarily cut off from one another and that there was no right to criticize another culture is simply false, but this kind of philosophical folklore continues to persist in arguments against what is imagined to be the position of relativism.

The philosopher Jerry Fodor (1985, 5) once said, "I hate relativism more than anything, excepting, maybe, fiberglass powerboats." This tells us a great deal about the elitist assumptions of those who decry what they construe as relativism, but like many objects of hatred, it is often an aesthetic construction of the hater. It would be difficult to find a self-identified relativist, and it is less what individuals such as Wittgenstein, Winch, and Kuhn said that has led critics to label them as relativists than what they did *not* say about the existence of universal reason. What is sometimes referred to as the "specter" of relativism is, indeed, a phantom, but one that, for the most part, seems to evoke fear only among philosophers, social theorists, and a few others who have taken onto themselves the burden of this philosophical anxiety. Natural scientists are actually seldom visited by this apparition, which is primarily an image of the abyss that supposedly would follow the demise of metaphysical realism. Just as some philosophers, in the course of seeking to demonstrate how a real human being is defined by subjective qualia, seriously imagine zombies as a contrast model, others imagine relativism as a position lacking rational bases of judgment. Both, however, are images of the walking dead. Part of what is involved here is the belief that practical judgment and the right and capacity to criticize rest on a philosophical warrant. There is, however, no need for what Wittgenstein spoke of as a philosophical "rider" attached to claims and judgments about what is right, true, and real. Natural science long ago left such codicils behind, but many philosophers continue to suggest, even in the case of natural science, that they can provide such endorsements—and social theorists continue to believe them.

Although Wittgenstein said that philosophy "leaves everything as it is," this is no reason to attribute to him some version of extreme philosophical quietism. Even though he was not particularly optimistic about his ability even to change the taste of his students, he did not refrain from critically analyzing either philosophy itself or other practices such as mathematics, natural science, anthropology, psychology, and everyday forms of speech and action. He did not, however, claim any special authority for doing so. Still, his image of philosophy continues to be worrisome to many social theorists, because it did *not* provide a philosophical answer to the practical relationship between inquiry and its subject matter.

Although it is easy to understand the concerns of social theorists who are seeking the kind of intellectual authority that would yield practical results, what seems "passing strange," in the sense that Shakespeare's Desdemona used the phrase, and what I want principally to explore, is why a philosopher such as Cora Diamond, who is a champion of Wittgenstein and a sensitive and respected reader of his work, believes it is necessary to save him from himself by interpreting him as vouchsafing some special capacity for making critical judgments about what is true and real in social practices. Her characterization of the "realistic spirit" in Wittgenstein's work (Diamond 1991) may have seemed to suggest the absence of such authority, but, in the end, she could not let go of what seem to be the vestiges of traditional philosophical realism.

The Problem of Criticizing from "Outside"

The first thing to ask is why such criticism should be considered a problem. We frequently criticize others on the basis of criteria outside their systems of thought and action. The real issue is whether there is some universally authoritative basis for such criticism. Diamond (2013) posed the questions of "whether we can have rational grounds for criticizing practices and beliefs very different from our own, and whether Wittgenstein held that we could not" (114). The content of what she referred to as "rational" was not initially specified, but it implied more than making coherent arguments and giving reasons. She claimed that "our understanding of *what is real* cannot be adequately elucidated if we consider only its role within language-games" (114). It is difficult to understand what would constitute a concept of reality that is outside language-games, but she maintained that, contrary to what many have assumed, Wittgenstein provided support for such a standard of reality. She framed her discussion by describing what she claimed was "a disagreement between Elizabeth Anscombe, on the one hand, and Peter Winch and Ilham Dilman, on the other hand, about whether it is legitimate to call something an error that counts as knowledge within some system of belief" (114). It is, however, important to be clear from the outset that there was less any actual "disagreement" between these individuals than what she suggested might hypothetically be construed as a disagreement. Her purpose was to use these individuals as a foil for exploring "what Wittgenstein's view" of this matter may have been. She acknowledged that although Anscombe had raised the question of whether Wittgenstein's philosophy allowed for outside criticism, Anscombe had not given a definite response and answer. Diamond maintained, however, that Anscombe's "implicit response" to what might seem to have been his denial of this possibility, was "Don't be too sure!" and that her "implicit answer" was that he did allow a basis for such criticism (115).

Diamond claimed that Anscombe's implicit answer had been "disputed by Dilman," whom Diamond interpreted as maintaining that in the case of conflict between different systems of belief, "we cannot here speak of right or wrong." And she maintained that Winch, in his essay "Understanding a Primitive Society," had gone even further and said that an outside observer does not have the "right" to judge another society or system of beliefs as wrong and that it is "illegitimate" to do so (Diamond 2013, 118). Diamond's basic concern was to counter the positions she ascribed to Dilman and Winch, and to make Anscombe's answer explicit. Because the "disagreement" in question was a construction by Diamond, it is important to clarify exactly what her *dramatis personae* actually said and the context in which they said it.

In Anscombe's work, the issue had emerged somewhat tangentially in the course of discussing the "question of linguistic idealism" and how this question might relate to Wittgenstein (1981). Anscombe suggested that certain things that he had said about how our concepts might not be the only possible ones and how essence is a function of grammar might imply linguistic idealism. She insisted, however, that there is a need to confirm that what we call real "actually exists and is not a mere projection of the forms of our thinking upon reality." She did not specify what concept of reality was at issue, but she maintained that we must "avoid the falsehoods of idealism" but also the "stupidities of empiricist realism," which, at least in the case of Locke, implied that concepts were creations of the mind rather than direct specifications of things in the world (114–16). She was, however, ambivalent about whether or not Wittgenstein provided an answer. Although she interpreted him as saying that the sense of expressions is dependent on language, she suggested that it was less evident that he believed that the "human possession of concepts is so dependent." She doubted, even if "the metaphysical necessities belonging to the nature of such things . . . *seem* to be regarded by him as 'grammatical rules,'" that he would have maintained that things such as horses, the color red, shapes, and the number 2 were products of linguistic practice (121). But, in the end, she felt forced to conclude that in some respects Wittgenstein actually "was a linguistic idealist" or, at best, a "partial idealist" (118, 122). Wittgenstein never argued that such objects were "products" of linguistic practice but only that was where we could locate them. Anscombe was even more ambivalent when she considered "another way of raising the question of a sort of idealism," which was prompted by Wittgenstein's question about whether language and human agreement decide what is true or false (Wittgenstein 2009, 241). She interpreted his answer as recognizing that we are always operating within language, but she maintained that the implication was not "that he never sees grounds for criticism." She claimed that his work clearly allowed for immanent criticism, such as pointing out unsatisfied criteria of correctness or even a more serious "reproach" involving a "superstition" created by a "grammatical illusion." The crux of the matter, however, was reached when she asked whether his position would preclude someone's saying that another person's picture of the world was simply wrong. Although she noted that it would not preclude simply making such a claim, she asked "does it preclude having grounds, being right?" She suggested that "in his work up through *On Certainty* we might think we could discern a straightforward thesis: There can be no such thing as 'rational grounds' for our criticizing practices and beliefs that are so different from our own. These alien practices and language-games are simply there. They are not ours, we cannot move in them" (125). So "isn't it as if Wittgenstein were saying: there isn't a right or wrong—but only the conflict, or persuasion, or decision?" (132). It is important to recognize how she posed this question, because the criteria of "right" and "wrong" are what conflict and persuasion are all about. It is not one versus the other.

Anscombe, however, basically left the matter at that point and decided that maybe his ultimate position was after all "not an idealistic one," because "*that some-one knows something is not guaranteed by the language-game*" but instead, as he had noted in *On Certainty*, is a "favour of nature" (133). She did not explain what he meant by that phrase, but she nevertheless claimed that in this respect, he had succeeded in his difficult enterprise and "achieved 'realism without empiricism.'" She maintained that for Wittgenstein, "the 'language-game' of assertion, which for humans is so important a part of the whole business of knowing and being certain, depends for its character on a 'general fact of nature'" (133). This was, I suggest, a very dubious interpretation of *On Certainty* and of what Wittgenstein spoke of as a "favour of nature," but exactly how even her reading would sustain the philosophical authority of outside criticism or make it possible to adjudicate a conflict between beliefs remained, in her own words, "unfinished business" (133).

The primary concern of Dilman's (2002) book on Wittgenstein was actually also with the issue of linguistic idealism, and although he did offer some criticism of what appeared to be Anscombe's attempt to ground linguistic meaning on the givenness of natural objects in the world, his basic concern was that, with respect to idealism, she had been "unable to give Wittgenstein a completely clean bill of health" (14). Dilman argued that Wittgenstein had managed to solve the problem of the relationship between "language and reality without embracing linguistic realism and without courting any form of linguistic idealism." Although Dilman noted that one might have the impression that Wittgenstein "at times sails close to the wind" as far as avoiding idealism, he maintained that a rejection of linguistic idealism was the core of Wittgenstein's "Copernican Revolution" (7). He pointed out that Wittgenstein's basic answer to the question of the relationship between language and the world was that when we acquire language, we acquire the objects in the world toward which language is directed. Although he agreed with Anscombe that language may in various ways be conditioned by certain facts independent of our language, he claimed that what counts as such facts "has evolved hand in glove with the life human beings live," which is a "life lived with language" (5).

In a chapter on Diamond, Dilman (2002) basically applauded what she had referred to as the "realistic spirit" in Wittgenstein and his attention to the "particular case," and the actual use of language. He also agreed with Anscombe and Diamond that Wittgenstein had achieved what Wittgenstein considered to be the "hardest thing, that is, 'realism without empiricism.'" He did, however, disagree with Anscombe's interpretation of Wittgenstein as saying that essence is not created, but rather only expressed, by grammar. He argued that what Wittgenstein meant, when he said that grammar tells us what an object is, was not, for example, what specific biological object an animal such as a horse is but the grammatical or logical category to which it belongs. Although Dilman agreed that there were ways that one might reasonably say that there were horses before language, for example by projecting our current account of natural history backward, he claimed that this was "not actually *relevant* to the question of linguistic idealism" (112). And the same was true in the case of Anscombe's claim about the color red and the numeral 2 existing before language.

He also stressed that Anscombe's worry about the possibility that Wittgenstein's work might imply that people were trapped in language was misplaced, because Wittgenstein did not view language as static and immutable. The language-games of one culture might change, for example, by contact with other cultures, and Dilman argued that when Wittgenstein "depreciates thinking that people with different concepts *must* be missing something that we realize, he doesn't mean that they *could* not be supposed to miss something we realize." But such supposing takes place in "*our* language" and "*our* concepts" (116). Dilman agreed with Anscombe that what is true is not simply a matter of human agreement, not even in the case of moral issues, but he insisted that the criteria for applying the word "truth" *is* a matter of such agreement.

When it came to the crucial problem of how *On Certainty* bore on the question of criticizing beliefs and practices in alien cultures, Dilman's response cut a little closer to the bone. He noted that Anscombe had asked if this was not parallel to Wittgenstein's claim that it is not interpretation but practice that determines the meaning of a rule. Anscombe had resisted on the ground that this would imply that Wittgenstein was an idealist and denied that there are external grounds of judgment. But Dilman noted that if interpretations required making judgments about what was considered true and real in the practices that were interpreted, it raised the question of how one should approach an issue such as Winch had broached in his disagreement with Alasdair MacIntyre about how to understand a society such as the Zande. MacIntyre had argued that to interpret an alien culture, it is necessary to judge the extent to which its beliefs are logically and substantively rational, and that whereas rational beliefs are understandable and self-explanatory, irrational beliefs must be causally explained. And MacIntyre's standard of rationality was Western formal logic and natural science. Anscombe had exempted Wittgenstein from reducing conflict resolution to a matter of persuasion and decision because, she claimed, with little evidence, he conceived of most of our judgments as less functions of our language-games than of general facts of nature and life. But Dilman asked how, even if this were the case, it related to an issue such as disagreement between cultures. He concluded that "it is not a disagreement that could be resolved by appealing to mutually acceptable criteria. It is a conflict in which there is no agreed method for settling it" (2002, 126). He insisted that Wittgenstein recognized that there are "*incommensurabilities*" both within and between cultures (126). Dilman maintained that this did not entail the impossibility of understanding people who hold different beliefs and, much as Winch had, that such understanding might even lead to broadening one's own beliefs. He argued that although Wittgenstein acknowledged that our reasons for holding our beliefs may run out, there is "nothing in Wittgenstein to suggest, that these limits cannot be transcended" or "extended" (127–28). He noted, however, that it was the notion of incommensurability with respect to conceptions of what is real and true that made Anscombe "nervous."

The notion certainly made Diamond nervous. Her anxiety led not only to misleading interpretations of Dilman and Winch but also to some actual misstatements about what they had said. For example, Dilman never stated, nor attributed to Wittgenstein, the view that, in the case of conflicting beliefs, "we cannot speak of right or wrong." Dilman, like Diamond, was addressing a situation in which beliefs come into conflict, and the issue was whether either a party to the conflict or an outside critic could call upon decisive and neutral grounds of adjudication that could, in both principle and practice, resolve the matter. Although Dilman had only briefly mentioned Winch, Diamond implicated Winch in the "disagreement" by noting that his essay was "complex and not easy to understand" and that it was "hard to sort out what his criticisms are of both Evans-Pritchard and MacIntyre" (2013, 117). But she nevertheless claimed that he had maintained that it was "illegitimate" to judge the Zande as wrong and the European as right, and that he insisted that someone from one culture has no "right" to make such judgments about another culture or assert that a particular concept is the "correct" one (117–18). Winch, however, had never said that it was illegitimate to call the Zande wrong or that one did not have the right to judge another society and to deny the correctness of its beliefs. What he actually said was that it was "illegitimate" to use the anthropologist or the philosopher's worldview as a paradigm for "understanding" the Zande. He was only concerned with judging with respect to the issue of whether it was necessary to judge in order to understand. This was the basis of his clearly specified disagreement with Evans-Pritchard and MacIntyre.

Diamond's extrapolation (2013, 119) of "a possible Anscombean view" of how to resolve a conflict that arises when "two principles really meet, principles that cannot be reconciled with each other," was, at least in this article, quite far removed from Anscombe's suggestion that rational grounds for adjudication might be based on certain general facts of nature. And Diamond was not clear about the locality and identity of a hypothetical outside critic, and to whom the frequently used pronouns "we," "us," and "you" referred. She seemed to choose the perspective of a philosopher or social theorist observing a conceptual conflict, and her basic argument was that in the process of observing, describing, and analyzing a conflict,

> "we" as outsiders are giving a logical shape to the conflict; we are making a conception of reality, of what is real, that is not internal to either of the two forms of thought that provide the initial understanding of the conflict-situation. That is, we take the situation here to be one in which what is real is contested; and this idea of *reality as contested* is a different notion of reality from that involved in either of the two forms of thought themselves. If the conflict is understood in this way, the *space* for the dispute between the two forms of thought is not given in advance; it is not provided by either of the two modes of thought that are in conflict. (119)

Diamond interpreted Winch's mention of conflicting modes of thought as "established" to mean that they could not be disestablished. This was, however, clearly at odds with anything Winch had said. But she asked why we should necessarily view them in this manner and "why can one not be making, giving articulation to, a kind of thought about reality *in thinking about the conflict*?" (119). Diamond analogized what she characterized as "the disagreement between Anscombe and Winch" as the difference between proving a theorem in mathematics when there is an accepted method and standard of validity for such a proof as opposed to a case of solving a mathematical problem by a new method of proof when the standard emerges in the course of the reasoning itself, that is, "we" are creating a new understanding of what is real and unreal (120).

It was unclear exactly how this analogy applied to Anscombe's question, but Diamond claimed that it is not "illegitimate to appeal to the standards of science," and that "our understanding of what is real and what is unreal can be in part shaped by how we take such conflicts and by how we reason in response to them" (120). Neither Dilman nor Winch had denied that a third-party observer of a conflict could conjure up an image of a third world of reality and rationality that might either mediate the dispute or provide an alternative perspective, but Diamond's proposal was not in any way an answer to what had been originally defined as the problem of criticizing from outside and providing an objectively rational assessment of what was real and right. The unanswered question was still how the outside contribution of a third party, such as a social theorist or philosopher, could resolve a conflict between incommensurable beliefs within a practice, between practices such as science and religion, or between different cultural pictures of the world. But Diamond still argued that "we" cannot assume that, because there may be a lack of agreement on what is persuasive to both parties, there are no "rational grounds for judging that the people's system of thought involves pervasive error" (120).

At times, it appeared as if Diamond's outsider was formulating standards of judgment that surpassed, or were at least an alternative to, those of the parties to a conflict. At other times, the outsider appeared to be acting as a sort of mediator who would aid the parties in finding a common space of reasons. With respect to the Zande, who had been described by anthropologists as believing in witches, Diamond claimed that both approaches were at once possible. She went to great length to urge how "we" might find rational grounds arising out of the conflict, which would allow "us" to not only hold the Zande in error but also "persuade" them to think differently. This, however, would seem to present exactly the dilemma that Diamond attributed to Anscombe, that is, whether it is possible to go beyond persuasion to something more universally demonstrable in claiming that a belief is in error or in achieving a resolution of conflicts between incommensurable principles. When Wittgenstein talked about persuasion, he was not talking about something that was an alternative to giving reasons. It did not imply a lapse into intimidation and rhetoric. Although persuasion can take many forms, reasons are already a means of persuasion, and when one's stock of reasons has been exhausted, persuasion becomes a matter of attempting to convince others to accept those reasons. It is difficult to understand why Diamond tended to pose "persuasion" and "reason" as mutually exclusive.

A significant problem with Diamond's essay was that the individuals with whom she chose to argue simply did not exemplify the positions that she attributed to them. Winch, for example, was only saying that there was a certain logic and form of rationality peculiar to the Zande vision of the world, and although it might not be perfectly coherent, this would also be the case in a less "primitive" society. What Diamond wanted to demonstrate was that we are not imprisoned in our "language-games," but neither Dilman nor Winch subscribed to such a position. It was actually Diamond who treated Wittgenstein's signature reference to language-games as if they inherently presented such a problem. For Wittgenstein, "language-game" did not refer to a specific object or element of social practice. It was a term of art, a tool of interpretation, and a "perspicuous representation." It was an ideal typification, a concept that denoted a *kind* or *class* of things. Language-games were a category for what he referred to as "regions of language," of various types and scope, and Wittgenstein also offered them as modes of representation devised for talking about such regions. In neither case was there an implication that they were fossilized. Some might be more bounded than others, but they did not designate isolated provinces with settled perimeters. Various language-games were quite different in character and were, congenitally and historically, susceptible to invasion as well as internal revolution.

The Elusive Spirit of Realism

Diamond's argument about how to complete Anscombe's "unfinished business" was neither in any obvious way derived from Anscombe nor adequately responsive to Dilman and Winch. And it was certainly not beholden to Wittgenstein. It did, however, although not mentioned by Diamond, resemble Frank Ramsey's "heuristic maxim" (1925) that when faced with two disputed positions, the truth does not lie in either but in conceiving a third possibility that contains an element of both positions, which can be a basis for claiming that while both are in error, there is basis for criticism or reconciliation. But, from the outset, the problem, for both Anscombe and Diamond, *was actually Wittgenstein himself.* They both worried that his philosophy was potentially vulnerable to the charges that it did not allow communication across language-games and that it not only failed to provide grounds for external rational criticism but also blocked the possibility. They believed that his work required remedial circumvention or supplementation. This was the actual "unfinished business."

In her 1991 book, Diamond had been determined, like Dilman and Winch, to demonstrate that Wittgenstein was not an anti-realist, but she also insisted, again like Dilman and Winch, that he did not subscribe to any form of traditional philosophical realism, which, she noted, had largely been an attempt to establish a transcendental position analogous to "elementary realism." What she instead attributed to Wittgenstein was a "realistic spirit," which, she claimed, sustained his wish to achieve realism without empiricism. Much of what identified this spirit was what it rejected, which included not only the reductionism of empiricism but also attempts to lay down philosophical conditions such as a "logical must," specify "determinative sense," and posit "real generals in nature." On the more positive side, it involved giving up metaphysics and philosophical theories and instead paying attention to what people say and do, and focusing on how things really are in practice and on how the realities of a particular situation might lead us to revise our typical ways of thinking. Notwithstanding the presence of this spirit, she worried that his later work implied that rationality is limited to operating "inside a system," and that "movement to a new system" is only possible through "persuasion or conversion" rather than by a "genuine exercise of thought or reason" (Diamond 1991, 7). She claimed that there remained in Wittgenstein's work a definite "'verificationist' element," which tied the meaning of language and the content of truth-claims to available methods of investigation and systems of belief. It seems that in her 2013 essay, what she was attempting to do was to rescue Wittgenstein from what she believed to be a consistent problem in his work.

In 1996, she had continued to urge "resisting the attractions" of traditional realism, but in the course of a critique of Sabina Lovibond's version of moral realism, she insisted that we can resist such realism and still find it "possible to speak of 'responsibility to reality' in the case of linguistic resources." She maintained that this would be "different from what is the case of ordinary experimental propositions," but she asked if "the world, and our nature makes the resource in question one that we should want and need?" (249). She pursued this theme more fully in a 1999 article in which she posed the problem of how we could acknowledge the existence of problems in Wittgenstein's philosophy, but still defend both the possibility of communication between people with different beliefs and of engaging in rational outside criticism. In answering this question, she took a cue from Putnam's opposition to what he had once characterized as "tired pseudo" interpretations of Wittgenstein, which had implied the impossibility of compatibility between truth-claims in languages belonging to different historical periods. Although Diamond did not directly attempt to appropriate what was, at that point, Putnam's answer to this problem, she claimed that it was possible to reject metaphysical realism, and still not give way to the kind of relativism that Putnam and others had attributed to Rorty. By the turn of the century, however, Putnam's latest take on realism did nothing to support Diamond's case.

Diamond's own answer to the problem of incommensurability was that, at least in principle, *there is no such problem.* She claimed that in the case of a conflict between beliefs, it is our interpretation of the situation that can ultimately "fix" or determine meaning. She maintained that criteria of meaning are not limited to the grammar of the particular language-games. Meaning can emerge when we raise a question for which we have no set method of answering. It is this question that guides our search for a meaning that is different from that of the existing grammars. This argument adumbrated her 2013 article, but the problem left hanging was still how such inventive outside critical interpretation could effectively be brought to bear on what it criticized as well as resolve conflicts between beliefs.

Diamond also, much like Anscombe, worried that Wittgenstein's conception of grammar as "showing" what we are talking about could lead to reading him as a linguistic idealist and relativist. Diamond argued, however, that we can get beyond this worry by recognizing that there is a natural propensity to ascribe to others the same beliefs as ours, even if their language is different. This, as she had implied in 1996, is simply a "human phenomenon" and "one of the characteristic features of our relation to the thought of other people" (2013, 118). She did not really explain this kind of claim, which has been advanced by others on various grounds, but she argued that this assumption allows us to find a degree of sameness of meaning between the beliefs of different cultures and historical periods as well as between levels of meaning in the same culture. She suggested that "if there is incommensurability between the languages, it is a matter of refusal to accept conventions allowing translation" (125). Although she rejected the idea of being "imprisoned in our forms of life and language," she did, however, allow that there was "room for a kind of incommensurability" that might arise from a resolute refusal to see sameness of belief and meaning. But she claimed that "such a view does not remove objectivity from our practice of translation, any more than Wittgenstein's treatment of mathematics removes objectivity from our practices of proof" (125), by which she presumably meant that Wittgenstein's rejection of logical foundations of mathematics did not destroy the standard of objectivity that was internal to the practice of mathematics. But pointing to such internal standards of objectivity did not speak to the issue in question.

This all sounded a great deal like Davidson's claim about the existence of "massive agreement" in beliefs, and the need, when interpreting others, to apply the principle of "charity" and assume congruity, but Diamond seemed wary of directly enlisting Davidson's support. This may have been because his concern was with how we can interpret others rather than how we can judge them. He had rejected not only traditional realism but also the assumption that there is a universal truth in terms of which particular claims to truth are either confirmed or falsified, and he denied that philosophers are the guardians of truth.

Although Diamond's assumptions about commonality of belief might seem to have lent support to her concerns about how to achieve communication across language-games, it is less clear how they could sustain her claims about outside criticism. In a 1999 interview (published in 2000), she admitted that, after all, there is, in practice, "no short way with the kinds of clashes that arise between people who think in different ways." She maintained, however, that this does not mean that "you cannot contradict" one of these ways or that you "cannot get a genuine clash" such as in the case of Jewish and Christian views of the Messiah (73). Although she acknowledged that Winch (1964) had said "that you can't say because they're playing different language-games there isn't a genuine conflict of view," she still maintained, but without specification, that he had "said some things which lead into grave difficulties about truth and how it is established in various language-games," which would seem to question how we can think of truth as "one thing" (79–80). Winch might well have questioned thinking of truth as one thing, even though he maintained that there were universal norms inherent to human practices.

It would be difficult to point in his work to anything that suggested the impossibility of making connections between language-games or the denial of genuine disagreement. Diamond maintained that simply because "two people have different circumstances in which they make assertions," such as the conflict between the theory of intelligent design and that of evolution, this "does not mean that they are making statements that do not, in some sense or other, clash" (80). But this was neither Winch's nor Dilman's position, and it would be difficult to point to anyone who held such a position. What worried Diamond, however, was that we might "lose this notion of, let's put a heavy philosophical word here, *'objective reality'—the reason all truths are compatible is because of reality*" (81, emphasis added).

In this statement, it seems that the less than fully articulated assumption that hovered over her arguments was finally expressed. She claimed that we can put aside Platonism and still hold on to "notions of truth as one" (81). It is difficult, however, to see how this argument was compatible with Wittgenstein. But, whatever the merits of her argument, neither Dilman nor Winch had suggested that communication between different systems of belief was impossible, that there could not be significant clashes, or that someone outside a system could not object to the beliefs of another system and claim that they were wrong.

The questions of exactly who Diamond could be interpreted as arguing against and what her specific position involved were ultimately left unanswered. What does seem clear is that she was struggling toward at least a functional substitute for the very thing for which she had praised Wittgenstein's "realistic spirit" as rejecting, that is, traditional forms of philosophical realism. But what she offered was less a substantive alternative than an image of the outsider as occupying a more objective and privileged position, which would allow either somewhat neutral grounds for external critical judgments or at least insights that might aid compromise between contending parties.

What Anscombe worried might be interpreted as the "straightforward thesis" of *On Certainty*, that is, that there is no *philosophical* answer for how to resolve a conflict between different systems of belief, was actually exactly what Wittgenstein had in fact said. Such principles might not necessarily clash, or even meet, but when they do, there comes a point at which there is an end to advancing reasons that might be plausible to both parties. This is particularly the case when the contenders, such as in the case of the theory of evolution, are not really talking about the same concept, even when they both use a word such as "human being." It is a matter of persuading one party to change its view of how things are, but such persuasion does not, despite Anscombe and Diamond's implication, simply entail, or result in, a lapse into irrationality and decisionism. The problem that Diamond was seeking to answer was that of how to make outside criticism credible and effective, but it is not a problem for which there is a philosophical answer. What seems to lurk behind this whole controversy is, as noted in the beginning, what would appear to be the bizarre assumption that criticism requires, and must be grounded upon, some sort of philosophical authorization and that just as a philosopher such as Winch can be construed as withholding it, others can be interpreted as stepping in to issue it. Wittgenstein's "view" of criticizing from outside seems quite straightforward, whether it is a case of a social theorist judging a social practice, one practice coming into conflict with another, or even one scientific theory clashing with another theory. Such criticism is always possible, but it cannot be philosophically validated. It is something that takes place with great frequency and in a variety of venues, but neither its possibility nor its success depends on philosophical guarantees.

In the end, it was Diamond who could not resist elevating words such as "truth" and "reality" to the level of what Wittgenstein (2009, 97) referred to as a "*super*-order" of "*super*-concepts," when in fact such words, he said, have only a variety of more "humble" uses. They are, I have already suggested, what Austin claimed as "substantive hungry" and what Toulmin described as modal signifiers that have a general semantic force but diverse criteria of application. They are not the names of things. Although Wittgenstein noted that a word such as "truth" may, through usage, take on a certain general "face," it is a face capable of many, and sometimes incompatible, expressions. Diamond's essay is an example of how difficult it is to let go of a concept of realism that somehow hovers behind all substantive claims about what is real.

Finally, it is worth noting that Wittgenstein (1998a, 11) once said that when someone discerns a certain "spirit" in a book, there is "a great temptation to want to make the spirit explicit." There is a realistic spirit in his work, much like that Diamond had described in 1991, but she nevertheless ultimately remained captured by a picture of the transubstantiation of that spirit.

Conclusion

> At the end of reasons, comes persuasion.
>
> WITTGENSTEIN

The previous chapters might seem to some readers as lacking, because I do not offer a substantive normative direction for either political theory or political practice. And, for the most part, that perception would be quite correct. My concern has been primarily the problem of understanding politics rather than seeking a philosophical ground of political judgment. My principal purpose has been to free political inquiry from the residual bonds of representational philosophy and to accept conventional realism. It would, however, be fair to raise the question of whether conventional realism has, at least in principle, any normative political significance. I believe that it does and that the significance is democratic. When Wittgenstein talked about persuasion after the end of reasons, it is worth mentioning once again that he did not mean that persuasion was an alternative to reasons but only that it was a matter of the reasons on one side convincing those on the other side. But for persuasion as something other than coercion, there must be space in which it can be freely practiced, and that is a democratic space, which is often not available even in science and what we might think of as other rational activities, let alone politics. But, given what Wittgenstein claimed is the ultimate "groundlessness of our believing," the concept of such a space is a benchmark.

At the point that I was completing the final draft of the manuscript for this book, an edited collection of Hannah Arendt's essays (from 1953 to 1975) was published under the title *Thinking without a Banister* (2018). It seemed to me that this metaphor could be construed as relating to aspects of the argument I have been making, that is, that we do not need trans-conventional banisters, but there is the question of how to interpret this metaphor, derived from what Nietzsche had referred to as thinking in the absence of the "handrails" or "banisters" (*Denken ohne Geländer*). The phrase was used by Arendt and has continued to be employed by others as a way of describing what is often considered to be a modern predicament (e.g., Strong 2012; Bernstein 2013). But what, exactly, is the nature of that predicament? The real issue, which I believe reflects Nietzsche's concern, was not so much the presence or absence of banisters as it was their place in metaphysical stairways to nowhere. But despite Nietzsche's rejection of traditional metaphysics, his "perspectivism" still seemed to assume two worlds, that is, the assumption that behind our perspectives there is a "world" that is, itself, ultimately unrepresentable. My argument is that there is, so to speak, no such "elephant" in the room and that this has democratic implications.

The metaphor might seem to imply, as someone such as Lukes has specifically argued, that with the loss of metaphysical foundations we are left, in politics and morality, without support for our judgments, but such an assumption is what I have been attempting to dispel. There are many areas in which we might come to believe that there is a predicament involving a breakdown of standards of judgment and even what counts as judgment, but it is not a matter of the demise of philosophical foundationalism, which is actually a problem conjured up by philosophy and those who seek philosophical backing for practical judgment. We make a mistake if we assume that in a putative post-metaphysical era we are left to wander without direction. We do not usually lack support in our first-order practices, and there, as Wittgenstein indicated, the banisters are actually often so entrenched that it is difficult to dislodge them. And without these supports, and the walkways of which they are a part, the practices would not exist. There are sometimes ruptures in politics, science, and so on, but these are indigenous matters and not problems in, or solvable by, philosophy. People can attempt to change practices, or move from one to another, but the grounds and context of our thinking are within them. We can engage in second-order thinking *about* first-order practices, but it is easy to fall into the trap of assuming that second-order thinking can provide the foundations for first-order practices and discourses, which is the snare in which much of philosophy and political theory has been caught. Whatever the metaphor might mean for some commentators, I believe that Arendt can best be interpreted as claiming that we must find meaning and support *in* human practices rather than *outside* them, not in some transcendental reality or some hidden sphere of the mind, whether conceived as psychological or physiological.

Although Arendt in her later work turned to Kant, it would be a mistake to interpret her, in any wholesale manner, as a Kantian. Like her erstwhile mentor, Heidegger, she claimed to be contributing to the "destruction," or, in her words, "dismantling," of metaphysics and returning us to the world of practices in which we primarily live and act. Just as Heidegger had wished to recover a pre-Platonic image of Being, Arendt was seeking to recapture what she claimed was the essence of a pre-Platonic democratic image of politics. The problems she attributed to modern politics had, in her view, originally stemmed from philosophical intrusions and a failure to recognize what was peculiar to political judgment and what was fully expressed in democratic judgment.

In *The Human Condition* (1958), she claimed that it was, beginning with Plato, the rise of the *vita contemplativa* that had derailed the *vita activa*, and especially its manifestation in politics. This, she argued, had set Western society on a fateful course by conspiring with *poiesis*, and eventually *homo faber*, in an attempt to overcome the inevitable uncertainty and frailty of human affairs. This had involved turning against what she had idealized as the public life of speech and action, which had momentarily taken shape in the Greek *polis* and not only constituted the institution of the *polis* but, through speech and action, provided individuals with a space for self-constitution. She argued that in the contemporary age, the last vestiges of a "tradition" that had begun with the ancient Greeks had dissipated, if not altogether self-destructed. This, she claimed, had ushered in an era of "world alienation" that propelled us toward radical subjectivity, relativism, historicism, nihilism, and, in politics, totalitarianism. She claimed that this modern "crisis," capped off in the work of Marx, had not only marked the end of authentic political life but also debased philosophy by reducing it to ideology.

For Arendt, however, the saving grace that attached to the modern crisis spawned by the break in tradition was that, although setting us adrift, it also freed us by opening up a space between "past and future" in which we could creatively think and, hopefully, act. Because the tradition was no longer available to help us traverse an intellectual abyss and aid in both descending into the past and ascending into the future, what was required in these "dark times" was, as a first step, charting how we had come to this situation as well as mining the past for remnants of the original meaning and spirit of politics and political concepts.

After her attributing the decline of the tradition to the ascendancy of the *vita contemplativa*, it is difficult to ignore what might seem to be the irony in her later valorization of the "life of the mind" (1961, 260). But she conceived that life as the life of a "truthteller." Preeminent among such an "outsider" was the philosopher who would inevitably come into conflict with politics, because truth and politics had always been on "bad terms" with each other (227). The kind of truth with which she was concerned in her essay "Truth and Politics" was what she referred to as "factual truth," or as Detective Joe

Friday said, "just the facts, ma'am." These, "once perceived as true and pronounced to be so," are "beyond agreement, dispute, opinion, or consent," even if, as in the case of the German concentration camps, denied but publicly known. Nevertheless, unlike mathematical axioms, they are "fragile" and in modern life had given way to mere "opinion" in "the affairs of the world" (1961, 235–36, 240).

It seems that Arendt conceived herself primarily as a truthteller and that the life of the mind was aimed at informing political action. In a well-known 1964 interview, she identified herself, in the American idiom, as a "political theorist" and not a "philosopher." The significance of this remark has been interpreted in a number of ways, but I suggest that in part it was, first of all, an attempt to signal that her ultimate concern was with practical matters, as her essays during this period would seem to indicate. Second, she wished to separate herself from the arguments of Leo Strauss, despite their mutual intellectual debt to Heidegger and his diagnosis of modernity. Strauss, in opposition to American empirical political science, insisted on identifying himself as a "political philosopher." But they were also separated by their political values.

Many of the émigré scholars who were involved with the study of politics saw themselves, at least potentially, as public intellectuals and wrote in a rhetorical style, but while Arendt often spoke quite directly about contemporary issues in a manner that valorized democratic principles, Strauss cloaked his elitist claims about "natural right" in complex esoteric historical/philosophical commentary that concealed his specific political position. His major criticism of the Nazi jurist Carl Schmitt was that he had not gone far enough in his critique of liberalism, and in a highly controversial and widely discussed 1933 letter to Karl Löwith, Strauss had claimed that, despite the treatment of Jews by the new regime, only on the basis of "a principle of the right—fascist, authoritarian, imperial—is it possible, in a dignified manner, without the ridiculous and sickening appeal to the 'unwritten rights of man,'" to effectively oppose the "monster" of Nazism. At the point of the 1964 interview, however, Arendt probably still had little sense of what the academic field of political theory had been all about, but she was correct in recognizing its practical and democratic concerns.

Academic political theory was, from its beginning, notwithstanding its roots in an imported German idealism, an American enterprise (Gunnell 1993) founded on celebrating the very tradition that Arendt would claim had run its course and self-destructed. This "tradition," however, was the reification of a retrospective, analytical, and rhetorical construction in which philosophers from Plato onward had been assigned roles in a quasi-historical narrative of political progress. Arendt, like Strauss, Eric Voegelin, Sheldon Wolin, and others (Gunnell 1979), transformed the story into a tale of a fall from grace, and the role Arendt ascribed to figures such as Plato was no more historically credible than what had been projected in political science and political theory since the mid-1800s. What characterized all these narratives, whether of progress or decline, was, strangely, a lack of actual political explanations for what had happened in politics. They were all stories about the path of ideas in the work of iconic commentators on politics, and the influence of these ideas on politics was more assumed than documented.

What distinguished Arendt's own dramatic rendition, however, was her admission that it was not "literally true" but instead, as she put it, an interpretive "metaphorical approximation" of what, she claimed, "had actually happened" below the surface of events (1961, 9, 15). Her just-so story had a point, which was that we must rethink the nature of politics and political judgment, but her basic answer to the modern crisis was not a new or resuscitated metaphysical vision. Linda Zerilli (2016) has argued in detail that the key to understanding Arendt's turn to Kant's work was not his claims about a human capacity for making determinatively or objectively universal true judgments in science and morals, but his discussion, in the *Critique of Judgment*, of reflective "subjective universal" judgments, such as those in aesthetics, which were not grounded in the sense to which philosophy had traditionally aspired. These were "representative," "reflective," "plural," "enlarged" judgments that took into account the perspectives of others and might arise from a confrontation between individual conscience and the particulars of a practice in the context of a *sensus communis*. Arendt had noted in her essay "Truth and Politics" that "the hallmark of all strictly political thinking" had been discovered by Kant in the first part of his *Critique of Judgment*, but "he did not recognize the political and moral implications of his discovery." This "very process of opinion formation is determined by those in whose places somebody thinks and uses his own mind, and the only condition for this exertion of the imagination is disinterestedness, the liberation from one's own private interests" (1967, 54). She claimed that under fully democratic conditions deception without self-deception was nearly impossible.

Parenthetically, it is worth noting that Arendt's formulation seems very similar to how Wittgenstein construed aesthetic judgments and value judgments as well as to what I have referred to as presentational claims. In pointing to historical instances that indicated these possibilities, Arendt also seemed to suggest that a democratic form of political life was endemic to the human condition.

It may be difficult to make perfect sense of what Arendt had to say about the relationship between philosophy and politics, but she seemed to have been suggesting that, from the beginning, the Western tradition had been devoted to finding standards of political judgment that were external to politics. I believe that she recognized, as Marx claimed in his critique of Hegel's *Philosophy of Right*, that there is a sense in which "democracy is the essence of every political constitution" and that all other forms are derivative. Marx was not the first to suggest something of this sort. He was in some ways echoing a theme present in at least the work of Hobbes, Locke, and Rousseau. If we look carefully at their texts, we can see that they never actually defended the existence of a baseline of "natural rights" (which is either a metaphor or self-contradictory phrase) grounded in a pre-conventional condition. Their essential implication was actually that *there are no natural rights*, but, despite the arguments of someone such as Strauss, this included the crucial fact that *there is no natural right to domination.* If there is no such right, then the only legitimate basis of political order is free individual consent, participation, persuasion, and conventional agreement—in short, something that would be a form of popular government. In addition, they all maintained that because human beings have a capacity for creating and participating in a political society, they are, if deprived of free and equal access to that opportunity, denied what Aristotle spoke of as their essential nature as political animals or what Marx referred to as their "species being." But even more broadly, despite the diversity among these philosophies, it seems that something like democracy could be construed as the logical implication of conventional and linguistic life (Gunnell 2003).

Arendt pointedly rejected talking about "human nature" and instead chose to speak about the "human condition." And that condition is conventionality. Humans are, one might say, naturally unnatural and cannot escape from language into either an abstract "world" or a mysterious realm of the "mind." There have been, and continue to be, many attempts to link language and democracy, such as Habermas's claim that language use contains universal standards of rationality and truth, but this was little more than an argument for a kind of immanent transcendentalism. Others such as Chantal Mouffe seek democratic implications in the porousness, undecidability, and diversity of language, but she also postulates something like a metaphysical universality of "the political." Although Taylor views language as the core of a pluralistic public realm, he, as I have already discussed, opted for universal grounds of rational judgment. In nearly all of contemporary political theory, there is, to say the very least, continuing reluctance to face up to the fact of conventional realism. Many see this as a danger to an image of democracy, but I suggest that it is actually the premise of such an image.

The banisters that support our practices are only to be found within our practices. And this was Wittgenstein's message. He had little or nothing specifically to say about politics, and it would be a strain to picture him as what we typically identify as a political philosopher—or, some might say, even a philosopher in the sense that philosophy had been, and often still is, practiced. But he was a theorist of the kind of stuff of which politics consists and of philosophy as an enterprise devoted to understanding human practices, which included understanding the kinds of understanding that takes place within those practices. What philosophy could provide was no longer metaphysical supports, which were in fact illusory, but, instead, confidence in our ability to find our way around in the world of convention where reasons and persuasion dominate.

Although philosophy may help us understand politics, it cannot provide, and never has, any more than in the case of science and other first-order discourses, a foundation for politics. Wittgenstein said that philosophy, as an activity, leaves "everything as it is" in the sense that philosophy has no intrinsic connection to any first-order practice, even though it may have intentional and unintentional effects and consequences. But philosophical recognition of the depth of conventionality points toward democracy as the essence of all aspects of public life, no matter in some cases how inconvenient, inappropriate, or even impossible democratic practice may be. But the fact that it is meaningless to talk about a standard of reality and truth that stands outside our language and conventions entails that we are responsible, and the final authority, for our judgments. There are no metaphysical justifications and excuses.

Acknowledgments

I very much appreciate Chuck Myers's editorial interest in this project and his sticking with it through many months of my largely self-instigated revisions. Although the manuscript was, for the most part, written in isolation, Peter Breiner and I have discussed, and sometimes argued about, these matters for many years, and Linda Zerilli's extensive comments on what might be considered the penultimate version of the manuscript were immensely helpful in pruning the content and articulating the final distribution of emphasis. I thank my longtime friend Gene Poschman for his insight into why it has been consistently difficult to transform the word "politics" into an abstraction, despite the efforts of many political theorists to do so. And I thank Jeff Isaac for helping clarify how the form of "critical realism" discussed in chapter 3 was insinuated into the American conversation. Finally, the manuscript has benefited significantly from the careful and skillful copyediting of Kathryn Krug.

An earlier and abbreviated version of chapter 2 was published in the inaugural issue of *Teoria Polityki* (Polish Review of Political Theory) 1 (2017): 187–201; chapter 3 is a revision of "Social Scientific Inquiry and Meta-theoretical Fantasy: The Case of International Relations," *Review of International Studies* 37, no. 4 (2011): 1447–69, © British International Studies Association 2011, published by Cambridge University Press; chapter 8 is a revision of "Social Inquiry and the Pursuit of Reality: Cora Diamond and the Problem of Criticizing from 'Outside,'" *Philosophy of the Social Sciences* 46 (2016): 584–603.

References

Unless otherwise indicated, references to Wittgenstein are to numbered remarks. References to *PPF* are to what has often been designated as Part II of the *Investigations* but in the 2009 edition cited here is "Philosophy of Psychology—A Fragment."

Anscombe, G. E. M. 1981. "The Question of Linguistic Idealism." In *The Collected Philosophical Papers of G. E. M. Anscombe*, vol. 1, 112–33. Oxford: Basil Blackwell.

Archer, M. A., R. Bhaskar, A. Collier, T. Lawson, and Alan Norrie. 1998. *Critical Realism: Essential Readings*. New York: Routledge.

Arendt, Hannah. 1958. *The Human Condition*. Chicago: University of Chicago Press.

———. 1961. *Between Past and Future*. New York: Viking.

———. 1967. "Truth and Politics." *New Yorker*, February 25, 1967.

———. 2018. *Thinking without a Banister: Essays in Understanding, 1953–1975*. Edited by Jerome Kohn. New York: Penguin.

Austin, J. L. 1961. *Philosophical Papers*. Oxford: Clarendon Press.

———. 1962a. *How to Do Things with Words*. Oxford: Clarendon Press.

———. 1962b. *Sense and Sensibilia*. Edited by G. J. Warnock. Oxford: University Press.

Barfield, Owen. 1957. *Saving the Appearances: A Study in Idolatry*. London: Faber and Faber.

———. 1963. *Worlds Apart: A Dialogue of the 1960s*. Middletown, CT: Wesleyan University Press.

Bell, Duncan, ed. 2008. *Political Thought and International Relations: Variations on a Realist Theme*. Oxford: Oxford University Press.

———. 2017. "Political Realism and International Relations." *Philosophy Compass* 12:1–2.

Bernstein, Richard. 2013. *Violence: Thinking without Banisters*. Cambridge: Polity Press.

Bhaskar, Roy. 1973. *A Realist Theory of Science*. New York: Humanities Press.

———. 1986. *Scientific Realism and Human Emancipation*. London: Verso.

Blackmore, Susan. 1999. *The Meme Machine*. Oxford: Oxford University Press.

Boyd, Richard, Philip Gasper, and J. D. Trout, eds. 1991. *Philosophy of Science*. Cambridge, MA: MIT Press.

Brodbeck, May, ed. 1968. *Readings in the Philosophy of the Social Sciences*. New York: Macmillan.

Cavell, Marcia. 1993. *The Psychoanalytic Mind: From Freud to Philosophy*. Cambridge, MA: Harvard University Press.

Cavell, Stanley. 1979. *The Claim of Reason*. New York: Oxford University Press.

Chauviré, Christiane, and Sabine Plaud, eds. 2012. Symposia. "Wittgenstein and Pragmatism." *European Journal of Pragmatism and American Philosophy* 4:6–174.

Chernoff, Fred. 2005. *The Power of International Theory*. New York: Routledge.

———. 2007. *Theory and Meta-Theory in International Relations: Contending Accounts*. New York: Palgrave Macmillan.

Collier, David. 1993. "Conceptual 'Stretching' Revisited: Adapting Categories in Comparative Analysis." *American Political Science Review* 81:845–55.

Collier, David, Fernando Daniel Hidalgo, and Andra Olivia Maciuceanu. 2006. "Essentially Contested Concepts: Debates and Applications." *Journal of Political Ideologies* 2:211–46.

Connolly, William. 1993. *The Terms of Political Discourse*. New York: Wiley-Blackwell.

Damasio, Antonio. 1994. *Descartes' Error: Emotion, Reason, and the Human Brain*. New York: Putnam and Sons.

Danermark, Berth, Mats Extröm, Liselotte Jakobsen, and Jan Ch. Karlsson. 2002. *Explaining Society: Critical Realism in the Social Sciences*. London: Routledge.

Davidson, Donald. 1963. "Actions, Reasons and Causes." *Journal of Philosophy* 60:685–700.

———. 1980. *Essays on Action and Events*. New York: Oxford University Press.

———. 1984. *Inquiries into Truth and Interpretation*. New York: Oxford University Press.

———. 1994. "Post-analytic Visions: Donald Davidson." In *The American Philosopher*, edited by Giovanna Borradori, 41–54. Chicago: University of Chicago Press.

———. 2001. *Subjective, Intersubjective, and Objective*. Oxford: Clarendon Press.

———. 2004. *Problems of Rationality*. Oxford: Clarendon Press.

———. 2005. *Truth, Language, and History*. Oxford: Clarendon Press.

Dawkins, Richard. 2006 [1976]. *The Selfish Gene*. Oxford: Oxford University Press.

Deacon, Terrence. 1997. *The Symbolic Species: The Co-evolution of Language and the Brain*. New York: Norton.

———. 2012. *Incomplete Nature: How Mind Emerged from Matter*. New York: Norton.

Dennett, Daniel C. 1977. "Critical Notice." *Mind* 86:265–80.

———. 1991. *Consciousness Explained*. Boston: Little, Brown.

———. 1995. *Darwin's Dangerous Idea: Evolution and the Meaning of Life*. New York: Simon and Schuster.

———. 2005. *Sweet Dreams: Philosophical Obstacles to a Science of Consciousness*. Cambridge, MA: MIT Press.

———. 2017. *From Bacteria to Bach and Back*. New York: Norton.

Devitt, Michael. 1984. *Realism and Truth*. Oxford: Blackwell.

Diamond, Cora. 1991. *The Realistic Spirit: Wittgenstein, Philosophy, and the Mind*. Cambridge: MIT Press.

———. 1996. "Wittgenstein, Mathematics, and Ethics: Resisting the Attractions of Realism." In *Cambridge Companion to Wittgenstein*, edited by Hans D. Sluga and David Stern. Cambridge: Cambridge University Press.

———. 1999. "How Old Are These Bones? Putnam, Wittgenstein and Verification." *Proceedings of the Aristotelian Society*, supp. vol., 73:99–134.

———. 2000. "What Time Is It on the Sun? An Interview with Cora Diamond." *Harvard Review of Philosophy* 8:69–81.

———. 2013. "Criticizing from 'Outside.'" *Philosophical Investigations* 36:114–32.

Dilman, Ilham. 2002. *Wittgenstein's Copernican Revolution: The Question of Linguistic Idealism.* New York: Palgrave Macmillan.

Dreyfus, Huber, and Charles Taylor. 2015. *Retrieving Realism.* Cambridge, MA: Harvard University Press.

Dummett, Michael. 1978. *Truth and Other Enigmas.* Cambridge, MA: Harvard University Press.

———. 1991. *The Logical Basis of Metaphysics.* Cambridge, MA: Harvard University Press.

Dworkin, Ronald. 1972. "The Jurisprudence of Richard Nixon." *New York Review of Books* 18: 27–35.

Easton, David. 1965. *A Framework for Political Analysis.* Englewood Cliffs, NJ: Prentice-Hall.

Eddington, Arthur. 1928. *The Nature of the Physical World.* Cambridge: Cambridge University Press.

Edmonds, David, and John Eidinow. 2001. *Wittgenstein's Poker.* New York: Ecco.

Fierke, Karin M., and Eric Knud Jørgensen, eds. 2001. *Constructing International Relations.* Armonk: Sharpe.

Fine, Arthur. 1984. "The Natural Ontological Attitude." In *Scientific Realism,* edited by Jarrett Leplin, 83–107. Berkeley: University of California Press.

Fodor, Jerry. 1975. *The Language of Thought.* Cambridge, MA: Harvard University Press.

———. 1985. "Précis of the Modularity of the Mind." *The Behavioral and Brain Sciences* 8:1–42.

———. 1998. *Concepts.* Oxford: Clarendon Press.

Freeden, Michael. 2008. *Ideologies and Political Theory: A Conceptual Approach.* Oxford: Clarendon Press.

———. 2013. *The Political Theory of Political Thinking: The Anatomy of a Practice.* Oxford: Oxford University Press.

Gallie, W. B. 1956. "Essentially Contested Concepts." *Proceedings of the Aristotelian Society* 56:167–98.

Geuss, Raymond. 2008. *Philosophy and Real Politics.* Princeton, NJ: Princeton University Press.

Giddens, Anthony. 1984. *The Constitution of Society: Outline of the Theory of Structuration.* Berkley: University of California Press.

Gladwell, Malcolm. 2005. *Blink: The Power of Thinking without Thinking.* New York: Back Bay Books.

Goertz, Gary. 2005. *Social Scientific Concepts: A User's Guide.* Princeton, NJ: Princeton University Press.

Goodman, Nelson. 1978. *Ways of Worldmaking.* Indianapolis, IN: Hackett.

Grafstein, Robert. 1998. "A Realist Foundation for Essentially Contested Concepts." *Western Political Quarterly* 41:9–28.

Grice, H. P. 1982. "Meaning Revisited." In *Mutual Knowledge,* edited by Neil Smith, 223–43. New York: Academic Press.

Gunnell, John G. 1975. *Philosophy, Science, and Political Inquiry.* Morristown, NJ: General Learning Press.

———. 1979. *Political Theory: Tradition and Interpretation.* Boston: Winthrop.

———. 1986. *Between Philosophy and Politics: The Alienation of Political Theory.* Amherst: University of Massachusetts Press.

———. 1987 [1968]. *Political Philosophy and Time: Plato and the Origins of Political Vision.* Chicago: University of Chicago Press.

———. 1993. *The Descent of Political Theory: The Genealogy of an American Vocation.* Chicago: University of Chicago Press.

———. 1998. *The Orders of Discourse: Philosophy, Social Science, and Politics.* New York: Rowman and Littlefield.

———. 2003. "The Language of Democracy and the Democracy of Language." In *Governance as Social and Political Communication,* edited by Henrik Bang and R. Rhodes, 161–79. Manchester: University of Manchester Press.

———. 2004. *Imagining the American Polity: Political Science and the Discourse of Democracy.* University Park: Pennsylvania University Press.

———. 2006. "Dislocated Rhetoric: The Anomaly of Political Theory." *Journal of Politics* 68:771–82.

———. 2007. "Are We Losing Our Minds? Cognitive Science and the Study of Politics." *Political Theory* 13:480–87.

———. 2009. "Ideology and the Philosophy of Science: An American Misunderstanding." *Journal of Political Ideologies* 14:317–37.

———. 2011. *Political Theory and Social Science: Cutting against the Grain.* New York: Palgrave Macmillan.

———. 2012. "Unpacking Emotional Baggage in Political Theory." In *Essays on Political Theory and Neuroscience,* edited by Frank Vander Valk, 91–116. New York: Routledge.

———. 2014a. "Reorienting Political Theory." Review of *The Political Theory of Political Thinking: The Anatomy of a Practice,* by Michael Freeden. *European Journal of Political Theory* 14:480–87.

———. 2014b. *Social Inquiry after Wittgenstein and Kuhn: Leaving Everything as It Is.* New York: Columbia University Press.

Hanson, Russell Norwood. 1958. *Patterns of Discovery.* Cambridge: Cambridge University Press.

Harré, Rom. 1986. *Varieties of Realism.* Oxford: Blackwell.

Hatemi, Peter K., and Rose McDermott, eds. 2001. *Man Is by Nature a Political Animal: Evolution, Biology, and Politics.* Chicago: University of Chicago Press.

Hempel, Carl. 1965. *Aspects of Scientific Explanation.* New York: Free Press.

Hindress, Barry. 1977. *Philosophy and Methodology in the Social Sciences.* Hassocks: Harvester.

Hirsch, E. D., Jr. 1976. *The Aims of Interpretation.* Chicago: University of Chicago Press.

Isaac, Jeffrey. 1987 "After Empiricism: The Realist Alternative." In *Idioms of Inquiry: Critique and Renewal in Political Science,* edited by Terence Ball, 187–205. Albany: State University of New York Press.

Jackson, Patrick Thaddeus. 2010. *The Conduct of Inquiry in International Relations: The Philosophy of Science and its Implications for the Study of World Politics.* New York: Routledge.

Jackson, Patrick Thaddeus, and Daniel Nexon. 2013. "International Theory in a Post-Paradigmatic Era: From Substantive Wagers to Scientific Ontologies." *European Journal of International Relations* 19:543–65.

Joseph, Jonathan, and Colin Wight. 2010. *Scientific Realism and International Relations.* Basingstoke: Palgrave Macmillan.

Keat, Russell, and John Urry. 1975. *Social Theory as Science.* London: Routledge.

Koselleck, Reinhart. 2002. *The Practice of Conceptual History: Timing History, Spacing Concepts.* Stanford: Stanford University Press.

Kratochwil, Friedrich. 1989. *Rules, Norms and Decisions: On the Conditions of Practical and Legal*

Reasoning in International Relations and Domestic Society. Cambridge: Cambridge University Press.

Kuhn, Thomas. 1962. *The Structure of Scientific Revolutions.* Chicago: University of Chicago Press.

Lakoff, George. 2008. *The Political Mind: A Cognitive Scientist's Guide to Your Brain and Politics.* New York: Penguin.

Laudan, Larry. 1977. *Progress and Its Problems.* Berkeley: University of California Press.

———. 1990. *Science and Relativism.* Chicago: University of Chicago Press.

Layder, Derek. 1990. *The Realist Image in Social Science.* London: Macmillan.

Lenin, V. I. 1950 [1909]. *Materialism and Empirio-criticism.* London: Laurence and Wishart.

Lowi, Theodore, and Mario Calise. 2011. *Hyperpolitics: An Interactive Dictionary of Political Science Concepts.* Chicago: University of Chicago Press.

Lukes, Steven. 1970. "Some Problems about Rationality." In *Rationality*, edited by Bryan Wilson, 194–213. Oxford: Oxford University Press.

———. 1974. *Power: A Radical View.* New York: Macmillan.

———. 1982. "Relativism in Its Place." In *Rationality and Relativism*, edited by Martin Hollis and Steven Lukes, 261–305. Cambridge, MA: MIT Press.

———. 2000. "Different Cultures, Different Rationalities?" *History of the Human Sciences* 13:3–18.

———. 2003. *Liberals and Cannibals.* London: Verso.

———. 2006. "Searle and His Critics." *Anthropological Theory* 6:5–11.

———. 2008. *Moral Relativism.* New York: Picador.

MacIntyre, Alasdair. 1973. "The Essential Contestability of Some Social Concepts." *Ethics* 84:1–9.

Manicus, Peter. 1987. *A History and Philosophy of the Social Sciences.* Oxford: Basil Blackwell.

———. 2006. *A Realist Philosophy of Social Science: Explanation and Understanding.* Cambridge: Cambridge University Press.

Mason, Andrew. 1990. "Explaining Political Disagreement: The Notion of an Essentially Contested Concept." *Inquiry* 33:81–98.

McDowell, John. 1996. *Mind and World.* Cambridge, MA: Harvard University Press.

McGuinness, Brian, and G. H. von Wright, eds. 1997. *Ludwig Wittgenstein: Cambridge Letters.* Oxford: Blackwell.

Mill, James. 1878. *Analysis of the Phenomena of the Human Mind*, vol. 2. London: Longmans, Green, Reader, and Dyer.

Monk, Ray. 1990. *Ludwig Wittgenstein: The Duty of Genius.* New York: Penguin.

Morgenbesser, Lee. 2014. "Elections in Hybrid Regimes: Conceptual Stretching Revived." *Political Studies* 62:21–36.

Morris, Errol. 2018. *The Ashtray: Or the Man Who Denied Reality.* Chicago: University of Chicago Press.

Mouffe, Chantal. 1996. "Deconstruction, Pragmatism, and the Politics of Democracy." In *Deconstruction and Pragmatism*, edited by Chantal Mouffe, 1–12. London: Routledge,

Moyal-Sharrock, D. 2003. "Logic in Action: Wittgenstein's Logical Pragmatism and the Impotence of Scepticism." *Philosophical Investigations* 26:125–48.

Niiniluoto, Ilkka. 1999. *Critical Scientific Realism.* Oxford: Oxford University Press.

Onuf, Nicolas. 1989. *World of Our Making: Rules and Rule in Social Theory in International Relations.* Columbia: University of South Carolina Press.

———. 2002. "Worlds of Our Making: The Strange Career of Constructivism in International

Relations." In *Visions of International Relations*, edited by Donald J. Puchala. Columbia: University of South Carolina Press.

Outhwaite, William. 1975. *Realism, Hermeneutics, and Critical Theory.* New York: St. Martin's.

Patomäki, Heikki. 2001. *After International Relations: Critical Realism and the (Re)construction of World Politics.* London: Routledge.

Philp, Mark. 2010. "What Is to Be Done? Political Theory and Political Realism." *European Journal of Political Theory* 4:466–84.

———. 2012. "Political Theory without Illusions." *Political Theory* 40:629–49.

Pinker, Steven. 2007. *The Stuff of Thought: Language as a Window into Human Nature.* New York: Viking.

Pitkin, Hanna Fenichel. 1972a [1967]. *The Concept of Representation.* Berkeley: University of California Press.

———. 1972b. *Wittgenstein and Justice.* Berkeley: University of California Press.

Putnam, Hilary. 1987. *The Many Faces of Realism.* La Salle, IL: Open Court.

———. 1999. *The Three-Fold Cord: Mind, Body, and World.* New York: Columbia University Press.

———. 2005. *Ethics without Ontology.* Cambridge, MA: Harvard University Press.

Radaelli, Claudio M. 2000. "Whither Europeanization?: Concept Stretching and Substantive Change." *European Integration online Papers* 4:1–28.

Ramsey, Frank. 1925. "Universals." *Mind* 34:401–17.

Rawls, John. 1971. *A Theory of Justice.* Cambridge, MA: Harvard University Press.

Rorty, Richard. 1972. "The World Well Lost." *Journal of Philosophy* 69:649–65.

———. 1979. *Philosophy and the Mirror of Nature.* Princeton, NJ: Princeton University Press.

Ryle, Gilbert. 1931. "Systematically Misleading Expressions." *Proceedings of the Aristotelian Society*, n.s., 32:139–70.

———. 1949. *The Concept of Mind.* New York: Barnes and Noble.

———. 1953. *Dilemmas.* Cambridge: Cambridge University Press.

———. 1966. *Plato's Progress.* Cambridge: Cambridge University Press.

———. 1979. *On Thinking.* Edited by K. Kolenda. Oxford: Blackwell.

Satori, Giovanni. 1970. "Concept Formation in Comparative Politics." *American Political Science Review* 64:1033–53.

———. 1984. *Social Science Concepts: A Systematic Analysis.* Thousand Oaks, CA: Sage.

Sayer, A. 2000. *Realism and Social Science.* London: Sage.

Searle, John. 1992. *The Rediscovery of the Mind.* Cambridge, MA: MIT Press.

———. 1995. *The Construction of Social Reality.* New York: Free Press.

———. 2006a. "Reality and Relativism: Shweder on a Which? Hunt." *Anthropological Theory* 6:112–19.

———. 2006b. "Social Ontology: Some Basic Principles." *Anthropological Theory* 6:12–29.

———. 2009. *Making of the Social World: The Structure of Human Civilization.* New York: Oxford University Press.

———. 2015. *Seeing Things as They Are.* New York: Oxford University Press.

Sellars, Wilfrid. 1956. "Empiricism and the Philosophy of Mind." In *Minnesota Studies in the Philosophy of Science*, vol. 1, edited by H. Feigl and M. Scriven, 253–329. Minneapolis: University of Minnesota Press.

———. 1963. *Science, Perception, and Reality.* New York: Humanities Press.

Shapiro, Ian. 1980. *Political Criticism.* Berkeley: University of California Press.

———. 2005. *The Flight from Reality in the Human Sciences.* Princeton, NJ: Princeton University Press.

Skinner, Quentin. 1972. "Motives, Intentions, and the Interpretation of Texts." *New Literary History* 3:400–407.

———. 1978. *Foundations of Modern Political Thought.* Cambridge: Cambridge University Press.

Smith, Steve, and Martin Hollis. 1990. *Explanation and Understanding in International Relations.* Oxford: Clarendon Press.

Strauss, Leo. 1957. "Machiavelli's Intention: *The Prince.*" *American Political Science Review* 51:13–40.

Strawson, P. F. 1964. "Intention and Convention in Speech Acts." *Philosophical Review* 73:439–60.

Strong, Tracy B. 2012. *Politics without Vision: Thinking without a Banister in the Twentieth Century.* Chicago: University of Chicago Press.

Swanton, Christine. 1985. "On the Essential Contestedness of Political Concepts." *Ethics* 95:811–27.

Taylor, Charles. 1964. *The Explanation of Behaviour.* London: Routledge and Kegan-Paul.

———. 1967. "Neutrality in Political Science." In *Philosophy, Politics, and Society,* edited by Peter Laslett and W. G. Runciman, 58–90. New York: Barnes and Noble.

———. 1970. "Explaining Action." *Inquiry* 13:54–89.

———. 1971. "Interpretation and the Sciences of Man." *Review of Metaphysics* 25:3–51.

———. 1982. "Rationality." In *Rationality and Relativism,* edited by Martin Hollis and Steven Lukes, 3–18. Cambridge, MA: MIT Press.

———. 1983. "Political Theory and Practice." In *Social Theory and Political Practice,* edited by Christopher Lloyd, 61–85. Oxford: Clarendon Press.

———. 1984. "Foucault on Freedom and Truth." *Political Theory* 12:152–83.

———. 2016. *The Language Animal: The Full Shape of the Human Linguistic Capacity.* Cambridge, MA: Harvard University Press.

Topper, Keith. 2005. *The Disorder of Political Inquiry.* Cambridge, MA: Harvard University Press.

Toulmin, Stephen. 1958. *The Uses of Argument.* Cambridge: Cambridge University Press.

Trigg, Roger. 1989. *Reality at Risk.* New York: Harvester Wheatsheaf.

van Fraassen, Bas C. 1980. *The Scientific Image.* Oxford: Oxford University Press.

Waldron, Jeremy. 2002 "Is the Rule of Law an Essentially Contested Concept (in Florida)?" *Law and Philosophy* 21:137–64.

Wendt, Alexander. 1992. "Anarchy Is What States Make of It: The Social Construction of Power Politics." *International Organization* 46:391–425.

———. 1999. *Social Theory of International Relations.* Cambridge: Cambridge University Press.

———. 2015. *Quantum Mind and Social Science: Unifying Social and Physical Ontology.* New York: Cambridge University Press.

Wight, Colin. 2006. *Agents, Structures, and International Relations.* Cambridge: Cambridge University Press.

———. 2012. "Philosophy of Social Science and International Relations." In *Handbook of International Relations,* edited by Walter Carlsnaes, Thomas Risse, and Beth A. Simmons, 23–51. Thousand Oaks, CA: Sage.

———. 2013. "The End of International Relations Theory." *European Journal of International Relations* 19:405–25.

Williams, Bernard. 1986. *Ethics and the Limits of Philosophy.* Cambridge, MA: Harvard University Press.

———. 2005. "Realism and Moralism in Political Theory." In *In the Beginning Was the Deed: Realism and Moralism in Political Argument,* edited by Geoffrey Hawthorn, 1–17. Princeton, NJ: Princeton University Press.

Winch, Peter. 1958. *The Idea of a Social Science.* London: Routledge.

———. 1959. "Nature and Convention." *Proceedings of the Aristotelian Society* 60:231–52.

———. 1964. "Understanding a Primitive Society." *American Philosophical Quarterly* 1:307–24.

Wittgenstein, Ludwig. 1958. *The Blue and Brown Books.* New York: Harper.

———. 1969. *On Certainty.* New York: Harper and Row.

———. 1974. *Philosophical Grammar.* Edited by Rush Rhees. Translated by Anthony Kenny. Oxford: Basil Blackwell.

———. 1975. *Philosophical Remarks.* Edited by Rush Rhees. Translated by Raymond Hargreaves and Roger White. Oxford: Basil Blackwell.

———. 1978. *Remarks on the Foundations of Mathematics.* Edited by G. H. von Wright, R. Rhees, and G. E. M. Anscombe. Translated by G. E. M. Anscombe. Oxford: Basil Blackwell.

———. 1980. *Remarks on the Philosophy of Psychology,* vol. 1. Edited by G. E. M. Anscombe and G. H. von Wright. Translated by G. E. M Anscombe. Oxford: Basil Blackwell.

———. 1981. *Zettel.* Translated by G. E. M. Anscombe and G. H. von Wright. Oxford: Basil Blackwell.

———. 1992. *Last Writings on the Philosophy of Psychology,* vol. 1. Edited by G. H. von Wright and Heikki Nyman. Translated by C. G. Luckhardt and Maxmillian A. E. Aue. Oxford: Blackwell.

———. 1998a. *Culture and Value.* Edited by Georg Henrik von Wright with Heikki Nyman. Translated by Peter Winch. Oxford: Blackwell.

———. 1998b. *Notebooks 1914–1916.* Edited by G. H. von Wright and G. E. M. Anscombe. Translated by G. E. M. Anscombe. Oxford: Blackwell.

———. 2009. *Philosophical Investigations.* Edited by P. M. S. Hacker and Joachim Schulte. Translated by G. E. M. Anscombe, P. M. S. Hacker, and Joachim Schulte. Oxford: Blackwell.

———. 2012 [1922]. *Tractatus Logico-Philosophicus.* Side-by-side-by-side edition, prepared by Kevin C. Klement and translated by F. P. Ogden/C. K. Ramsey and D. F. Pears/B. F. McGuinness.

Wolfe, Tom. 2016. *The Kingdom of Speech.* Boston: Little, Brown.

Wolin, Sheldon. 1960. *Politics and Vision.* Boston: Little, Brown.

Zerilli, Linda M. G. 2016. *A Democratic Theory of Judgment.* Chicago: University of Chicago Press.

Index